PRAISE

10TH ANNIVERSARY EDITION

IF YOU LOVED ME YOU'D STOP!
What you *really* need to know when your loved one drinks too much.

"If You Loved Me, You'd Stop!" is an essential read for understanding the science behind alcohol addiction. You'll discover things about yourself and your loved you didn't realize needed to be discovered. Lisa Frederiksen presents this powerful information in a concise, easy-to-understand way. As an adult child of an alcoholic on a healing journey, I learned more from this book than the dozens of clinical books I've read on the topic. It also provides practical coping and healing tactics for all those who love an alcoholic. "If You Loved Me, You'd Stop!" belongs in the library of all adult children of alcoholics and all those who are worried about a loved one's drinking.

—Jody Lamb, adult child of alcoholic and author of 7 *Things That Change Everything*

This book is outstanding and should be a seminal read for all families. Period. Alcohol plays too large a role in our lives and society and the consequences of untreated alcohol use disorders are too horrific and common for us to lack the understanding of subtle differences between healthy and unhealthy drinking behaviors, disease progression, treatment options, and the stages and lifestyles of recovery.

—Fay Zenoff, Executive Director of Open Recovery

Lisa's user-friendly book gives the reader hope and a better understanding of how a loved one's drinking or other drug use disorders turn families upside down and how they may regain their balance.

—Carolyn Younger, MFT, Family Program Director Muir Wood Adolescent and Family Services

Lisa brings 50-years of very personal and heart-wrenching experience to this 10th Anniversary Edition of her fine book. In assisting the secondhand drinker with finding their own recovery, Lisa shares cutting-edge scientific information from the best minds and leading researchers, as well as addressing emotional and mental health dynamics. Lisa will convince you that you aren't alone, and the best part is she does it because she cares. For anyone wanting to understand secondhand drinking and emerge from its impact, look no further.
—Bill White, MS, LLPC, Founder of Chipur.com

Lisa Frederiksen's book, "If You Loved Me, You'd Stop!," is an excellent resource for families concerned about a loved one's drinking. A thorough explanation of the difference between social drinking, alcohol abuse, and alcoholism and how excessive drinking affects the brain is included. Family members will have a much better understanding of their loved one's drinking habits not to scold or confront, but rather to work towards finding a recovery process that makes sense for them. Lisa's coined term, secondhand drinking, so clearly puts into focus what a family member goes through as they navigate the choppy waters of alcohol use disorder. With personal anecdotes, research, and tips on how family members can help themselves, this book is a must-read for anyone struggling with their loved one's excessive drinking.
—Cathy Taughinbaugh, Certified Parent Coach, Founder of CathyTaughinbaugh.com

"If You Loved Me, You'd Stop!" belongs in the toolbox of everyone who loves someone with a drinking problem; there is help and hope for a better way on every page. In this handbook for loved ones, Lisa Frederiksen tackles the shame, misunderstanding, and dysfunction, breaking it into manageable bites of understanding and action. Practical, compassionate and real, she explains without excusing and guides without accusing, helping to bridge the chasm between heart and head. Just open the pages and let the healing begin.

—Sandy Swenson, author of *The Joey Song: A Mother's Story of Her Son's Addiction* and *Tending Dandelions: Honest Mediations for Mothers with Addicted Children*; Founder of MomPower.org.

This book offers extremely powerful information for anyone suffering from a loved one's drinking – whether that person is an alcohol abuser, alcoholic, or week-end binge drinker. And though she focuses on drinking, her research and concepts can be applied to a loved one with a drug use problem, as well. Helping people understand the science behind drinking problems and toxic stress, which is what can happen to family members and friends, and her tools and tips for reclaiming one's life are very empowering. A must-read!

—Michael Herbert CASAC, ICADC, CIP, Founder of Recovery Guide

Lisa Frederiksen's book, "If You Loved me, You'd Stop!," is a book of hope. It leaves the reader with the understanding that resiliency and dignity can emerge out of facing adversity.

Through her voice of experience coupled with her extensive research, she provides an extraordinary book of knowledge and wisdom that is written in a clear and understandable manner for those navigating the painful path when a loved one is in the grasp of addiction or abuse of alcohol/drugs.

—Elizabeth Holt, Psychotherapist, LPC, ATR-BC, SEP

This is a great book and a must read for anyone dealing with a loved one who drinks too much or has developed alcoholism. Lisa's extensive research and knowledge of both and the toxic effects they have on family members is presented in a way which is easy to understand. She also includes updated research on adverse childhood experiences (ACEs), childhood trauma, and the correlation they have to someone developing a severe alcohol use disorder and why addressing them is necessary in order to fully recover. The real bonus is she offers practical, everyday tools and resources to help family members learn better ways of coping with a loved one's drinking behaviors and to improve their own health and quality of life. I have added this book to the list of other books I recommend to my clients who have loved ones suffering from the disease of addiction.

—Rosemary O'Connor, Author of *A Sober Mom's Guide to Recovery: Taking Care of Yourself to Take Care of Your Kids* (Hazelden 2015) and Founder of SoberMomsGuide.com

Please read this book. If you have a drinking problem, read the book. If you know or love someone who has a drinking problem, read this book. This book is full of information about alcohol use disorders and secondhand drinking that will help you understand your loved one, as well as yourself. Updated to include the most recent discoveries in brain science and social investigations, it makes clear that it is time to step into recovery and drop the stigma and shame. Truly a "must read" for anyone in the treatment industry, for the families of those in treatment centers, and for those realizing it isn't "just me."

—Kyczy Hawk, Yoga Instructor, Founder of YogaRecovery.com, and Author of *Yoga and the Twelve Step Path, Yogic Tools For Recovery,* and a series of word puzzle books combining recovery and yoga.

*Reading "If You Love Me, You'd Stop!" opened my eyes to the
reality that addiction, whether to alcohol or other drugs, is a devastating,
all encompassing, family disease. How I wish I had the knowledge this
book would have provided during the height of my son's addiction. If
your loved one has a drinking problem, I urge you to purchase this book.
Purchase this book for everyone you know whose life has been affected
by someone's alcohol or other drug abuse. "If You Loved Me, You'd
Stop!" is a lifeline full of the newest scientific research that gives you the
knowledge base to not just survive your loved one's addiction but to
thrive in finding yourself again.*

—MaryBeth Cichocki, RN, Creator of the blog, MothersHeartBreak,
Founder of Support After Addiction Death and A Hug From Matt

*Lisa Frederiksen has done an impressive job of integrating research
and current scientific findings into readable text about addiction and its
impact on families – through multiple generations. Everyone working
with families traumatized by child abuse/neglect, family violence, and
addiction needs to read this book as it links brain development, trauma,
and addiction and what we can do. My agency will definitely list this
book as recommended reading.*

—Rosemary Tisch, M.A., Director, Prevention Partnership
International, Program Developer *Celebrating Families!*™

*As a person who needs to see the scientific proof, I appreciated that
Lisa's book provides the latest information about the impacts of alcohol
use disorders, ACEs (adverse childhood experiences), trauma, stress,
environment, and genetics on brain and mental health. I also appreciated
the easy-to-understand manner in which it was presented. The way Lisa
wove her personal experiences throughout the chapters to demonstrate
the concepts made it relatable, human, and interesting. This is a must-
read for anyone whose life has been impacted by alcohol.*

—Debbie Hampton, Author, Writer, and Creator of The Best
Brain Possible.

...It answers so many questions – Lisa's understanding of alcohol use disorders and the family member's experience – aka secondhand drinking – and the way she presents the latest research in a conversational manner – it's just really a fine piece of work!

—Caroll Fowler, M.A., LMFT, Certified Addiction Counselor, 35 Years Recovery

Reading "If You Loved Me, You'd Stop!" has been a pleasure for me and more importantly, sharing it with two ex-wives of alcoholics, one who was in a 20-year marriage and another in a 10-year marriage. Both said to me, "I asked that very same question a multitude of times and learned that he loved his alcohol more then he loved me." Through therapy they both have learned to forgive and to hate the disease and not the person.

—Eddie deRoulet, MA, LBSW, LCDC

10TH ANNIVERSARY EDITION

IF YOU LOVED ME, YOU'D STOP!

What you *really* need to know when your loved one drinks too much.

BY

LISA FREDERIKSEN

KLJ PUBLISHING

FAIR OAKS, CA

KLJ Publishing
www.kljpublishing.com

All rights reserved

No part of this book may be reproduced, translated, stored in a retrieval system,
or transmitted, in any form or by any means, electronic, mechanical,
photocopying, microfilming, recording, or otherwise, without written permission
from the Publisher.

Printed in the United States of America

©2019 Lisa Frederiksen

ISBN: 978-0-9816844-8-2

Library of Congress Control Number: 2019901807

Developmental Editor: MC Blakeman
Author Photograph: Hilary Hausman
Cover Design and Typesetting: Jennifer Patankar
Cover Photo: Torn Paper by Andrey Kuzmin/123RF
Cover Photo: Jeans by Dmitry Naumov/123RF

WARNING AND DISCLAIMER

The purpose of this book is to provide general information. Every effort has been made to
supply accurate information to the reader and to accurately cite and credit sources, but no
warrant of fitness is implied. The information provided is on an "as is" basis. It represents
reference material only and is not intended as medical advice or a substitute for
professional advice, treatment, and/or guidance. You should not use this information to
diagnose or treat a health problem or disease without consulting a qualified health care
professional or expert. The author and the publisher shall have neither liability nor
responsibility to any person or entity with respect to any injury, loss, or damage caused or
alleged to have been caused, directly or indirectly, by the information contained in this
book. Additionally, the memoir-type pieces interspersed throughout this book are the
author's perspective and remembrance, and she fully appreciates and accepts others may
have different perspectives and remembrances of the same events. These memoir-type
pieces are shared solely to help frame the larger issues, namely, what happens to the
family members and friends when their loved one drinks too much.

Dedicated To

the nearly 80 million Americans whose loved one drinks too much

those loved ones who are struggling themselves

and

my mom and daughters for their courage, strength, love, and support, and their work to help break the cycles.

CONTENTS

PART 4
The Family Member's Experience
...and the Concept of Secondhand Drinking

PART 5
Reclaiming Your Life

10TH ANNIVERSARY EDITION

IF YOU LOVED ME, YOU'D STOP!

What you *really* need to know when your loved one drinks too much.

PART 1

How Things Got So Bad

Chapter 1
"If You Loved Me, You'd Stop!"

How many times have you said, pleaded, or screamed these words – *"If you loved me, you'd stop!"* – after a particularly nasty bout of drinking by your loved one? How many times has your husband, sister, or daughter promised to stop or cut down…drink no more than two a day…drink only on the week-ends? How many times has your heart been broken by your mom or dad, brother, wife, or son when *this* time turned out to be just like all of the times before?

Those of us who love someone – a relative or friend, a grandchild or grandparent, a girlfriend or boyfriend – whose drinking has become an all-consuming problem in our own lives will likely have spent years trying to fix things. That's why we'd pick up a book with a title like this one. We are desperate.

I understand. I was desperate too.

I was desperate for an answer to the question I'd churned over and over in my mind for years: "Why? Why if they love me, why won't they stop the drinking that's ruining our lives?" I'd been so sure that if I could just find the answer, if I could just use their love for me as leverage, I could make them stop. Or I could at least get them to limit their drinking to a level *I* considered acceptable.

I believed, like tens of millions (yes, tens of millions!) of wives, husbands, parents, grandparents, brothers, sisters, children, and significant others who love someone who drinks too much that *I* had the power to help my loved ones get a grip on their drinking. I believed *I* had the power to return our lives to normal. And so, I'd spent years trying to roll back the present to a time past – a time that had started out so happily – until I was consumed with anger and frustration, as each "last time" became the new next.

And "I" Slowly Disappeared

The more my loved ones drank or broke their promises not to drink or to cut back on their drinking, the more vigilant I'd become. I knew the next "fix" would be the one that would finally work. When that didn't happen, I would step up my efforts – nagging, pleading, fixing, denying, arguing, crying, pouting, rationalizing, and so on. My common theme was, "If you loved me, you'd stop!"

I honestly believed that if I just managed our household more efficiently or went along with their excuses (or made up my own) or believed their promises or _____ (fill in the blank, I'm sure I tried it), then my loved one would quit drinking so much and our lives would finally be happy. When those attempts failed, as they invariably did, I'd step up my vigilance to manage the next inevitable crisis as a way of wresting control of the situation. And, in a complex life of marriage, jobs, children and children's school/sports/and after school activities, ex-spouses, in-laws, friends, and family, there was an endless source and variety of crises and drama.

As I would come to understand decades later, focusing "over there" on other people, allowed me to deny the underlying problem right in front of me – alcohol – my loved ones' use and my reactions to their use. And it wasn't just my reactions. It was also the reactions of my other loved ones (children, parents, grandparents, siblings) to the drinking…or their reactions to me because of the way I behaved when they were drinking…and then my reactions to their reactions…and then their reactions to one another! All of it creating a vicious cycle of bad reactions that allowed the crises and drama to continue unchecked for years.

For you see, I was unknowingly living in the dangerous world of "enmeshment." In that world, I had absolutely no concept of boundaries. I didn't know where "I" ended and "someone else" began. In my world, the "I" and the "someone else" were one and the same. This made it impossible to have a straightforward, mature relationship with clear, healthy boundaries, let alone understand what in the heck a "boundary" was supposed to be.

Instead, my identity was thoroughly entangled in the notion that it was my job to make sure others were happy, toed the line, and succeeded at work, in school, and life in general. It was my job to see the world as my loved ones saw it or to make sure they saw it the way I did. I'd reduced my world to rigid absolutes – good or bad, right or wrong, the truth or a lie, you're with me or you're not.

With absolutes, there was a target, an objective; something that could be argued and fought for until a "winner" and a "loser" could be declared. And, by gosh, I was going to win this battle over my loved one's drinking because my whole being was caught up in the notion that we had to agree on the "truth" of what was going on. And if we didn't, then it was up to me to try harder, be smarter, accommodate more, and move faster to fix it so we could.

In the end, "I" disappeared…numb, scared, confused, sad, resigned, angry, fed-up… which brings me to my loved ones.

Meet My Loved Ones, "Alex"

As I would later understand, I'd had several loved ones over the years, both friends and family, male and female, whose drinking affected my life on deeper levels than I realized. To protect their privacy, I will not be speaking about any specific loved one in particular, with one exception – my mom (for reasons you'll soon read). Rather, I will use a composite. My composite's name is "Alex" (or loved one), and I will use the pronoun "he" for simplicity's sake. At times, I will refer to them all collectively as "loved ones."

But Alex is a composite, and the scenarios I attribute to Alex in this book are drawn from assorted experiences I had with one or more of them at various times over the years. These experiences were the result of their *drinking behaviors* – the things they said or didn't say and the

If You Loved Me, You'd Stop!

things they did or didn't do when they drank too much. And it wasn't just their behaviors while they were drinking. It was their behaviors before and after they'd had too much drink, as well.

These *drinking behaviors* included things like:

- countless broken promises to stop or cut down

- driving under the influence (DUI), arrests for drunk driving

- health and/or financial problems

- being loving and friendly while drinking and then cold and distant the next day

- deflecting, minimizing, denying the problems caused by drinking

- lost friendships

- handling a gun while under the influence

- bankruptcy

- "disappearing acts"

- insane circular arguments about what constituted "drinking too much"

- passing out on the couch long before bedtime

- school, family, and work problems

- verbal abuse

- even physical intimidation and violence.

For each item on this list, I could recount dramatic scenes, countless tears, and sleepless nights. Perhaps you've witnessed some of these kinds of drinking behaviors in your own loved ones.

I've often wondered if I would still be tolerating Alex's drinking behaviors had I not gotten the kind of help I did nor discovered the 21st

Century research that's revolutionizing what we now know about the human brain and drinking problems. Based on the stories shared with me by my clients, readers who comment on my blog posts or call me with questions, and family members of loved ones in treatment at the centers where I've lectured over the years, it is very likely that I would. Fortunately for me, there was a defining moment...

Alex Decides to Get Help

It was 2003 – the year of my 50th birthday. I will never forget following Alex up a steep flight of stairs into a small, cramped waiting area. He was checking himself into a residential treatment program for alcoholism. Finally! I thought.

Finally! I would be proven right – his drinking really was a problem. Finally! Someone else would take over my job of trying to get him to stop. Finally! Alex would get fixed, all would be well, and life could return to normal. But nowhere in that "finally" was I thinking, "Finally – I'm going to start my *own* recovery."

In short order after Alex's admittance to the treatment center, I was labeled a codependent and an enabler and told that *I* needed to get help for myself. "What? Me?! You can't be serious. I don't need help – it's Alex who has the problem," I'd argue. "And what in the world do you mean I'm an enabler, a codependent? I'm just trying to keep everything that's falling apart somehow together!"

I was told alcoholism was a disease, as were other drug addictions. I really balked at that one. "Cancer is a disease," I would argue, "all they have to do is put down the bottle!" And I was told alcoholism (and addiction to other drugs) was a family disease. "Oh brother, you've got to be kidding!" I'd grumble to myself.

But I was also done! Done! *Done with what*, I didn't know. But I knew something had to change. I was done...after seemingly thousands of broken promises and zillions of crazy-making arguments over issues

I'd thought resolved or considered so picky I couldn't figure out why I was talking, let alone arguing, about them – again! I was done...after countless times of being accused of things I hadn't said or done and then being wrapped in the warmth of his heart-felt apology the next day, only to be accused of those very same things a month later! I was done...after years of trying to protect and shield my children from Alex's and my behaviors – behaviors that made no sense because we were fighting a losing battle and didn't understand the reasons why. I was done...after loaning Alex money, overlooking his promise to be home by midnight, or convincing myself it was just a "little white lie"...after countless hours defending myself against accusations, such as "What, don't you trust me?" or "If you'd just stop nagging – it's not that big of a deal" or "Can't a guy stop by a bar with his buddies after work?" or _____ (fill in the blank – likely you have experiences similar to mine). After all of that, I was so broken, so tired, so despondent, and oh so very frustrated, angry, and bitter. I was done!

You see, by 2003, it had been decades of this craziness because, as I explained, it was not just one but many Alexes with whom I'd been having these exchanges. Over the years, I had moved so many, many boundaries established in fits of threats, "Never again or I'm leaving!" ...Or in moments of remorse on Alex's part, "I'm so sorry. I don't know what happened. I didn't mean to. I promise, it will never happen, again." ...Or in desperation on my part to make it work because I didn't want to face what it meant if it didn't.

But by 2003, I was finally ready to concede that my way was not working.

Fortunately, I took to heart what the family therapist at Alex's treatment center said to do. I attended as many family group programs at the center as were available and started participating in Al-Anon, a 12-step program for family and friends of a loved one who drinks too much. I found a therapist who specialized in helping people on the family side of this disease and spent three years in Cognitive Behavioral Therapy

(CBT) with him. (I will share more of my recovery journey in later chapters.)

And in the midst of all this, I did what I do – I researched. I had to understand how I went so far down and why I'd tolerated my loved ones' drinking behaviors for so, so long. I had to know why treatment professionals could possibly call alcoholism (and other drug addictions) a disease.

As I did more research, my defenses started to crack. Maybe the professionals were right. Maybe the impact of alcohol could change the health and functioning of the brain and maybe those changes could lead to a person "developing" alcoholism. Maybe alcoholism could be considered a brain disease.

But then I'd counter with something like, "Wait a minute. How could excessive drinking cause that? And what is 'excessive drinking,' anyway?" So, I kept digging and each discovery led to more questions and more digging. I had to understand and answer the questions that kept bothering me: "But why?" "How?" "Is this true for everyone?" "Can it be fixed?"

It was four years into my study of this research that scientists and medical professionals were able to explain why alcoholism is a brain disease. Let me repeat that, because it is one key to understanding what you *really* need to know when a loved one drinks too much: alcoholism is a brain disease. It was these developments in brain science, which have advanced even further in the past 10 years, that made it "okay" for me to accept the concept that alcoholism is a disease.

I learned why and how a person develops the disease. I learned that people with alcoholism couldn't stop their excessive drinking as long as they consume *any* amount of alcohol. Simply put, they can't drink anymore. I learned that as long as they even *think* they can drink successfully at some point in the future, there is no amount of willpower nor good intentions that can help them avoid a "next time." All of this new knowledge meant it was pointless for me to keep ranting, "If you loved me, you'd stop!"

I also learned that alcoholism develops in phases and stages just like other chronic diseases, like cancer. I learned that the stage referred to as alcohol abuse (which starts with "excessive drinking") always precedes alcoholism. I learned that a person in this stage of drinking *might* be able to learn to "re-drink." If they do, they may possibly avoid *developing* alcoholism.

Most importantly, I learned that the insanity of my loved ones' drinking behaviors was not about me or my children or the guys at the office or other family members and friends or what I had or had not done. It was about the behaviors that occur as a result of the brain changes in someone who drinks too much. It was also about the toxic stress consequences a person can suffer when coping with a loved one's drinking behaviors over and over and over again.

In my early research, I also learned there was little that focused specifically on the family experience and what it takes to help family members cope and eventually do things differently in order to improve their own physical and emotional health and quality of life. Instead it was more about the experiences of the drinker or the alcoholic – protecting *their* anonymity, finding treatment for *them*, supporting *their* recovery – plus the pervasive belief that if the alcoholic gets well, everything else, including the family, will somehow get well too.

Which is why I wrote the first edition of *If You Loved Me, You'd Stop!* published in 2009. That edition combined the most current research on alcoholism and alcohol abuse with information on what coping with a loved one's drinking behaviors does to family members. That book was set against the backdrop of my almost 40-years-experience in dealing with these problems and the research available at that point in time.

But a decade later, there is so much more to share – not only of my own recovery story but of the new and advanced scientific research about the brain – the organ that is at the root of both the drinker's and the family member's experiences. Research that explains:

- why alcoholism is considered a brain disease[1]

- why treatment for alcoholism is not "one size fits all," nor does it necessarily have to involve residential rehab or a 12-step program

- what adverse childhood experiences (ACEs) and the CDC-Kaiser ACE Study have to do with alcohol use disorders and their impacts on the family

- why dealing with a loved one's drinking behaviors can cause toxic stress, and why toxic stress can change a family member's physical and emotional health and quality of life

- and why society's common belief that alcoholism is a choice, a lack of willpower, and/or a moral failing is utterly absurd.

Even the terminology has changed. In the mental health diagnostic field, these issues are no longer simply labeled "alcohol abuse" and "alcoholism." Rather it's "alcohol use disorders," and within this classification a person can have a mild, moderate, or severe alcohol use disorder. These terms are more fully explained in Chapter 2.

All of this and so much more of what I share in this 10th Anniversary Edition is rooted in brain science that was not widely known in 2009 or has been newly discovered or advanced since, which brings me to…

My Mom's Story and Why I Can Tell It Now

My mom was one of my loved ones who drank too much. She didn't stop drinking until age 79. She died in 2017 when she was 84. There was no warning, no lingering illness. She died two days after an unsuccessful emergency surgery. But we had five-plus years during which she did not drink, after 45 years during which she did.

You see, my mom knew she had a drinking problem. So did we, the rest of her family. There were times when she fought mightily to stop or control it. There were times when the rest of us fought mightily to help her get help or to try make her stop or to shame her into stopping. She even succeeded in cutting back or not drinking for periods of time, which convinced her and us that she really wasn't an alcoholic.

None of us knew alcoholism was a developmental brain disease. None of us knew the key risk factors for developing the disease include genetics, social environment, childhood trauma, having a mental illness, and early use (drinking before age 21). None of us knew that it was alcohol abuse that made her brain vulnerable to these key risk factors. These facts had yet to be discovered in the manner they are known today. None of her primary care doctors who saw her over the four-plus decades her disease developed and advanced ever diagnosed it. They didn't know this, either.

This is because it was not until "The Decade of the Brain" (the 1990s) and "The Decade of Discovery" (2000-2010) that these facts were identified through advances in imaging technologies that were used to study the live human brain in action and over time. Examples of these imaging technologies included SPECT (single-photon emission computerized tomography, which allows scientists and medical professionals to analyze how an organ is functioning), and fMRI (functional magnetic resonance imaging, which allows scientists and medical professionals to measure brain activity). Thus, the revolutionizing scientific studies that explained how a person develops and treats alcoholism (and other drug addictions) and how they are prevented had yet to be conducted when my mom was in the midst of her disease.

Ironically, my mom was also a 17-year cancer survivor when she died. She knew to do self-breast exams and consistently did them. She found a lump and immediately contacted her doctor; her doctor immediately ordered a biopsy; and she was diagnosed with breast cancer in 2000. She had a mastectomy, went through radiation and chemotherapy, lost her hair, and showed such courage and grace in her battle to recover. (If you've ever witnessed someone recovering from cancer, you know what I mean by "battle.")

But cancer is a disease rooted in scientific research that people and their doctors understand. Symptoms are openly talked about and medical protocols are routine. There is no denial, secrecy, judgment, or shame surrounding the disease of breast cancer.

That was not the case with my mom's other disease – alcoholism.

It wasn't until my mom's third alcohol-related collapse and ambulance ride to the ER within a one-week period in the summer of 2012 that she was finally diagnosed with acute alcoholism. The ER doctor said she was too sick to go home and referred her to a skilled nursing facility.

When she was admitted to the facility, she couldn't walk but a few shuffling steps without someone on both sides holding her up. She had difficultly recognizing her family and didn't know how to follow the normal sequence of steps for washing her hands or going to the bathroom without help. She ate like a toddler – mostly shoveling food into her mouth with her hands – the idea of using a napkin and utensils didn't register.

Her treatment included intensive occupational therapy, physical therapy, speech therapy, sleep, exercise, and eating nutrient rich foods and vitamins. By the end of her stay, as her clarity returned, she felt great shame, guilt, and remorse. She wanted desperately to go home and promised never to drink again. She never did.

During the last years of her life, mom and I talked a great deal about the work and research I'd been doing since 2003. She'd known the gist of it. I had offered my expertise and help over the years and couched it in terms of the other "Alexes" in my life. She'd get uncomfortable and gloss over my giving a presentation or completing a book or an article on alcohol misuse with a vague, "That's nice dear. I'm happy for you." There were times after a particularly bad bout or a disastrous consequence of drinking that she'd express a willingness to get help, but she never wanted to go to rehab, nor back to Alcoholics Anonymous (AA), something she'd tried in the mid-1980s. Back in the mid-1980s, it was generally presumed that participating in AA was "the" way to get and stay sober.

After she stopped drinking and had months of clarity, my mom didn't cut me off as quickly when I shared a new talk or blog post topic. She eventually started asking questions about the research I'd been studying and would think about my answers and then would ask more questions.

I will share the highlights of how my mom developed alcoholism and how she recovered in later chapters. But for now, I want to share one of her greatest gifts to breaking the cycles of this family disease; for it is a family disease because it affects just about every member in a family in some way or another.

It happened during one of our phone calls. She said to me, with deep emotion, "Lisa – *please* – *please* use my story – our story – to help others."

And so, I am.

For My Mom, Myself, and the Nearly 80 Million Family Members and Friends Whose Loved One Drinks Too Much...and for Those Loved Ones Who Are Struggling Themselves

I want to share my own and my mom's stories because they reflect the stories of the hundreds of people with whom I've worked over the years. I also want to share the explosion in research that has been discovered, refined, or expanded since I published the first edition of this book in 2009. To put this explosion into perspective, think about the first smartphone introduced in 2007. If you had one, you know how basic it was compared to the smartphone of 2019. There's no comparison, really. Today's versions have advanced so far that our smartphones have just about everything and more that we need to run our lives.

So, my intention with this 10th Anniversary Edition is to not only share these important research advances, but also to offer suggestions for helping *yourself* – something you can't imagine needing to do right now – after all, it's your loved one who has the problem! Right? Yet it will likely be these suggestions that will help you thrive, whether your loved one stops drinking or not or whether or not you continue your relationship with them, end it, or redefine it.

This book is by no means exhaustive, and I've purposefully tried to keep it relatively short and simple – well, as simple as it can be when explaining the complex workings of the brain! I know, myself, that when I started looking for information, I was overwhelmed with trying to understand so many terms and concepts, such as: the differences between excessive drinking, alcohol abuse, and alcoholism; "co-occurring disorders" (having an alcohol use disorder and a mental health disorder); adult children of alcoholics; and codependency. I also wanted to know how to help the alcoholic stop drinking, how to talk to my children, and how to support the family in recovery. The list went on and on.

If You Loved Me, You'd Stop!

At the time, I just wanted something that could help me grasp the overall picture. And that's what I've attempted to do in this 10th Anniversary Edition, because no matter how much you love someone whose drinking is affecting your life, nor how much they love you back, love will not and cannot make them stop. But the good news is that it's possible for you to truly enjoy your life regardless. For today, I can honestly say I've never been happier, more fulfilled, and more at peace with myself.

It may not seem like it now, but I promise you things can and will change. I invite you to keep reading because life – *your* life – really can be better.

Chapter 2
You're Not Crazy, Something Really *Is* Wrong

When Alex finally entered the residential treatment program for alcoholism, I experienced a giddy – "I knew it, I knew it! I'm not crazy" – kind of a feeling. Finally, he was admitting what I'd been trying to get him to acknowledge all along: namely, he really *could not* control his drinking. So why had I put up with it if it bothered me so much?

The short answer: I deeply, deeply loved him.

The longer answer: he refused to admit he couldn't control it, and if he couldn't control it, did that mean he was an alcoholic? I wasn't about to call him that. Instead, I set out to prove he wasn't because I'd always thought alcoholics were people who lost their families, their homes, or their jobs because of their drinking. Alex still functioned well. He went to work, exercised, joined us on vacations, made me feel loved and appreciated much of the time, and had many periods of being a truly great person. He'd even stopped drinking for years at one time so it seemed obvious he could do it, again. And as I've said, I loved him – that deep, down, in your heart and soul, "love will conquer all," brand of love. So, I spent years trying to convince myself he could get control of his drinking – somehow.

Complicating it for me was the fact I'd already spent decades rationalizing various loved ones' destructive drinking habits and excusing their behaviors. At most, I thought they drank too much sometimes and were out of control. But certainly, they were not alcoholics. That's because I thought a person's drinking had to be either "normal" or "alcoholic." I didn't understand there is another stage of drinking known as alcohol abuse. I didn't understand that alcohol abuse is always a precursor to alcoholism but that it doesn't always have to develop into alcoholism.

Since I was not about to label my loved ones as alcoholics, I tried to convince myself their drinking was normal or excusable, in spite of all the problems it caused. Why? Because I was conditioned, like most of us, to believe that being an alcoholic was "bad." It was a sign of "weakness," "a lack of willpower," and perhaps most importantly, a sign they did not love me enough to stop. And, if they wouldn't stop, what would I do? I couldn't begin to face answering that question.

So, I spent hours and then years and then decades arguing with my loved ones about the finer points of their various drinking patterns. Each one denied their drinking was really *that* bad. And, with each one, I denied to myself it was really out of their control. Instead, I rationalized their behaviors (and mine), saying things to myself like:

- He stopped drinking before, so of course he can control his drinking and have just a glass of wine or two on weekends or at holiday celebrations.

- I drank. Often, I drank a lot and partied right along with him but that doesn't mean I have a drinking problem *or does it*?

- It could be worse. At least he's not mean when he drinks.

How "Rational" Can You Be?

(Excerpts from a family member's journal – notice how close the dates are in these entries.)

April 14 *You came home and said you were going to go on a controlled drinking program for the rest of your life – only 4 drinks per day. You said you probably wouldn't do it if it weren't for us...that if you were alone, you would probably go on as you had been, but that we were too important – you had to do it.*

May 21 *You played golf and came home drunk. Insisted Susan, [a 5-year-old] should learn what a tape measure "really" does and how to use it. Ended up in the back yard with her counting dead snails (killed by* *the snail bait). You were doing the "high five" hand slap with her and hit her so hard, tears sprung to her eyes...blamed me for it because I exclaimed... "Why'd you do that?" You said it hadn't hurt her until I'd said that...You started yelling the usual...said you were leaving... Didn't come home until the next morning after I'd gone to work—never did call. That night, when I got home from work you said, "I'm sorry about last night, I overreacted a bit." I said, "Overreacted???!!!???..." and the fight was on.*

Why Did I Excuse Them for So Long?

One of the forces driving my pattern of minimizing and rationalizing my loved ones' drinking was the fact that I, myself, had struggled with eating disorders for 12 years (including one year of anorexia and eleven years of bulimia starting at age 16). I knew the self-loathing, the shame, the fear, and the desperation my loved ones felt over breaking the promises they had made to themselves to stop or cut back because I had felt those same things myself.

I knew the insanity of wanting and believing each purge was the last, only to find myself crazed in a food binge two hours later, followed by the mental volley of loathsome, self-hating slams, "You swore the last time was the last time! You worthless piece of sh*%!" But, since I had learned to re-eat successfully, and a person needs food to survive but doesn't need alcohol, I thought people who had problems with drinking could simply stop or learn to re-drink and overcome those problems. I would later learn that, on one level, I was basically correct. But there's a big catch. Some people *might* be able to cut back on their drinking – but only as long as their drinking hasn't progressed to alcoholism. (You'll learn more about this concept later in this chapter). For many, many people, though, that option is not available and overcoming drinking problems is not a simple matter of "putting down the bottle."

The idea that simple willpower could prevent or reverse alcoholism is only one of the misconceptions that blinded me to the realities of the problems caused by my loved ones who drank too much. Over the years, my excuses and rationalizations morphed, absorbed, blurred, and merged until I had simply made the unacceptable acceptable – for decades!

With all of that muddled thinking, the first information that helped me begin to sort out my life was learning there are three kinds of drinking patterns: alcohol use (low-risk or what we might call "normal" drinking), alcohol abuse (an outcome of excessive drinking), and alcoholism (alcohol dependence). The following information about these patterns and terms is not meant to help you try to label your loved one in hopes he or she will "see the light." Rather, it is provided to better equip you in validating what you likely already know – your loved one really *does* drink too much and their drinking really *is* the cause of a lot of problems for you and for them.

But first…

Why So Many Terms?

You will hear a lot of different terms when it comes to people talking about a drinking problem. In everyday conversations, it's not uncommon for people to say things like "he's a drunk," or "she's such an alcoholic." In the medical, therapy, legal, education, and treatment worlds, as examples, you'll hear terms such as alcohol abuse, binge drinking, alcoholism, alcohol dependence, addiction, and alcohol use disorder, to name a few.

But there is a book used by psychiatrists and other clinicians to give them a common language for understanding, diagnosing, and talking about a range of mental health conditions – including conditions afflicting our loved ones who drink too much. It is called the *Diagnostic and Statistical Manual of Mental Disorders (DSM)*, and it is developed, updated, and published by the American Psychiatric Association (APA).

The terms "alcohol abuse" and "alcoholism" were two of the mental health conditions included in the fourth edition of the DSM, referred to as the DSM-IV, which wasn't updated until 2013. This is why those two terms are still the most commonly used today. But in May 2013, the APA released a new edition of this manual, called DSM-5. This revised edition put both alcohol abuse and alcoholism into one classification and called it "alcohol use disorder (AUD)." Then, the psychiatric professionals further divided the alcohol use disorder classification into three sub-classifications: mild, moderate, and severe.[2] You might think of it as the way health conditions like asthma or arthritis are classified as mild, moderate, or severe.

As far as the clinical and psychiatric community is concerned, what we commonly call "alcoholism" is technically classified as a "severe alcohol use disorder." And what we commonly call "alcohol abuse" is technically classified as a "mild or moderate alcohol use disorder." I'll explain more about these terms and the different classifications as you continue reading so don't worry about learning the definitions for new words or changing your vocabulary right now.

Besides clarifying terms for health professionals, the publication of the DSM-5 also helped fuel a movement within the treatment and recovery field to change the "label" given to people with a drinking problem. This movement is to no longer label people with alcohol use disorders as alcohol abusers or alcoholics. Instead, there's now a concerted effort to refer to them as people with a mild | moderate | or severe alcohol use disorder. These distinctions help make the point that individuals are not defined by their drinking pattern – so they are not alcoholics or alcohol abusers, for example. If you think about it for a moment, you'll see it's similar to the way we describe people who have cancer. They are people with cancer; they are not "cancerics." [Note: For many people in 12-step programs, self-identification as an alcoholic is important to their recovery, which of course is their choice.]

All of this may seem a bit confusing, I know. But I share it because I use the term alcohol use disorder often in this book. At the same time, I also continue using society's more commonly recognized terms, alcohol abuse and alcoholism. I do that for two reasons. The first is because those are the terms most people know and use. The second is to make it easier to explain and understand the differences between alcohol abuse (a mild or moderate alcohol use disorder) and alcoholism (a severe alcohol use disorder).

Note: As if this could get any more confusing, in addition to "alcohol use disorder," there is one more term you'll likely hear: substance use disorder. Substance use disorder is the umbrella term for any alcohol or drug use problem, with the same classifications of mild, moderate, or severe within the substance use disorder classification. When the "drug of choice" – as it's often referred to – is identified – as in the case of alcoholism, the drug of choice is alcohol – then the substance use disorder term is modified to and becomes "alcohol use disorder."

Why Understanding the Differences Between Alcohol Abuse and Alcoholism is So Important for Family Members

In my opinion, it is critical to understand the differences between alcohol abuse and alcoholism, because the way a person stops their *alcohol abuse* is very different than the way a person develops and treats their *alcoholism*. Yet, both cause drinking behaviors like those I described in Chapter 1, under "Meet My Loved Ones, 'Alex'" (and like those you've no doubt experienced in your own life). And, it is coping with those drinking behaviors that causes harm to family members and friends.

This harm is typically related to toxic stress – the kind of stress a family member or friend experiences when repeatedly coping with a loved one's drinking behaviors. Toxic stress can cause a number of physical and emotional health consequences, like anxiety, migraines, headaches, depression, sleep problems, stomach ailments, tension/muscle aches in one's neck/shoulder/back, vertigo, hair loss, and the like. (The impact of a loved one's drinking on the family member or friend's mental and physical health is more fully explained in Part 4, The Family Member's Experience.)

Additionally, a person with alcohol abuse may be able to learn to "re-drink" and thereby stop their drinking behaviors, whereas a person with alcoholism must *never* drink, period. The why and how of this is explained as you continue reading.

All of this is to say, it doesn't matter how much or how often a person drinks or whether they can be labeled an alcoholic or an alcohol abuser. What matters is the answer to this simple question, *"Do my loved one's behaviors change when they drink?"* What to do with your answer is also explained as you continue reading.

You should know that most people who exhibit drinking behaviors are alcohol abusers. They are not alcoholics.[3]

You're Not Alone – They're Not Alone

Sometimes it can feel like you're the only one with a loved one whose drinking is making your life and the lives of other family members miserable. So, it may help you to know you're not alone.

It is estimated that *one* person who has an alcohol use disorder affects at least *five* other people[4][5] (moms, dads, husbands, wives, children, brothers, sisters, grandparents, grandchildren, boyfriends, girlfriends….). Given almost 16 million Americans had an alcohol use disorder in 2016, according to the National Institute on Alcohol Abuse and Alcoholism (NIAAA)[6], that means nearly *80 million* Americans were affected by a loved one's drinking. That's more than one-fourth the American population!

Think about that…nearly 80 million Americans are affected by a loved one's drinking. Like me, that fact may make you want to scream,

"Then WHY isn't this talked about?" "Why isn't this diagnosed by our family doctors?" "How is it possible the general population has no idea there are millions of family members seriously harmed by a loved one's drinking?"

I understand the frustration. I felt it too, and it's one reason I've been committed to getting this information into the hands of as many people as possible. The main thing to remember, though, is that you are not alone! There is help and hope, as you'll see when you progress through this book.

Now back to explaining the first information that helped me begin to sort out my life. It included:

- learning there is actually a definition of "normal" drinking

- learning how the body processes alcohol and why this matters

- learning drinking is not only "normal" or "alcoholic."

What's Considered "Normal" Drinking?

Sometimes it is easier to get a sense of what is abnormal by understanding what is considered "normal." In the case of alcohol consumption, "normal" is the definition of "low-risk" drinking or alcohol use. This means the amount a person drinks is *not* likely to cause drinking behaviors or other alcohol-related problems. People in this category are sometimes called "social drinkers" or "casual drinkers." These types of drinkers, for example, may have a glass of wine at a meal but then stop for the evening.

Definition of "Low-Risk" Drinking Pattern – also referred to as "Normal" Drinking and Alcohol Use

The National Institute on Alcohol Abuse and Alcoholism (NIAAA) defines "low-risk" drinking[7] (aka "normal" drinking) as:

- no more than 4 standard drinks a day [daily limit] AND no more than 14 standard drinks a week [weekly limit] for men, and

- no more than 3 standard drinks a day [daily limit] AND no more than 7 standard drinks a week [weekly limit] for women.

What Is a "Standard" Drink?

Notice I kept referring to "standard drinks" above. A "standard drink" means there is the same amount of ethyl alcohol in one alcoholic beverage as there is in another – whether it's a cocktail, a glass of wine, can of beer, or other type of drink. (Note: in addition to the term "standard drink," you may also see the term "Alcohol by Volume" (ABV) – which is another way of describing how much ethyl alcohol there is in an alcoholic beverage or drink container.)

Why is knowing the amount of ethyl alcohol in a drink important?

Ethyl alcohol is a chemical. It is what makes a person feel good when they drink an alcoholic beverage because of how it works in areas of the brain responsible for a person's feelings of pleasure. It is also what makes a person exhibit drinking behaviors when they drink too much – due to the impact of ethyl alcohol on *other* areas of the brain responsible for motor control, memory, and reasoned thinking.

Each of the drinks shown in Image 2.1 below is considered <u>one</u> standard drink.[8] This means each beverage (drink) contains the same amount of ethyl alcohol as is contained in the drink pictured before it and the drink shown after it.

If You Loved Me, You'd Stop!

Image 2.1 "What Is a Standard Drink?" Source: National Institute on Alcohol Abuse and Alcoholism (NIAAA) – *Rethinking Drinking*

There are two other things related to standard drinks that are important to understand.

The first is that drinks served at bars, restaurants, or parties often contain *more* than one standard drink. For example:

- an IPA beer may contain 1 ½ – 2 standard drinks

- a margarita may contain 1 ½ – 2 standard drinks

- a martini may contain 1 ½ – 2 standard drinks

- a good, "stiff" scotch on the rocks may contain 2 – 3 standard drinks.

So, when someone enjoys the latest IPA beer on the market and says they "only had two beers," they actually may have consumed *three* beers worth of ethyl alcohol – not just two. Similarly, downing three margaritas at Happy Hour could really be the equivalent of having *five to six* standard drinks worth of ethyl alcohol.

The second important thing is to get a sense of the number of standard drinks in common drink containers. For example:

- a bottle of table wine contains 5 standard drinks

- a tall, 24-ounce, regular beer contains 2 standard drinks

- a fifth (750 ml) of 80-proof spirits (vodka, gin, scotch, bourbon, tequila) contains 17 standard drinks.

How This Information Relates to Your Loved One's Drinking

Think about your loved one's typical drink. Pour the amount of alcohol your loved one typically pours as "*a* drink" into a measuring cup. Then compare that measurement with the standard drink measurements just explained. That is how you'll know how much your loved one typically drinks as their version of "*a* drink."

Similarly, if your loved one finishes off a fifth of vodka in a week, you'll know they have had 17 standard drinks that week, which for a woman exceeds "low-risk" limits by 10 drinks! Or if a man drinks most of one bottle of table wine a night, you'll know he's drinking about 5 drinks a night or 35 drinks a week – more than *double* the 14 standard drinks per week considered "low risk" drinking for men.

I'm not suggesting you try this exercise in measuring how much alcohol your loved one consumes so you can double your efforts to police their drinking or use this information to win an argument or start a confrontation. Rather, I want to give you these basic facts to help cut through some of the fog and confusion that typically plagues those of us who love someone who drinks too much. Arming yourself with this information about standard drinks – and that which I share next on how the body processes alcohol – may help you accept there is absolutely no point in engaging with your loved one when they are drinking excessively. Nor should you take to heart the things they say or do while drinking. You are dealing with a brain that can no longer function normally no matter how much the person wants to or thinks they can.

How the Body Processes Alcohol and Why This Matters

This information is another piece to the puzzle that helps explain why a person's behaviors change when they drink.

Alcohol is not processed like other foods and liquids through the digestive system, which is, in part, why drinking too much can be a problem. Instead it passes through the stomach and enters the bloodstream through the walls of the small intestine. Because alcohol dissolves in water, the bloodstream carries it throughout the body, which is 60-70% water. As the alcohol flows through the bloodstream, it is absorbed into body tissues and organs that are high in water concentration and highly vascularized (meaning lots of blood vessels). One such organ is the brain.

Enzymes in the Liver

What happens next, once alcohol reaches the bloodstream? Enzymes produced only in the liver, called ADH and ALDH, break down (metabolize) the ethyl alcohol so it can leave the body. These liver enzymes can only metabolize a certain amount of ethyl alcohol per hour, which means ethyl alcohol leaves the bloodstream more slowly than it enters. This rate of metabolism explains why a person's Blood Alcohol Concentration (BAC) can continue to rise long after that individual has stopped drinking or passed out. Their liver is still processing the ethyl alcohol even though the person is not ingesting any more of it.

Contrary to popular belief, then, we cannot rid our bodies of the ethyl alcohol in the alcoholic beverages we drink by peeing, sweating, or vomiting. Similarly, drinking coffee or lots of water or eating a big meal or taking a walk around the block will not get rid of it. The only thing that can sober a person up is TIME.

As a *General* Rule

It takes the liver about **one hour** to metabolize (get rid of) the ethyl alcohol in **one standard drink**. So, after a person drinks *six* drinks, it will take their liver *six* hours to rid the body and clear the brain of ethyl alcohol chemicals – even if the drinks were consumed back-to-back in a short period of time.

While "waiting their turn" to be processed out of the liver, these ethyl alcohol chemicals interrupt the brain's normal cell-to-cell communication process (explained in Chapter 4). These changes, in turn, are what cause a person to engage in drinking behaviors, such as saying mean things, getting into a fist fight, or thinking that having unprotected sex is a good idea. Or why a person may "choose" to drink and drive because they "feel fine." And it's likely true. At the point they gather their keys and head out, they may be "fine." But as the ethyl alcohol backs up in the body, waiting its turn to be processed out of the liver, the blood alcohol concentration continues to rise, and these chemicals interrupt normal brain functioning. This interruption causes people to slur their words, ignore the speed limit, delay their braking reflexes, and find their vision is blurred.

Keeping in mind the general rule that it takes the liver about one hour to rid the body of the ethyl alcohol in one standard drink, you can judge how compromised your loved one is based on how much they've had to drink over what period of time.

You may also want to get an even better sense of your loved one's blood alcohol concentration level after one of their drinking sessions. This will help you gauge how long it will likely take their liver to rid their brain and body of ethyl alcohol, which is what allows their thoughts,

If You Loved Me, You'd Stop!

feelings, and behaviors to return to "normal." One way to do this is to go to the NIAAA Rethinking Drinking website, select *Calculators*, and then select *Blood Alcohol Concentration (BAC) Calculator*.

Variables That Can Change Things

Frustratingly, however, there's a wrinkle in the simplicity of all this that I need to explain. It is the personal, individual variables and the way in which those variables affect how a person's liver, brain, and body "handle" ethyl alcohol. People who weigh less, for example, have less body water as compared to someone who weighs more. Thus, drink for drink, a person who weighs less will have more alcohol concentration in their body water than someone who weighs more. People who have lower amounts of the liver enzymes that metabolize ethyl alcohol will take longer to metabolize the same amount as someone else. The stage of brain development also has an influence on how alcohol works in one person's brain as compared to another's. There are other variables, as well, such as taking medications, lack of sleep, stress, or the existence of a mental illness that can also influence how much is "too much" for one person as compared to another or for the same person from one drinking episode to the next.

Just an Explanation, NOT an Excuse for Drinking Behaviors

The information on how standard drinks are measured and how the body processes alcohol that's just been explained should not be considered an excuse for drinking behaviors. NOTHING excuses them. Rather, this information is meant to help you understand how and why they happen in the first place. It is also to help you understand how important it is to speak about the behaviors and not the person.

And that's because, generally, the drinking behaviors of your loved one do not represent the person they really are. Typically, drinking behaviors are the result of the excess ethyl alcohol waiting to be processed out of the liver and interrupting the brain's normal cell-to-cell communication process in the meantime. This is why blaming and shaming, for example, do not work. [Note: If your loved one behaves badly *without* alcohol, you may need to seek professional counseling or help beyond the scope of this book. Or, if *their drinking has progressed to alcoholism*, other factors are involved, which you will learn about as you continue reading.]

Beyond "Normal" Drinking: What is "Excessive Drinking," Alcohol Abuse, and Alcoholism?

So you've learned what's considered "normal" or "low-risk" drinking. But there are other kinds of drinking patterns you need to know about, and they will be explained in this section. First, we'll look at "excessive drinking," which can develop into the drinking pattern identified by the term "alcohol abuse." Then, you'll see introductory information about the drinking pattern described as alcoholism. You'll learn much more about the specifics of alcohol abuse and alcoholism in upcoming chapters.

Drinking Pattern Identified as "Excessive Drinking," Which Can Develop Into Alcohol Abuse

Alcohol abuse is an outcome of "excessive drinking."

But what defines "excessive drinking?"

According to the Centers for Disease Control and Prevention (CDC), **"excessive drinking"** includes binge drinking, heavy drinking, and any drinking by pregnant women or people younger than age 21,[9] as explained below:

- Binge drinking is the most common form of excessive drinking and is defined as 4 or more standard drinks during a single occasion for women and 5 or more for men.[10]

- Heavy drinking is another common form of excessive drinking and is defined as consuming 8 or more standard drinks a week for women and 15 or more for men.[11]

When you look back at the low-risk drinking limits you see that binge drinking exceeds the daily limit, and heavy drinking exceeds the weekly limits.

- Any drinking by pregnant women is considered a problem because of the fetal brain developmental processes occurring in utero (explained in Chapter 4).

- Drinking under age 21 is a problem because of key brain developmental processes occurring ages 12 through roughly 25 (also explained in Chapter 4).

Alcohol abuse develops when a person repeatedly engages in binge drinking and/or routinely engages in heavy drinking. It is critically important to understand, here, that just knowing these drinking limits does not fully explain alcohol abuse and why it can be such a huge problem for the drinker and the family member. I'll give you a general overview in the next chapter, but the more complete explanation is presented in Part 3.

Drinking Pattern Identified as Alcoholism

Unlike the other drinking patterns, there is no quantity of drinks to help explain alcoholism, which is especially frustrating to family members and friends. The reason for this is that alcoholism is now defined as a brain disease (also referred to as brain disorder). Yes, that's right – a brain disease. So, what are you supposed to do with this information?

At this stage, there isn't much you can do because there is so much more for you to understand before this definition can even remotely make sense. As with explaining alcohol abuse, I'll give you a general overview in the next chapter, but the more complete explanation is presented in Part 3.

All of This Was a Wake-up Call for Me...

When I learned about the concepts of standard drink sizes, "low-risk" limits, how the body processes alcohol, and the fact that drinking is not just "normal" or "alcoholic" – it was a huge wake-up call for me to look at my own drinking. I was clearly in the alcohol abuse stage.

Given I have several of the risk factors for developing alcoholism (risk factors explained in Chapter 6), I was grateful for the timing in my learning this information before I crossed the line. Very likely, my developing eating disorders and my recovery work to get over those were reasons I hadn't done so already (more on my recovery work is shared in later chapters).

Summarizing the Three Drinking Patterns: Alcohol Use, Alcohol Abuse, and Alcoholism

You've just read through a lot of terms (again), so let me summarize these three drinking patterns before I continue:

Alcohol Use = low-risk drinking; "normal" drinking; "social" drinking; "casual" drinking.
  – *NOT classified as an alcohol use disorder.*

Alcohol Abuse = an outcome of excessive drinking that includes repeated binge drinking and/or routine heavy drinking.
  – *Classified as a mild or moderate alcohol use disorder.*

Alcoholism = alcohol dependence; addiction to alcohol; a brain disease; a brain disorder.
  – *Classified as a severe alcohol use disorder.*

One of the things you'll learn is that a person develops alcoholism. This development occurs when a person's drinking progresses from alcohol use to alcohol abuse to alcoholism. Or said another way, it develops as a person's drinking *crosses the line* from alcohol use to alcohol abuse to alcoholism. This "line" is illustrated below:

Alcohol Use ➜ Alcohol Abuse ➜ Alcoholism

So where do you go from here? Likely you're wondering where is your loved one's drinking on this line? In other words, "How much is too much?"

Chapter 3
How Much is "Too" Much?

As someone who is investing your time in reading this book, you are no doubt hoping to find out – or at least get a sense of – whether your loved one's drinking pattern is *really* problem. And if it is, how bad is it?

Using one of the assessment tools now available can help you answer this question.

Assessing Your Loved One's Drinking Pattern

The reason it is useful for *you* to assess your loved one's alcohol use is to help you understand what you and they are up against. It is not so you can make your loved one stop drinking nor help them see the slippery slope they are headed down (although they may be open to the information and to making their own assessment).

Rather, assessing helps you better understand the differences between alcohol use, alcohol abuse, and alcoholism, as they relate to your loved one's drinking.

There are several alcohol use assessments. I am sharing the World Health Organization's (WHO) Alcohol Use Disorders Identification Test (AUDIT) below.[12] It was developed and evaluated over a period of two decades by the WHO's Department of Mental Health and Substance Dependence. It was created primarily for health care practitioners around the world as a simple method of screening for excessive drinking.

The AUDIT – Alcohol Use Disorders Identification Test

Instructions: Circle the answer that best applies to your perception of your loved one's drinking. In other words, the "you" is your loved one. And don't forget, the "size" of a drink matters – refer to Image 2.1 in the previous chapter.

1. How often do you have a drink containing alcohol?

   (0) Never
   (1) Monthly or less
   (2) 2 to 4 times a month
   (3) 2 to 3 times a week
   (4) 4 or more times a week

2. How many drinks containing alcohol do you have on a typical day when you are drinking?

   (0) 1 or 2
   (1) 3 or 4
   (2) 5 or 6
   (3) 7, 8, or 9
   (4) 10 or more

3. How often do you have six or more drinks on one occasion [note: this is known as binge drinking, and in the U.S., binge drinking is five or more drinks on one occasion for men and four or more drinks on one occasion for women]?

   (0) Never
   (1) Less than monthly
   (2) Monthly
   (3) Weekly
   (4) Daily or almost daily

4. How often during the last year have you found that you were not able to stop drinking once you had started?

(0) Never

(1) Less than monthly

(2) Monthly

(3) Weekly

(4) Daily or almost daily

5. How often during the last year have you failed to do what was normally expected from you because of drinking?

(0) Never

(1) Less than monthly

(2) Monthly

(3) Weekly

(4) Daily or almost daily

6. How often during the last year have you needed a first drink in the morning to get yourself going after a heavy drinking session?

(0) Never

(1) Less than monthly

(2) Monthly

(3) Weekly

(4) Daily or almost daily

7. How often during the last year have you had a feeling of guilt or remorse after drinking?

(0) Never

(1) Less than monthly

(2) Monthly

(3) Weekly

(4) Daily or almost daily

8. How often during the last year have you been unable to remember what happened the night before because you had been drinking?

(0) Never

(1) Less than monthly

(2) Monthly

(3) Weekly

(4) Daily or almost daily

9. Have you or someone else been injured as a result of your drinking?

(0) No

(2) Yes, but not in the last year

(4) Yes, during the last year

10. Has a relative or friend or a doctor or another health worker been concerned about your drinking or suggested you cut down?

(0) No

(2) Yes, but not in the last year

(4) Yes, during the last year

Scoring the AUDIT: Now, look at the numbers in the ( ) for each answer you've circled and total those numbers. According to the AUDIT evaluation, total scores between 8 and 19 indicate alcohol abuse. Remember, alcohol abuse is an outcome of excessive drinking and is classified as a mild or moderate alcohol use disorder. Total scores of 20 and above indicate alcohol dependence. This higher score points to a person having a severe alcohol use disorder, or, in other words, alcoholism.[13]

The AUDIT recommendations from the World Health Organization go on to say that in the absence of a trained professional conducting this questionnaire, these guidelines and scoring must be considered tentative – NOT definitive. (That recommendation is made because trained professionals know how to ask the AUDIT questions and interpret answers accurately or to dig more deeply for accurate answers.)

Additionally, the AUDIT notes that in an ["official"] evaluation, it matters on which questions points were scored. So, it is important to review the entire AUDIT document and <u>not to draw any firm conclusions</u>. As with explaining the definition of a "standard drink" and the way the body processes alcohol, my goal in offering you the AUDIT tool is to help you begin to get a fuller picture of what type of drinking pattern or disorder is affecting your loved one's behavior – and your life.

To find the AUDIT online, search for WHO | *AUDIT: The Alcohol Use Disorders Identification Test*. The questionnaire is on page 17, and the scoring and interpretation explanations are on pages 19 and 20.

Other Assessment Options

I mentioned there are several alcohol use disorder assessments. Here are two more – both were created by the National Institute on Alcohol Abuse and Alcoholism (NIAAA).

- An anonymous, online, two question screening assessment found at *NIAAA Rethinking Drinking What's Your Pattern?* There you will also find suggestions and tips for cutting down or changing a drinking pattern.

- The *Alcohol Use Disorder Assessment* found online at NIAAA > Alcohol & Your Health > Alcohol Use Disorder. This one is especially helpful with trying to figure out the difference between mild and moderate alcohol use disorder.[14]

Why Assess a Loved One's Drinking Pattern?

What good does it do to complete a questionnaire like the one presented in the previous section to assess a loved one's drinking? Here's the answer, according to research on the AUDIT evaluation process:

- *"...the bulk of harm associated with alcohol occurs among people who are not dependent* [meaning they have not developed alcoholism].

- *"...people who are not dependent on alcohol may stop or reduce their alcohol consumption with appropriate assistance and effort. Once dependence has developed, cessation of alcohol consumption is more difficult and often requires specialized treatment.*

- *"Although not all hazardous drinkers become dependent, no one develops alcohol dependence without having engaged for some time in hazardous alcohol use.* "[15]

With this information, it may now be helpful to understand more about the differences between alcohol abuse and alcoholism.

What Distinguishes Alcohol Abuse from Alcoholism?

I explained the different drinking patterns in Chapter 2 and told you I would give you more general information about the difference between alcohol abuse and alcoholism. To that end, I am sharing an adapted version of the American Psychiatric Association DSM-IV's criteria for alcohol abuse and alcoholism.[16] Granted the DSM-IV criteria is no longer used given the changes in the DSM-5, but it is enlightening, nonetheless.

DSM-IV's Diagnostic Criteria Alcohol Abuse
- Recurrent use of alcohol resulting in a failure to fulfill major role obligations at work, school, or home (e.g., repeated absences or poor work performance related to alcohol use;

alcohol-related absences, suspensions, or expulsions from school; neglect of children or household)

- Recurrent alcohol use in situations in which it is physically hazardous (e.g., driving a car or operating a machine when impaired by alcohol use)

- Recurrent alcohol-related legal problems (e.g., arrests for alcohol-related disorderly conduct or driving while impaired)

- Continued alcohol use despite having persistent or recurrent social or interpersonal problems caused or exacerbated by the effects of alcohol (e.g., arguments with spouse about consequences of intoxication).[17]

It is no wonder most of us confuse alcohol abuse (mild or moderate alcohol use disorder) with alcoholism (severe alcohol use disorder)!

DSM-IV's Diagnostic Criteria for Alcoholism

- Need for markedly increased amounts of alcohol to achieve intoxication or desired effect; or markedly diminished effect with continued use of the same amount of alcohol

- The characteristic withdrawal symptoms for alcoholism; or drinking (or using a closely related substance) to relieve or avoid withdrawal symptoms

- Drinking in larger amounts or over a longer period than intended

- Persistent desire or one or more unsuccessful efforts to cut down or control drinking

- Important social, occupational, or recreational activities given up or reduced because of drinking

If You Loved Me, You'd Stop!

- A great deal of time spent in activities necessary to obtain, to use, or to recover from the effects of drinking

- Continued drinking despite knowledge of having a persistent or recurrent physical or psychological problem that is likely to be caused or exacerbated by drinking.[18]

Who Defines Alcoholism as a Brain Disease?

Alcoholism is now defined as a brain disease by hundreds of reputable institutes, agencies, and organizations, including: the National Institute on Drug Abuse (NIDA), the National Institute on Alcohol Abuse and Alcoholism (NIAAA), the Substance Abuse and Mental Health Services Administration (SAMHSA), the U.S. Surgeon General's Office, the American Medical Association (AMA), the American Board of Addiction Medicine (ABAM), and the World Health Organization (WHO), to name a few.

I'm highlighting below what some of these institutes, agencies, and organizations have to say about alcoholism being a brain disease (and remember, alcoholism is also referred to as an addiction [an addiction to alcohol], alcohol dependence, and a brain disorder):

Well-supported scientific evidence shows that addiction to alcohol or other drugs is a chronic brain disease that has the potential for both relapse (recurrence) and recovery.[19] (FACING ADDICTION IN AMERICA: The Surgeon General's Report on Alcohol, Drugs, and Health, 2016.)

Addiction is a lot like other diseases, such as heart disease. Both disrupt the normal, healthy functioning of an organ in the body, both have serious harmful effects, and both are, in many cases, preventable and treatable.[20] (NIDA, Drugs, Brains, and Behaviors: The Science of Addiction, 2018.)

For much of the past century, scientists studying drugs and alcohol and drug and alcohol use labored in the shadows of powerful myths and misconceptions about the nature of addiction. When scientists began to study addictive behavior in the 1930s, people addicted to drugs and alcohol were thought to be morally flawed and lacking in willpower. Those views shaped society's responses to drug and alcohol use, treating addiction as a moral failing rather than a health problem, which led to an emphasis on punishment rather than prevention and treatment. Today, thanks to science, our views and our responses to addiction and the broader spectrum of substance use disorders have changed dramatically.[21] (NIDA, Drugs, Brains, and Behaviors: The Science of Addiction, 2018.)

What the Distinction Between Alcohol Abuse and Alcoholism Means When It Comes to Drinking

It's important to restate, here, that individuals who have a severe alcohol use disorder (alcoholism) cannot drink *any* amount – *ever* – if they want to successfully treat their disease. Alcoholism (and other drug addictions) can absolutely be treated, however. This means the disease of alcoholism (or other drug addictions) can be managed, thereby allowing a person to live a "normal," healthy, joy-filled life. It cannot be "cured" in the sense that a person can go back to drinking after a period of time.

In Chapters 5 and 6, I'll explain more about how a person develops alcoholism, and in Chapter 7 you'll learn more about what it takes for a person to treat their alcoholism.

The reason for understanding which type of alcohol use disorder a person has at this stage of reading this book is perhaps best explained by one of the police captains attending a conference at which I was speaking. You'll see his story in the box below.

"I Knew I Wasn't an Alcoholic"

"I heard Lisa speak at a National Police Activities League Conference and was blown away to learn that alcohol abuse is not the same as alcoholism. Because I knew I wasn't an alcoholic, I didn't really worry about my drinking even though it bothered me (and my wife) sometimes. But learning about alcohol abuse and that my drinking was causing secondhand drinking* for my family made me want to cut way back. It took me a while, and I had set backs. But now I have it under control. This has given me a whole new perspective on what's important to me and strengthened my relationships with my wife and kids."

—*Police Captain attending law enforcement conference*

* Secondhand Drinking refers to the negative impacts of a person's drinking behaviors on others and is explained in Chapter 8.

So Why Doesn't Everybody Know This Information?

If some of the best minds and leading researchers know about the information shared in these last two chapters and have concluded that alcoholism is a brain disease, then why doesn't everyone know this?

The primary reason is the gap between the time when scientists make discoveries and the time when those discoveries become a part of common knowledge. For the general public, policy makers, medical schools, insurance companies, media, employers, teachers, treatment providers, legal professions, criminal justice systems, and community leaders – even medical professionals – this research and these study findings are still "new." As such, much of this new research and its implications are not fully understood by doctors, media representatives, clinicians, therapists, social workers, law enforcement officials, insurance underwriters, and… (the list could go on and on) – let alone in our workplaces, homes, schools, and communities. But there is finally great movement to change this – thanks to these scientific discoveries and people talking about and incorporating them into their professional work and conversations with others.

At this stage, you may have a good sense of your loved one's drinking pattern. But your next burning question may be something along the lines of, "How did this happen? How did their drinking get so out of control?" To answer these questions is to explain how alcohol can hijack a loved one's brain. And to do that, I first need to share some key brain facts with you, which is what I'll cover next.

These facts about the brain are part of the explosion in 21st Century research that is shattering the stigma, misinformation, and shame that surrounds alcohol use disorders. By grounding yourself with these facts, it will be easier to grasp the information in Part 3, "How Alcohol 'Hijacks' the Brain & What Can Be Done to Stop It." As importantly, it will be easier to grasp why family members and friends of a loved one who drinks too much are so deeply, deeply affected. This is explained in Part 4, "The Family Member's Experience."

PART 2

The Human Brain

Key to Understanding a Loved One's Drinking and Its Impact on Family Members and Friends

Chapter 4
Basic Brain Facts

As I've mentioned, advances in imaging technologies now allow scientists and medical professionals to observe and study the live, conscious human brain like never before. The resulting findings – some in just the last 10-15 years – are revolutionizing our understanding of this three-pound organ. Think of it. Just three pounds, just a fraction of our total body weight, and yet it controls *everything* we think, feel, say, and do.

If our brain doesn't work, we can't feel pain or love or run or drive a car. If our brain doesn't work, our heart can't pump, our lungs can't breathe, and our limbs can't move. If our brain doesn't work, drinking alcohol and toxic stress would have no effect on our thoughts, feelings, and behaviors. So, it's knowing the basic facts about how our brains work that will help you understand:

- how drinking alcohol can hijack a loved one's brain and what can be done to return their brain to health (explained in Part 3)

- how the physical and emotional health and the very quality of a family member's life is so dramatically changed by repeatedly coping with a loved one's drinking behaviors and what can be done to reverse these impacts (explained in Part 4).

Personally, I found these basic brain facts life-changing because they answered so many of the questions I had. "Life-changing" is also the description given by so many of the people with whom I've worked when they learn of this research, as well.

Take It Slowly and "Take Away" What's Important

You are going to be seeing a lot of "science-y" information in this chapter, so try reading it as you would a novel – nothing to struggle with, just a worthwhile read to pick up and set down as time and interest allows. The brain is complex, and no one expects you to grasp all of this information at once. But knowing some basic facts about how the brain works will give you a much better understanding of how alcohol and toxic stress get in the way of it working properly. I've included "Take Away" paragraphs at the end of each section to give you a quick summary of what you'd just read.

The Brain's Communication System

To gain a general understanding of the brain, it helps to start with recognizing the brain's extraordinarily complex neuron-to-neuron communications system. This system involves an electro-chemical signaling process. That process is commonly referred to as neural networks, neural circuitry – or more simply, as brain wiring.

It is through this electro-chemical signaling process that neurons in the brain (typically called brain cells) "talk" to one another and to and from other neurons throughout the body via the nervous system. This "talking" is how the brain controls *everything* a person thinks, feels, says, and does. That control includes walking, reading, reacting to emotions, talking, and worrying about a loved one, as examples. It also includes how a person develops a drinking problem or experiences toxic stress consequences as a result of repeatedly coping with a loved one's drinking behaviors.

How Neurons Talk to One Another

You can see how neurons "talk" to each other through the electro-chemical signaling process by looking at Image 4.1. The terms discussed below will give you more details on this process. Remember, you do not have to absorb all of this information; you only need to grasp the overall picture, so here are the terms that will be useful for gaining this insight:

Neurons. These are specialized cells designed to receive, process, and transmit information (in the form of an electrical signal) to and from other neurons. There are three types of neurons: *sensory neurons*, which bring information *into* the brain; *interneurons*, which process information *within* the brain; and *motor neurons*, which carry information *out* of the brain to the body's muscles via the nervous system.[22] When discussing the brain, neurons are often referred to as "brain cells." Basically, then, neurons generate or receive *the electrical signaling portion* of the electro-chemical signaling process.

Branch-like extensions. These carry outgoing and incoming electrical signals from one neuron to the next.

Neurotransmitters. These are *the chemical part* of the electro-chemical signaling process, located at the end of outgoing branchlike extensions. These chemical messengers change the electrical signal into something that can "float" across the gap, called a synapse, between two branchlike extensions.

Synapse. The gap between outgoing and incoming branchlike extensions. There can be hundreds to thousands of synapses on any one neuron, and there can be trillions of synaptic connections occurring at any one time.[23]

If You Loved Me, You'd Stop!

Receptors. These are located at the end of incoming branchlike extensions. They accept the neurotransmitter – like a "key in a door lock" – and change it back into an electrical signal that travels up the branchlike extension to the receiving neuron. That neuron may send its own electrical signal and continue the process or end the message.

Without Neurotransmitters and Receptors, One Neuron Cannot "Talk" to Another

Recall the description I gave in Chapter 2 about how ethyl alcohol is processed in the body and how when it backs up, waiting its turn to be processed out of the liver, it changes brain functioning. That's because the excess ethyl alcohol chemicals in alcoholic beverages change or interrupt neurotransmitter/receptor connections throughout the brain. When these "normal" connections are interrupted, the "normal" messaging of those neural networks are also changed. This is why drinking too much alcohol can change a person's thoughts, feelings, and behaviors and result in drinking behaviors like those I described in Chapter 1.

Electro-Chemical Signaling Process (Neural Network)

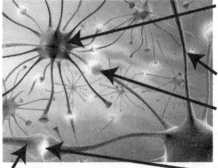

Neurons are the electrical signaling portion of the electro-chemical signaling process (neural network); when talking about the brain, they are also called "brain cells"

Branchlike Extensions carry the electrical signal to and from neurons

Neurotransmitters are the chemical portion of the electro-chemical signaling process; they are chemical messengers that "float" the neuron's message across the synapse

Receptors receive the neurotransmitters like a "key in a door lock;" change them back into an electrical signal that travels up the branchlike extension to the receiving neuron. That neuron may send its own electrical signal and continue the process or end the message.

Synapse is the gap (pathway) between outgoing and incoming branchlike extensions

©Lisa Frederiksen, BreakingTheCycles.com

Image 4.1 Illustration of the Electro-Chemical Signaling Process, also known as Neural Networks

Cues Start the Process – Sometimes as Fast as a Light Switch

Now that you've read the explanation of how neurons "talk" to each other, you may wonder what starts the "conversation." Those conversation starters in the brain are called "cues" or "triggers." These cues can be sound, sight, touch, smell, memories, emotions, or anything else that gets a neuron to start its electrical signaling.

The tricky thing about cues is they can trigger neural networks into action as fast as turning on a light switch. Think about that. If you flip the light switch on, before you can blink, the electrical current arrives at the light bulb, and the light is on. That is how fast some of our neural networks can activate. And therefore, that's how fast we can engage in a behavior without "thinking," like jumping out of the way of an oncoming car without taking time to ponder, "Oh my, that car is going to hit me. What shall I do?"

For someone with an alcohol use disorder, for example, a cue to start drinking, may be the sound of a beer can tab being popped open, the smell of a glass of wine, or the face of a timepiece showing it's 5:00 o'clock in the afternoon. For a family member coping with a loved one's drinking behaviors, a cue to start worrying or getting angry may be the sound their loved one's key makes when they're fumbling with trying to open the door, or the noise of their stumbling footsteps down the hallway, or the droop of their eyelids and the frequent licking of their lips when talking to you after stopping off with friends for drinks on the way home. All of this discussion about cues and triggers will make more sense when you understand brain wiring and mapping, and we'll get to that in the next section.

Thank Goodness for Synapses

Just think. If there were no synapses (gaps between branchlike extensions), then all of our neural networks would be stuck in the "on" position. We would be trying to sleep, sit, talk, run, read, do math, eat...ALL at once. Thus, the health of what happens at these synapses and along a neural network is critical to the brain's "motor control," "reacting," and "thinking," and thereby to the brain and body's overall health and functioning.

Too much or not enough of a neurotransmitter, not enough receptors, unhealthy neurons, or too much or not enough of some of the other key components to a successful neural transmission (which are too extensive to explain here) can drastically change how we think and feel and what we say and do.

Take Away: *The electro-chemical signaling process (neural networks) is (are) the first step in building a brain. If neurons can't or don't talk to one another in the brain, there is no way they can talk to and from others throughout the body.*

Location Matters: Regions of the Brain

Now that you know a little about how the brain "talks" through its neural networks, the next basic brain fact to understand is the concept of brain regions. Science has organized the brain into three general regions or "sub-brains" (see Image 4.2 below). These sub-brains are the Cerebellum, the Limbic System, and the Cerebral Cortex.

Each of these three sub-brains contains neural networks that are involved in a different part of the overall scope of human activity. And, they follow the human brain's evolution and development.

Note: Within each sub-brain, there are many, many parts or "sub-areas." In the Limbic System, for example, there is the amygdala, hippocampus, and hypothalamus, to name a few. In the Cerebral Cortex, there is the pre-frontal cortex, often referred to as the "executive center" of the brain. These sub-brains or "regions" are also referred to by various names. The Cerebellum, for example, is often called the Reptilian brain, and the Limbic System is also known as the Mammalian brain.

Where in the Brain the Neural Network Activity
Occurs Determies Thoughts, Feelings, Behaviors

The "3-Brain" Brain Complex

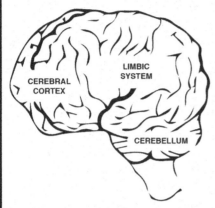

CEREBRAL CORTEX

LIMBIC SYSTEM

CEREBELLUM

Cerebral Cortex = higher level thinking
(referred to as the **"thinking"** part of the brain
because neural networks here control reasoning,
judgment, motivation, perception, decision-making)

Limbic System = survival-type functions
(referred to as the **"reactionary"** part of the brain
because neural networks here control fight-or-flight,
pleasure/reward, pain, and emotions)

Cerebellum = motor movements
(referred to as the **"motor movements"** part of the
brain because neural networks here control functions
like breathing, heartbeat, and motor skills)

There are many sub-areas within each area: Amygdala in the Limbic
System and Prefrontal Cortex in the Cerebral Cortex, as examples.

Image 4.2 – "3 Brain" Brain Complex – Regions of the Brain

I want to call your attention to the activity of the Limbic System in
particular. This is because it's the part of the brain that most concerns us
when it comes to alcohol use disorders and the toxic stress family
members typically experience when they repeatedly cope with a loved
one's drinking behaviors. This is because Limbic System neural
networks control our survival instincts and functions: pleasure/reward,
fight-or-flight, pain, and emotion.

Alcohol triggers the pleasure/reward neural networks. Coping with a
loved one's drinking behaviors triggers the fight-or-flight stress response

neural networks. As you continue reading, you'll learn more about the important role of the Limbic System. For now, however, the primary objective of Image 4.2 is to help you understand there are three general groupings of brain activity responsible for everything we think, feel, say, and do.

Take Away: The brain has three main regions or "sub-brains." They include the Cerebellum, responsible for "motor movements;" the Limbic System, which is the "reactionary" part of the brain; and the Cerebral Cortex, which is the "thinking" part of the brain. The neural networks in the Limbic System are of particular interest because they control survival instincts and bear the brunt of the impact of alcohol or toxic stress on our own or a loved one's thoughts, feelings, and behaviors.

Brain Wiring and Mapping for the Things We Do

When you look at Image 4.2, it becomes obvious that neural networks have to connect from one region of the brain to another and then to and from neurons throughout the body in order to make our lives possible. And this is where the concept known as brain wiring comes into play. Basically, brain wiring is the brain "hooking" together neurons/neural networks to make the things we think, feel, say, and do possible.

Picture Brain Wiring to be Like Plugging Strands of Holiday Lights Together

To give you a visual image of how this "hooking together" of neurons (this brain wiring) works, think of strands of holiday lights plugged into strands of holiday lights plugged into even more strands of holiday lights. People connect these strands to light the holiday scenes they set up in their front yards.

One series of strands may light the tree, another the Santa, another the reindeer, and several more illuminate the house trim and candy canes lining the walkway. Some are white, others red, and still others are multi-colored. When all are plugged in together, neighbors and visitors see an entire scene – not just *a* Santa, *a* reindeer, or *the* house trim. If the lights go out on the Santa or they go out on the tree or several of the candy canes lining the walkway, the holiday scene is dramatically changed.

Similarly, brain wiring connects a variety of neural networks to each other. Changes in one area of those connections can change the way the other connections work, which in turn changes the "original" thought, feeling, or behavior.

Brain Wiring

Some of our brain wiring is instinctual, hardwired, and built in to being human – meaning we don't consciously hook those neurons/neural networks together. These are the series of neural network connections that form systems between the brain and other organs in order to control our body's major functions. These are the systems we are born with. These include the fight-or-flight stress response system, for example, as well as the circulatory and digestive systems. They are what make our heart pump, our blood circulate, and our lungs breathe from the moment we are born. These systems control our instinctual drives to eat food when hungry, drink water when thirsty, sleep when tired, or fight or run when confronted with danger.

The majority of our neural networks, however, connect by repetitive activation. Meaning, we repeat the thought, feeling, activity, or behavior over and over, again, until the brain connects the series of neural networks so they engage without thought. This is the concept of "pushing new synapses" – connecting one neuron to another and another and another.

The process of learning to ride a bike is one example of the repetitive activation of a series of "strands" of neural networks. Riding a bike requires engaging the neural networks responsible for seeing, balancing, peddling, and listening for cars, as well as recognizing and knowing the meaning of road signs and rules, braking, and responding with reflexes to swerve out of the way of a dangerous object. The whole process of hooking together the neural networks – the brain wiring – needed to ride a bike takes some serious time. Think training wheels and a lot of skinned knees.

When practiced over and over, however, these neural networks eventually work together on autopilot, and the child, teen, or adult is now "riding a bike." Other examples of the repetitive activation of neural networks (brain wiring) include those involved with learning to walk, becoming a great athlete, speaking a new language, or typing on a computer.

Neuroscientist Carla Shatz summarizes this wiring process as: "Neurons that fire together wire together."[24]

Brain Mapping

Dr. Carla Shatz goes on to say that this "firing together, wiring together" process – whether it's instinctual or repetitively activated – causes the brain to form embedded "brain maps"[25] for the things we think, feel, say, and do regularly. These embedded brain maps, then, become our habits, our go-to-behaviors; they're how we move through our days.

And thank goodness we have brain maps. If we didn't, we would still be trying to get out of bed. The complex series of neural network connections needed to do that simple function would take forever to hook together if we had to first think of and then perform each next step in the connection series.

If You Loved Me, You'd Stop!

So, over the course of our lives, we create brain maps for walking, brushing our teeth, driving a car, swimming, operating equipment, handling stress, expressing our opinions and feelings (or not), playing an instrument, texting – just think about it! This also explains why a person who has learned to ride a bike can give it up for a while, but when they hop on that bike years later, their bike riding brain maps kick in. They may be a bit wobbly at first, but it's not long before they are again riding a bike. It was "mapped."

Another example is learning to read. It is a *years long* process to become an adult reader. But those adult-reading neural networks are so embedded that it's impossible not to instantly read when a piece of paper with words is put in front of you.

This same analogy is true for a person who has a severe alcohol use disorder (alcoholism). They can stop drinking for years, but if they start again, it's not long before they activate all their alcoholism-related brain maps, and they are back in it, again. Why this happens is more fully explained in Part 3.

Take Away: The phrase "brain wiring" refers to the brain's ability to "hook" together the neurons/neural networks that make the things we think, feel, say, and do possible. You can think of this wiring as being similar to strands of holiday lights all plugged together – where what happens to one strand affects all the others. "Brain mapping" is when sequences of brain wiring are repetitively activated, allowing us to form "brain maps" for the things we think, feel, say, and do regularly. Some of our brain wiring and brain mapping is already in place (hardwired) at birth to allow for survival-type functions, like breathing. But most are by repetitive activation, like those involved with riding a bike or reading. These same brain maps can also become distorted by the misuse of alcohol or toxic stress, explained in later chapters.

Brain Development: One of the Most Profound Influences on How Our Brains Wire and Map

Brain development – the growth of the brain from the time we are in utero until we mature – is one of the lesser-known factors that has a dramatic influence on how our brains wire and map.

I'm going to take a little time to explain brain development in this section, which is somewhat longer than others in this chapter. It has so many basic brain facts that will be useful for you – not only in regard to a loved one's drinking but also to many aspects of your own life.

The first thing is to look at Image 4.3 below. It is a 10-year time-lapse study showing scans of the brain taken at various stages of development from ages 5 through 20. Above the line are side views. Below the line are top-down views. The bluish, purple colors (darker colors when viewed in black and white) represent brain maturity (brain development).

I have added the approximate ages to the original images to give you an idea of how much change occurs. It is now understood the brain continues important developmental changes through age 22 on average for girls/women and 24 for boys/men. [Note: in general terms (not distinguished by gender) human brain development is referred to as occurring in utero through age 25.] I explain these developmental changes below Image 4.3.

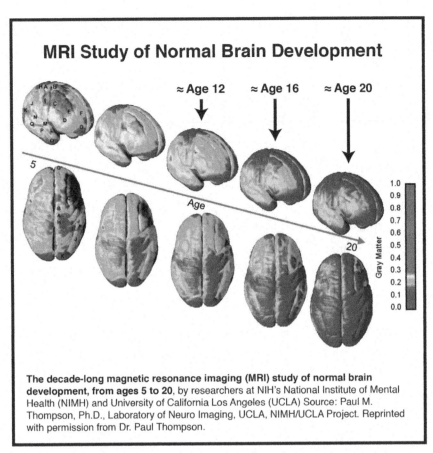

MRI Study of Normal Brain Development

≈ Age 12   ≈ Age 16   ≈ Age 20

The decade-long magnetic resonance imaging (MRI) study of normal brain development, from ages 5 to 20, by researchers at NIH's National Institute of Mental Health (NIMH) and University of California Los Angeles (UCLA) Source: Paul M. Thompson, Ph.D., Laboratory of Neuro Imaging, UCLA, NIMH/UCLA Project. Reprinted with permission from Dr. Paul Thompson.

Image 4.3 MRI Study of Normal Brain Development, ages 5 to 20. Courtesy Paul M. Thompson, Ph.D

The First Decade or So

We are born with approximately 100 billion brain cells (neurons), which is about the number of brain cells we have as adults. If the majority of our neural networks were wired at birth, we would come out doing what we do as adults. But about all a newborn baby's neural networks do is allow it to breathe, eat, sleep, cry, smile, and dirty the diapers – those instinctual, hardwired systems I explained previously. And by the way, the fact that a newborn arrives with these capabilities means there is brain development during pregnancy, as well.

About Drinking During Pregnancy

The fact a newborn comes out with the basic survival capabilities for breathing, eating, sleeping, etc., means there is brain development during pregnancy. This is why the Centers for Disease Control and medical professionals advise pregnant women not to drink during pregnancy. The alcohol in the mother's bloodstream passes directly to her fetus through the placenta. Because the growing fetus does not have a fully developed liver or other organs, it's unable to metabolize the ethyl alcohol, which is what makes a mother's drinking during pregnancy harmful to her baby.[26]

So, from birth to about age three, our neurons wire at an explosive rate, guided primarily by our responses to touch, sound, sight, smell, and taste. After all, we aren't reading at age two, so we cannot learn from a book or instructions on a computer. This means long before our conscious memories are formed, our brains are wiring in response to what is happening around and to us, as well as to our genetic (hereditary) traits.

Then from about age four until puberty, our neural networks continue to wire and rewire. Think of this in terms of our newfound abilities to engage in sports, do math, learn languages, or play music. In this first decade of life, a child's brain forms trillions of neural networks because everything a child thinks, feels, says, and does requires them.

This is why factors such childhood trauma (verbal, physical or emotional abuse, neglect, coping with a parent's drinking behaviors, being bullied), genetics (heredity), and social environment (home, school, friends, neighborhoods) have such a significant influence on the development of a child's brain and the brain maps that are forming at this time. These factors continue to have a profound influence on brain wiring and mapping through our early 20s. They are also key risk factors for developing alcoholism, by the way (also explained in Part 3).

And, then… just at the time when science used to think the work of brain development was "done" – hardwired – it turns out the brain goes through three more developmental processes beginning around age 12 with the onset of puberty and continuing through a person's early twenties (often through age 25!).

Pushing New Synapses

The idea behind brain development or changing an existing brain map is the concept of "pushing new synapses." When a child/teen/adult learns something new, they "push new synapses," meaning they connect the series of neural networks needed to perform this new function. If the new function is to replace an old one (like a bad habit) or create a new one altogether, the repetitively activated new series of neural networks becomes the embedded brain map.

Creating a new brain map by "pushing new synapses" is how a person changes a drinking pattern, including healing their brain of alcoholism. It is also how a family member changes the way they cope with a loved one's drinking behaviors. They push new synapses. Suggestions for how to do this are explained in later chapters.

Brain Changes with the Onset of Puberty Around Age 12

Puberty is an instinctual wiring process. We don't decide if or when to do it. And it is a wiring process that was critical to the survival of the human species back in the days of early humans. You have to remember that early humans had a very simple life – no cars, computers, jobs, schools, houses, books, or machinery. And they had a very short lifespan of about 25 years.

So, about the only neural networks they needed at the time were those in the Cerebellum and Limbic System. There was not a lot of

Cerebral Cortex wiring because the "needs" (the cues/triggers) to push those kinds of synapses weren't part of life for early humans. Early humans did, however, need the wiring that occurs with the onset of puberty, especially that which occurs in the Limbic System (the reactionary – not thinking – part of the brain). That's because the "purpose" of puberty is to cause brain changes that motivate humans to turn to their peers and take risks. It is also to take care of the obvious – causing humans to develop adult-like bodies capable of reproducing – and the not so obvious – to experience hormonal changes to "make" the brain/body want to have sex so that it did have sex and reproduce.

These three instinctual drives (take risks, turn to peers, and reproduce) were critical to the survival of the human species in earlier times when humankind had that simpler, shorter lifespan of about 25 years. That shorter lifespan meant parents were likely dead, unable to protect a child from around age 12 on; hence the importance of puberty to the survival of our species.

The problem for tweens and teens in modern times, however, is these brain wiring changes still occur with the onset of puberty, but the part of the brain needed to make "adult-like" decisions is not wired. That kind of wiring doesn't really get underway until around age 16.

Understanding the point of puberty was a real eye-opener for me when it came to understanding the dramatic shifts in interests and temperament I saw in my daughters as they moved from elementary school to middle school. It explained the sudden interest in body image, boys, and peer groups, and their seeming indifference to my wisdom and guidance. And what happens in the next phase of brain development explained even more reasons for this shift.

The "Thinking" Part of the Brain

There is about a four-year lag time between the start of puberty at around age 12 (on average) and the next stages of brain development that generally start around age 16 (on average). These next stages can take until age 22 on average for girls/women and 24 on average for boys/men. They include:

- continued wiring in the cerebral cortex, the "thinking" part of the brain, especially that which occurs in the prefrontal cortex, the "executive center" of the brain

- the "pruning and strengthening" process.

It is this continued wiring in the Cerebral Cortex, especially the prefrontal cortex, that allows a young person to engage in sound reasoning, good judgment, complex planning, and appropriate impulse control, as well as weighing the consequences of their actions, and learning from their mistakes.[27] This continued wiring also serves as the brakes on the risk-taking behaviors that started with puberty.

And it is the "pruning and strengthening" process that allows the brain to organize itself more efficiently. Because, let's face it, everything that child has been thinking, feeling, saying, doing repeatedly has been wiring as brain maps. To sort through and make the brain more efficient, then, the brain "strengthens" those being frequently used – the ones being repetitively activated. It does this by wrapping them in a fatty tissue called myelin to make the neural connections more efficient. The purpose of this myelin wrapping is similar to the idea of an insulated cable wire being a better conductor than a non-insulated one.

Those maps that are not being repeatedly activated get "pruned." It's not that they "die" necessarily. Rather, the brain misses some important neural network wiring, mapping, and strengthening opportunities.

Without the Experience / Memory, There Is No "There" There

Until a tween/teen's brain experiences something and has a memory of the outcome, that tween/teen has a difficult time believing or appreciating someone, like their parent, telling them how it's going to be if they don't do x, y, or z. I know I would give long-winded lectures to my daughters on the importance of doing something or ignoring the mean girls or not being hurt when a boy didn't ask them out because it "wouldn't matter in five years." I did not know then that until a child has had an experience and stored the outcome into long term memory in order to know or appreciate what you say is true, it's like talking to the wall. No wonder my girls would give me a blank look that expressed something like, "You have no idea!" And, frankly, no wonder I did the same to my parents. At age 14, that's as far as my daughters' (and my own) experiences/memories had mapped. We had no point of reference to understand (let alone believe) it wouldn't matter in five years.

Image 4.4 below was created by the National Institute on Drug Abuse (NIDA)[28] and is similar to Image 4.3, but it includes class pictures. These class pictures drive home these concepts. Notice, especially, how long it takes the prefrontal cortex (circled in red in the last scan) to develop. And as I've said, this prefrontal cortex is the "executive center" of the brain. It is the neural networks in this part of the brain that "powers the ability to think, plan, solve problems, make decisions, and exert self-control over impulses. This is also the last part of the brain to mature, making teens most vulnerable (NIDA)."[29]

The brain continues to develop into adulthood and undergoes dramatic changes during adolescence.

One of the brain areas still maturing during adolescence is the prefrontal cortex—the part of the brain that enables us to assess situations, make sound decisions, and keep our emotions and desires under control. The fact that this critical part of an adolescent's brain is still a work in progress puts them at increased risk for poor decisions (such as trying drugs or continuing abuse). Thus, introducing drugs while the brain is still developing may have profound and long-lasting consequences.

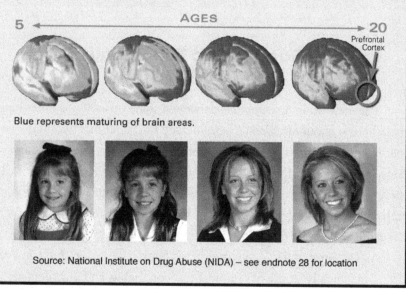

Blue represents maturing of brain areas.

Source: National Institute on Drug Abuse (NIDA) – see endnote 28 for location

Image 4.4 – Brain Changes Ages 5-20 With Class Pictures. Source: National Institute on Drug Abuse (NIDA) – see endnote 28 for location

Take Away: This lag time between the start of puberty and the completion of the Cerebral Cortex wiring and mapping (especially that which occurs in the prefrontal cortex) helps explain why tweens/teens make poor "decisions." When we think about it, there is no way we

would give our 12-year-old the keys to the car (class picture 2nd from left) and tell them to go practice driving, especially on the freeway and during commute hours, so they're good and ready when they take their driver's test at 16 (class picture 3rd from left). Well, the same is true of so many other adult-like decisions we expect from teens but which they are unable to fully execute without benefit of these final brain developmental stages.

This lag time also helps explain why "Just Say, 'No'" campaigns to deter destructive tween/teen behavior typically don't work and why early use (drinking before 21) is a key risk factor for developing alcoholism or other drug addictions as explained in Chapter 6.

The Good News: The Brain is Far From Hardwired

This new brain research has debunked some of society's other long-held beliefs about the brain. These include the belief that our brains were hardwired by around puberty and that from then on, it was in a long, slow process of decline; or that heavy drinking (or other drug use) "killed" brain cells; or that you only used a very small percentage of your brain's capacity. Debunking these kinds of long-held beliefs is the result of research around the concept known as "neuroplasticity."

As Dr. Norman Doidge writes in his book, *The Brain That Changes Itself*, "Ironically, some of our most stubborn habits and disorders are products of our [brain's] plasticity. Once a particular plastic change occurs in the brain and becomes well established, it can prevent other changes from occurring. It is by understanding both the positive and negative effects of [the brain's] plasticity that we can truly understand the extent of human possibilities."[30] In other words, our brains have an incredible capacity to repair, to heal, to rewire, and thereby we have the incredible capacity to change our thoughts, feelings, and behaviors. This includes those involved with an alcohol use disorder or coping with a loved one's drinking behaviors.

Neuroplasticity – Good and Bad

It is the brain's ability to wire and map that explains how a person *develops* an alcohol use disorder or toxic stress consequences when repeatedly coping with a loved one's drinking behaviors. At the same time, it is also the brain's ability to wire and map that gives a person the power to wire new brain maps to *stop* an alcohol use disorder or change how they cope with drinking behaviors.

Look at my mom and me. I was almost 50 years old when I started my brain rewiring recovery from almost four decades of coping with various loved one's drinking. My mom was 79 when she started her brain rewiring recovery from 45 years of alcohol use disorders. Thank goodness it's never too late to start!

Understanding the basic brain facts I've shared in this chapter lays the groundwork for understanding what happens when alcohol hijacks the brain. It also lays the groundwork for understanding what happens to family members and friends. And it is these understandings that can give you a road map for changing *your* life for the better, whether you continue your relationship with your loved one, end it, or redefine it.

If You Loved Me, You'd Stop!

PART 3

How Alcohol "Hijacks" the Brain & What Can Be Done to Stop It

Chapter 5
How Alcohol "Hijacks" the Brain

All of the fights, all of the arguments, and all of the times I screamed at or quietly pleaded with my loved ones to stop or cut down on their drinking might have been avoided if I had known this simple fact: when alcohol abuse becomes alcoholism, people drink because they *have* to drink. It is not a question of willpower, as many assume, because as the new brain research shows, alcoholism is a brain disease.

So how does someone's drinking move from use to abuse to alcoholism? In other words, "How does alcohol hijack the brain?"

Many factors contribute, not the least of which is ignorance about the risks of excessive drinking, as well as the concept of drinking limits – that is, what's considered "normal" or "low-risk" drinking and what's considered "a" drink, as explained in Chapters 2 and 3. Additionally, for the most part, society still views drinking as either normal or alcoholic and still considers alcoholism as somehow a "choice." So, family members and the drinker continue to rationalize excessive drinking as normal, for fear that not to is to admit their loved one is an alcoholic – as if abusing alcohol weren't problem enough! For all of these reasons, I found the information contained in this chapter and the next one especially helpful when I was starting to sort out my life after decades of dealing with loved ones who drank too much.

Where the Hijacking Begins

To explain how drinking alcohol can hijack a person's brain, I must first highlight two important brain facts shared in the last chapter:

1. Neural networks are the way the brain's neurons (brain cells) "talk" to one another. Our brains use these neural networks

to direct our bodies to do everything from blinking and coughing to breathing and eating. To function, the neural networks require an electrical component and a chemical component. The neuron (brain cell) is the electrical component, and the neurotransmitters and receptors are the chemical component. This "talking," then, is referred to as an electro-chemical signaling process (see Image 4.1).

2. The brain is made up of three general regions: Cerebral Cortex, Limbic System, and Cerebellum. The brain pays particular attention to neural networks located in the Limbic System because they control our most basic survival instincts and functions (see Image 4.2). And as you may recall from Chapter 4, pleasure/reward is one of those basic survival instincts and functions (along with pain, emotions, and the fight-or-flight stress response). It is the pleasure/reward neural networks that play a key role in how alcohol can hijack a person's brain.

One point I hadn't shared in the last chapter is these pleasure/reward neural networks rely on a neurotransmitter called *dopamine*.

These neural networks depend on dopamine neurotransmitters and dopamine receptors to perform the "chemical" function of the electro-chemical signaling process. In other words, without dopamine a person cannot feel pleasure/reward.

But, "Why is pleasure/reward critical to survival?" you may be asking.

Pleasure/reward is a survival instinct because its purpose is to give humans a pleasurable feeling as the reward for engaging in a particular behavior. This pleasurable feeling makes them want to repeat the behavior so they can get that pleasurable feeling – the reward – again.

In the days of early humans, experiencing a pleasurable feeling for eating food is what drove the species to eat again. Experiencing a pleasurable feeling for having sex is what drove the species to have sex again. Both were important outcomes for the survival of the human species, and they are still. Essentially, then, without the pleasure/reward neural networks, no one would be here!

In our modern, complex lives, our pleasure/reward neural networks go beyond basic survival-of-the-species types of instincts and functions that drove early humans. These networks now give us a pleasurable feeling as the reward for so many, many, many of our thoughts, feelings, and behaviors – all thanks to dopamine. Feeling love, laughing during a funny movie, enjoying a good meal, cheering wildly for a favorite sports team, feeling contentment while watching a sunset, dancing with abandon, getting an exhilarating rush skiing down a mountain, or any of the other things we may do that give us pleasure all require dopamine to make the pleasure/reward neural networks possible.

Bottom line: no dopamine, no pleasure.

To be clear, however, it's not only the pleasure/reward neural networks that depend on dopamine. Other neural networks in other areas of the brain also rely on dopamine neurotransmitters and receptors to perform the "chemical" portion of the electro-chemical signaling process. These other neural networks include those controlling memory, learning processes, and movement, as examples. In other words, these would be neural networks located in the Cerebellum and Cerebral Cortex regions of the brain.

Thanks to Dopamine, Drinking Alcohol Feels Good

Drinking alcohol works on these dopamine-reliant, pleasure/reward neural networks. The ethyl alcohol chemicals in the alcoholic beverage trigger a surge in dopamine neurotransmitter levels. *It is this surge in dopamine that gives a person the pleasurable feeling as the reward for drinking alcohol* – a feeling they may wish to repeat, causing them to want to drink alcohol again.

Let's face it, if drinking alcohol didn't make us feel good, it's unlikely we'd repeat the behavior and keep drinking it. It'd be about as "pleasurable" as drinking a glass of water, which of course, slays thirst (important to survival), but "feels good?" – not so much.

So, let's look, again, at the three consecutive stages of drinking – "the line" – introduced in Chapter 2:

Alcohol Use ➔ Alcohol Abuse ➔ Alcoholism

Alcohol Use = low-risk drinking; "normal" drinking; "social" drinking; "casual" drinking.
 – *NOT classified as an alcohol use disorder.*

Alcohol Abuse = an outcome of excessive drinking that includes repeated binge drinking and/or routine heavy drinking.
 – *Classified as a mild or moderate alcohol use disorder.*

Alcoholism = alcohol dependence; addiction to alcohol; a brain disease; a brain disorder.
 – *Classified as a severe alcohol use disorder.*

If a person stays within low-risk drinking limits, the dopamine surges caused by the ethyl alcohol in a standard drink are manageable by the liver's enzymes, and the person enjoys drinking without exhibiting drinking behaviors. There are always exceptions, of course, but for the most part, a low-risk drinker typically does not engage in the same kinds of drinking behaviors common to excessive drinkers, alcohol abusers, or people with alcoholism. It's when alcohol consumption becomes excessive that the dopamine surges start throwing the whole system out of whack.

It's Not Just Alcohol – Other Substances Affect Dopamine Levels Too

Alcohol is not the only substance that affects dopamine-reliant neural networks in the Limbic System. All drugs of addiction – opioids (which include drugs like prescription pain medications, heroin, and fentanyl), marijuana, meth, and cocaine, as examples – initially target the dopamine-reliant pleasure/reward neural networks in the Limbic System. This is why a person experiences a pleasurable feeling as the reward for using these other kinds of drugs, as well.

Dopamine Is Not the Only Neurotransmitter Affected

Dopamine is but one of the neurotransmitters in the brain affected by excessive alcohol consumption. Others include serotonin, norepinephrine, glutamate, and GABA.

Glutamate, for example, is an *excitatory* neurotransmitter (increases brain activity and energy levels), and GABA (gamma-aminobutyric acid) is an *inhibitory* neurotransmitter. GABA is the brain's "natural dampening circuit" and acts as a "chemical check on excitatory messages." It is what chemically "tells" the brain that enough is enough, satisfaction complete.[31]

When a person drinks more alcohol than their liver can metabolize, the ethyl alcohol suppresses the release of glutamate (slowing down neural network transmissions) and increases GABA production (also slowing down neural network transmissions), which together account for the depressant effects of drinking too much alcohol.

These are just some of the examples of how alcohol changes the way the brain works, and thus changes a person's thoughts, feelings, and behaviors.

If You Loved Me, You'd Stop!

And Then There Are the Cues, Triggers, and Possible Brain Maps

As explained in the last chapter, neural networks need more than just chemical messengers. They need cues, triggers – the "something" that activates the neuron to send it's electrical signal in the first place. As I've just explained, it's the electrical signal *plus* the chemical messengers that create the complete electro-chemical signaling process. From this process, the brain wires and then creates brain maps of repeatedly activated neural networks. (Recall the examples of learning to ride a bike or read – and the expression, "Neurons that fire together, wire together" to form embedded "brain maps.")

In the case of drinking alcohol, cues, often referred to as triggers, can be sound, sight, touch, smell, or emotions. They can be the alcohol ad on the billboard a person sees every day on their way home from work, angst over the confrontation they had with their boss, or the confidence they gained after having a couple drinks before meeting new friends for dinner.

For the person who is losing (or has lost) their ability to control their drinking, cues eventually can be just about anything. They can be celebrating a good day, letting go of a bad day, enjoying a child's first birthday at a family gathering, trying to forget a deep, deep hurt, hearing a song, or noticing the time of day. Cues can be the awfulnes of the boss, the rambunctiousness of the children, or the simple act of surviving another two-hour, traffic-jammed commute home after work.

When a person repeatedly finds cues to drink – and then drinks on "cue" – their brain is on its way to creating brain maps and memories of drinking alcohol as the "answer" to their cues. This process can also be the point at which they start their denial that drinking alcohol is the actual problem. Instead, they start their inner dialogue of excuses – such as their drinking behaviors were *really* the result of something other than too much alcohol. Or, "I'll cut back how much I drink after we've wrapped up this trial."

Crossing the Line From Alcohol Use to Alcohol Abuse

When a person's drinking moves up the line from alcohol use to alcohol abuse, the excessive drinking causes the brain to experience rapid, prolonged surges of dopamine in the synapses. What's the problem, you may wonder? Who wouldn't want prolonged feelings of pleasure? Let me lay out the steps in this process so you can better understand how these dopamine surges negatively affect the brain of your loved one:

1. If the excessive drinking pattern is regularly repeated, the brain – being the wonder that it is – automatically reduces the amount of dopamine it would normally produce in order to offset the overload.

2. This reduction causes dopamine receptors to be less sensitive.

3. Consequently, all of this leaves the brain wanting *more* alcohol in order to get that "feel good" feeling, again – the feeling it has mapped as the repeatedly experienced reward for drinking.

4. However, the "feel good" feeling becomes harder and harder to get because the brain has reduced its normal dopamine production, That, in turn, has caused its dopamine receptors to be less sensitive.

Remember: no dopamine, no pleasure.

These dopamine-reliant pleasure/reward neural network interruptions then ripple along to other neural networks, impacting other brain activities [recall the comparison to the strands of holiday lights in Chapter 4]. Not only do ethyl alcohol chemicals interrupt dopamine-reliant neural networks, but the neural networks responsible for other activities are also suffering their own difficulties. This is due to ethyl alcohol's independent impact on these other neurotransmitter/receptor connections, as well.

If You Loved Me, You'd Stop!

Not understanding the "mechanics" of what is happening leaves the brain of the alcohol abuser thinking *it's the lack* of alcohol that's responsible for the missing pleasurable feelings. In reality, it is the repeated alcohol abuse that's causing the repeated drop in dopamine production, that's causing dopamine receptors to be less sensitive – and *that's* causing the depleted feelings of pleasure when drinking alcohol. So the brain 'says,' "Give me more alcohol, then!" Talk about a Catch-22!

When loved ones get caught in the vicious cycle of drinking more to try to re-capture the "feel good" feelings that alcohol first gave them, it can lead them to cross the line from alcohol use to alcohol abuse and – potentially – to alcoholism.

Alcohol's Effect on the Brain – Seeing is Believing

In the previous section, you learned how the ongoing assault of ethyl alcohol affects the neural networks that rely on normal dopamine production. You also read about ethyl alcohol's independent impact on other neurotransmitter/receptor connections of neural networks that control other brain functions. With that information as background, you can begin to see why repeated alcohol abuse causes chemical and structural changes throughout the brain as you see in Image 5.1 below. Collectively, these changes alter the way the brain works, especially with regards to pleasure, problem solving, judgment, decision-making, learning, movement coordination, and memory.[32]

What Alcohol Does to the Brain

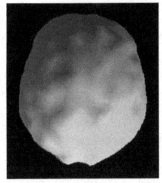

Surface SPECT of a
healthy brain

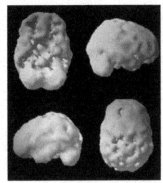

Surface SPECT Scan of a
56 year old brain with daily
use—3-4 drinks/day—but
NOT an alcoholic

SPECT Surface Scans Courtesy Amen Clinics, Inc., www.amenclinics.com

Image 5.1 – What Alcohol Does to the Brain.
Courtesy Amen Clinics, Inc.

What You Are Seeing in Image 5.1

As you may recall from Chapter 1, SPECT stands for single-photon emission computed tomography and is one of the imaging technologies commonly used today. It measures blood flow and brain metabolism. This ability of SPECT technology to give us images of the brains of live, functioning people is one of the great breakthroughs resulting in the explosion of brain research during the past couple of decades. It's also what has enabled scientists and medical professionals to make huge strides in understanding the effects of alcohol and other drugs on the brain.

Now let's take a closer look at the scans in Image 5.1.

What appear to be holes in the brain images on the right (in the four-scan series) are *not* lost brain matter. Rather they are areas of low blood flow; low brain metabolism. [And for comparison, the top-down view of

If You Loved Me, You'd Stop!

a healthy brain on the left is the same view as the bottom right image in the four-scan series on the right.]

Blood flow is critical to brain functioning and health – so that is why it is important to note the areas of low blood flow in the SPECT image. It is through the blood the brain gets the two things it needs to survive: *oxygen* and *glucose*.

Briefly, here are two points to remember about oxygen and glucose:

- When a person's brain is deprived of oxygen for several minutes, it can be damaged and even die, but the body can be kept alive by machines. That is how important oxygen is to the brain.

- Glucose is the brain and body's energy source. Glucose, which comes from the foods we eat, is to the brain what gasoline is to the car. The brain uses approximately 20% of the body's total glucose (energy) intake to do all of its work to control our thoughts, feelings, and behaviors. If a person eats nutrient-rich foods, then the brain also gets the nutrients it needs to function optimally, like vitamins, minerals, proteins, and amino acids. If a person eats less nutritious food (too much candy, pastries, etc.), the brain/body gets glucose (energy), but it doesn't get important nutrients for optimal functioning. As you'll read in Chapter 7, eating nutrient-rich foods is one of the brain healers a person treating their alcohol use disorder can use.

Note: It's important to understand that SPECT scans are not diagnostic in and of themselves. Medical professionals can't just scan a brain and conclude, "That's alcoholism." These scans are only one component of a complete clinical (medical) evaluation.

Seeing these visual images of changes in brain metabolism caused by alcohol abuse and/or alcoholism can help family members and friends realize their loved one's drinking behaviors were not those of the "real" person (unless that's how they behave without alcohol; or, once their drinking has progressed to alcoholism, that "real" person can only re-emerge after treatment due to reasons explained in the next chapter). That's certainly what I'd always assumed. And it was this belief that caused me so much confusion, hurt, frustration, anger, and endless hours of crazy-making arguments during and after one of Alex's heavy drinking bouts.

Rather, a person's drinking behaviors are the result of neural networks being changed by the overload of ethyl alcohol chemicals and any resulting brain wiring and maping changes, which will be described in the next chapter. (Remember – it's only through metabolism processes occuring in the liver that these chemicals can leave the body).

Bottom line: "Ethyl alcohol interferes with the way neurons send, receive, and process [electrical] signals via neurotransmitters."[33]

You've now seen clear pictures of how alcohol affects blood flow and metabolism in the brain, which in turn affects your loved one's thoughts, feelings, and behaviors.

Now it's time for the next question that's likely on your mind: "Why do some people become alcoholics and others do not, and what makes it a brain disease?" Those are the questions I'll answer in the next chapter.

Chapter 6
Crossing the Line from Alcohol Abuse to Alcoholism

When I started looking for answers in 2003, my burning question was, "How in the world can you call alcoholism a disease, let alone one that's like other diseases?" And, as you may recall from Chapter 1, I would push back when staff at Alex's treatment center claimed it was, saying things like, "Seriously! People with lung cancer or heart disease don't steal money from me or endanger my children by driving with them in the car while they're under the influence. All they have to do is put down the bottle!"

Since those early days, I've learned so much more about this issue thanks to all of the developments in brain research – much of which wasn't known to the extent it is today until the discoveries in the past 10-15 years. This scientific research disproved the widely-held belief that alcoholism was not a disease.

But what – exactly – makes alcoholism a brain disease? To answer that, I start with the basic definition of disease.

Disease, by its simplest definition, is something that changes cells in a negative way.

If you negatively change cells in a body organ, you change the health and functioning of that organ. For example, cancer cells in the lungs change the health and functioning of the lungs. Alcoholism changes cells in the brain, thereby changing the health and functioning of the brain.

In the Key Findings segment of his 2016 "Report on Alcohol, Drugs, and Health," the Surgeon General defined alcoholism (and other drug addictions) as "a chronic brain disease that has potential for recurrence and recovery."[34]

Other researchers in this field have included additional descriptions to the definition of alcoholism to explain it is also:

- developmental, in that a person is not born with alcoholism

- chronic, in that it has a prolonged duration

- not transmissible from one person to the next

- has a genetic influence, and

- has the potential for death or relapse unless treated and managed properly.[35] Note: the term "relapse" here means the person starts drinking again.

Granted alcoholism differs from other diseases, like cancer or heart disease. That's because these other diseases do not usually cause the *kinds* of behavioral changes that occur with alcoholism because they are not brain diseases (with the exception of brain cancer or things like traumatic brain injury, of course). But it's the symptoms of alcoholism vs. the symptoms of other diseases, like lung cancer, that make it especially difficult for people to accept the fact that alcoholism is a disease. Consider these comparisons. The symptoms of lung cancer include shortness of breath, persistent cough, hoarseness, a cough that produces blood, and unexplained weight loss. The symptoms of alcholism include continuing to drink even though it hurts the people one loves the most; relapsing after rehab; lying, cheating, stealing; and blaming, shaming, and denying/hiding the drinking, to name a few.

Therefore, it is normal and usually easy to feel sympathy for someone with lung cancer. It's not so normal or easy to feel sympathetic towards someone with alcoholism because the symptoms of that disease are so awful.

Three Reasons Why Some Alcohol Abusers Become Alcoholics and Others Do Not

Despite the fact that brain science now explains why alcoholism is classified as a disease, some may still wonder why one person who abuses alcohol develops alcoholism and others drinking the same amount do not. And notice I wrote, "develops alcoholism." People are not born with alcoholism, and it's not just drinking too much that causes it. Rather, a person develops the brain disease of alcoholism based on three key reasons:

- Brain wiring and mapping – electro-chemical signaling processes, "embedded maps," and influences on a child or adult's brain wiring and mapping.

- Characteristics of this disease – cravings, loss of control, physical dependence, and tolerance.

- Risk factors for developing this disease – genetics, early use, social environment, childhood trauma, and mental illness.

For the rest of this chapter, we'll take a closer look at each of these reasons because they are crucial to your understanding of alcoholism as a brain disease.

Brain Wiring and Mapping as Factors in Developing Alcoholism

Chapter 4 gave an in-depth explanation of brain wiring and mapping. Brain *wiring* is basically the process of "hooking" together neurons/neural networks to make the things we think, feel, say, and do possible in the first place. Brain *mapping* is the result of neurons "firing together, wiring together," to form "brain maps" for the things we think, feel, say, and do on a regular basis. These "brain maps" become our habits, our go-to-behaviors; they're how we move through our days.

And, as also mentioned in Chapter 4, deeply influencing brain wiring and mapping are key developmental processes occurring in the brain from the time a person is in utero through their mid-20s. Equally influential are the "inputs" / "influences" a brain receives along the way, such as nuturing, healthy foods, medical care, early use of alcohol, and childhood trauma.

As you read in the last chapter, consuming alcohol can lead a person to develop brain maps that get activated by certain cues/triggers (reasons) for drinking. So, when trying to understand why some people cross the line from alcohol abuse to alcoholism, the brain mapping and wiring of the individual must be taken into account.

For instance, once my mom's drinking crossed the line to alcoholism after years of alcohol abuse, she would still try to manage how much she drank. Sometimes she'd stop drinking all together. When she felt she had it under control, she'd convince herself that, *now,* she could drink just one or two and then stop. What she (and I) didn't understand is that drinking any amount kick-started her alcoholism-related brain maps and her drinking soon escalated to the quantities she'd been drinking before her latest attempt to control how much she drank. This is the same idea of what happens to a person who can climb back on their bike after years of not riding and soon find themselves riding their bike they same way they'd done back in the day.

Now let's move on to the second reason some people become alcholics: characteristics of the disease.

Characteristics of the Disease of Alcoholism

All diseases have characteristics. These are the "things" – symptoms and signs – that are common to a particular disease. For example, shortness of breath, persistent cough, hoarseness, a cough that produces blood, and unexplained weight loss are the characteristics – the symptoms and signs – of lung cancer. In the case of alcoholism, when a person's drinking crosses the invisible line from alcohol abuse to alcoholism, there is "an adaptation, that tells the brain alcohol is indispensable for survival."[36] This adaptation can be identified by the presence of one or more of the following characteristics of this brain disease: cravings, tolerance, physical dependence, and loss of control.[37] Here is more detail on each one of these:

Cravings. Cravings refers to the strong, overpowering need and urge to drink caused by the repetitive "hammering" on the dopamine-reliant pleasure/reward neural networks in the Limbic System. And remember – the brain considers neural networks repeatedly activated in the Limbic System as critical to survival. Alcoholism cravings can be three to *five times stronger than the [instinctual] cravings our brains evolved in the first place to be rewarded by, like food or water or sex,"* says Dr. Paula Riggs[38] in the HBO documentary, "Addiction."

These cravings explain why an alcoholic will lie, steal, cheat, sneak, intimidate a loved one – do anything to get and drink alcohol. Knowing this can perhaps help you understand that your loved one meant it when he or she tearfully told you with heartfelt sincerity for the umpteenth time, "I'm so sorry. I love you so much. I promise I'll stop. I promise."

Now you can better understand the reason your loved one couldn't keep their promise was: 1) the compromised dopamine-reliant pleasure/reward neural networks, among others, and the alcoholism-related brain maps that "told" them alcohol was "indispensable for survival," *and* 2) the changes in other areas of the brain critical for judgment, decision making, learning, memory and behavior control that, combined with #1, overrode your loved one's self control.

Loss of Control. In the case of alcoholism, "loss of control" means the inability of a person to predictably control and/or stop their drinking once they've begun. Loss of control is further defined by the persistent desires – but unsuccessful efforts – to cut down on drinking, as well as the crazed obsession with trying to obtain, use, hide, and/or recover from the effects of drinking.

Alcoholics – along with their family and friends – can be tricked into believing they can control how much and when they drink because they do not understand how their neural networks have been hijacked by ethyl alcohol chemicals, nor how deeply embedded their "all-things alcohol" brain maps have become. Recognizing and accepting this loss of control is what it means to be "powerless over alcohol." They are powerless over the functioning of their brain when alcohol (ethyl alcohol chemicals) is/are in it.

Physical Dependence. It is not just the brain, other body organs and tissues can also be affected. Recall the explanation in Chapter 2 of how alcohol "sits" in the body's tissues and organs that are high in water content and highly vascularized while it waits to be metabolized by the liver? If an alcoholic stops drinking, they may experience withdrawal symptoms, such as nausea, sweating, shakiness, and anxiety because other body organs and tissues "need" it, too. They may try using another substance to relieve or avoid the withdrawal symptoms. Physical dependence is why some alcoholics need to go through a medically supervised detoxification/stabilization process, commonly known as detox.

Tolerance. When a person has a severe alcohol use disorder, they have so drastically changed their brain's neurotransmitter/receptor connections and must consume greater amounts of alcohol to get the same "feel good" feeling their brain has mapped as the source of that feeling. But this pleasure is something the brain is unable to experience because of the way alcohol has hijacked the brain. And it's not only these pleasure/reward neural networks; it's so many others, as well. This is why a loved one hides and sneaks drinks from bottles of alcohol hidden throughout the house, car, garage, and yard – even in their children's bedroom.

If You Loved Me, You'd Stop!

Among the characteristics just described, notice the word, "predictably," in the "Loss of Control" description. Yes, alcoholics may be able to stop for days, weeks, or even years, or to drink intermittently. And at times, they may seem to hold it to a reasonable amount, all of which gives the alcoholic and their family members and friends the illusion that the alcoholic has their drinking under their control.

That was certainly the case in my situation with Alex. He had stopped drinking for 11 years, six of those were spent participating in AA. Then he decided he could drink an occasional glass of wine, now and then. That made sense to me, after all, I'd learned to re-eat after 11 years of bulimia. It worked for Alex for a while, until it didn't.

As I mentioned earlier, my mom also stopped drinking for periods of time. Or else she would go on a "controlled drinking" program now and then. That was proof to me that she could control it, which of course fueled my anger and frustration when she didn't.

Understanding these characteristics (cravings, loss of control, physical dependence, and tolerance) – this illusion of control – helped me understand why I'd believed my loved ones' promises to stop or cut down, time and again, because it appeared as if they could. As importantly, it helped me understand that once their drinking had crossed the line from abuse to alcoholism and they drank *any* amount, there could be no control over how much, how often, or when they drank. And that's because the ethyl alcohol chemicals would kick-start all their alcoholism-related brain maps, causing them to relapse into their disease.

It's the Characteristics That Make the Difference Between Alcohol Abuse and Alcoholism

Both alcohol abuse and alcoholism cause chemical and structural changes in the brain, which is what makes a brain more vulnerable to the risk factors for developing alcoholism (explained next). The key word here is *vulnerable*. Just because a person abuses alcohol and has risk factors does not necessarily mean they will develop alcoholism.

The brain disease of alcoholism differs from the condition of alcohol abuse because of the four characteristics of this disease: cravings, loss of control, physical dependence, and tolerance.

Risk Factors for Developing Alcoholism

In addition to brain mapping/wiring and characteristics, certain risk factors also contribute to the development of alcoholism. The same way there are risk factors for other diseases – like smoking is a risk factor for developing lung cancer.

The chemical and structural changes explained in the previous chapter are what set up the brain to be more vulnerable to these common risk factors. That vulnerability, then, increases the likelihood of a person's drinking moving up the line. As with other chronic diseases, not all risk factors need be present in order for a person to develop alcoholism. The more risk factors, however, the more likely a person who abuses alcohol is to cross the line to alcoholism if they don't reduce their drinking to low-risk limits or stop drinking all together. These common risk factors include: genetics, mental illness, social enviornment, childhood trauma, and early use.[39] Here is the detail on these risk factors:

Genetics. Genetics is responsible for about half the risk for developing an alcohol use disorder.[40] It's not that there is a specific alcoholism gene – at least not one that has been identified, yet. Rather it's the concept of genetic differences that underpins this risk factor. Just as we inherit certain genetic differences from our parents that determine our eye color, hair color, skin color, and body type, for example, so too are there genetic differences that influence how our brain/body interacts with ethyl alcohol. These differences may include higher or lower levels of dopamine neurotransmitters or higher or lower levels of the enzymes in the liver that break down the ethyl alcohol, as examples. These genetic differences are passed along from one generation to the next. So, looking at your loved one's family history – mom, dad, grandparents, siblings, aunts/uncles – to see if they had/have alcoholism (or other drug addictions) is one way to determine whether genetics is a risk factor for your loved one.

Mental Illness (also called mental health disorder). Mental illnesses, such as depression, anxiety, bipolar, PTSD, ADHD, are also brain changers / brain differences. In other words, the way the brain cells of a person with a mental illness communicate with one another is different (for a variety of reasons) than the way the brain cells of someone without that illness communicate with one another. This is important to understand because "[t]hirty-seven percent of alcohol abusers and 53 percent of drug abusers also have at least one serious mental illness."[41]

Why is this important to know? Because the person may turn to alcohol (or other drugs) to self-medicate the symptoms of their mental disorder – like drinking to relieve anxiety, for example. Drinking alcohol may also worsen the symptoms of their existing mental illness. Either way, their brain creates brain maps that connect the use of alcohol with the symptoms they experience because of their mental disorder.

When a person has both a mental illness and alcoholism, that person has two brain diseases (disorders). This is known as having *co-occurring disorders*, and both must be treated at the same time, in order for the person to succeed in long-term recovery. [These co-occurring disorders are similar to a person who has both cancer and diabetes. Doctors would not stop treating the diabetes while they treat the cancer, nor would the same treatment work for both diseases.] If not treated at the same time, the absence of the alcohol will likely trigger the brain to drink because that's what the brain mapped as its soother for the symptoms of the mental disorder.

Not treating co-occurring disorders at the same time is one of the key reasons people relapse (that is, they go back to drinking after they've stopped for a period of time).

Early Use. It is crucial to recognize this risk factor because the adolescent brain is not the brain of an adult, as was explained in Chapter 4. For example, the adolescent brain interacts with ethyl alcohol in a different way than does the adult brain for a number of reasons. Additionally, the key brain developmental processes occurring from ages 12 through early 20s makes the tween/teen/young adult's brain especially vulnerable to mapping an alcohol use disorder (or another drug use disorder).

For example, as you read in the last chapter, telling adolescents in the 12-15 age range to "just say, 'No'" doesn't typically work. This is because the onset of puberty is "telling" the adolescent brain to "take risks" and "turn to your peers." If their peers are saying, "yes" to risks, drugs and/or alcohol, it's likely that the adolescent will, too. This action does not mean they are bad kids. It simply means their brain's instinctual wiring – the wiring that activates during puberty – is in charge.

Additionally, early use – early abuse – of alcohol wires in brain maps around the finding, seeking, using, hiding, covering up, and getting over the effects of drinking at an especially vulnerable time. This vulnerability is the result of the brain's pruning and strengthening processes. Not only that, but early abuse teaches a developing brain that drinking is the way to "cope" with a host of teen- and life-in-general triggers, a pattern that can become a destructive coping behavior going forward.

It is estimated that 90 percent of adults who developed severe alcohol or other drug use disorders (addiction) started using before age 18 and half started using before age 15.[42] And, contrary to popular belief, the Europeans do not have underage drinking (or other drug) abuse prevention under control, either.[43] Check out the *European School*

Survey Project on Alcohol and Other Drugs online to learn more about this fact.

Social Environment. The home, neighborhood, peer groups, and community within which a child grows and lives also influences early brain wiring. [Remember: it's a combination of "inputs," genetics, and brain developmental stages that wires and maps a brain. By the same token, that wired and mapped brain is interpreting everything that comes at it from that mapped brain's perspective.] If it is stable, nurturing, and without excessive drinking, for example, a child's brain has the opportunity to wire and map "normal" thoughts, feelings, and behaviors and model "low-risk" drinking when (or if) they decide to drink as an adults.

On the flip side, if a child/teen/young adult lives or works or goes to school in an environment where heavy drinking (or other drug use) is the norm, they will likely drink or use other drugs to that same level. Unfortunately, that same level may not work in their brains the way it works in the brains of their co-workers, family members, fellow students, or friends (and frankly it's likely not working all that well in those other brains, either).

And lastly, if an adult is living in a social environment with heavy drinking or one wrought with stress (like living with a loved one who has an alcohol use disorder), they, too, may turn to alcohol for relief or the "thing to do" when living in that environment. Not only this, but people who abuse alcohol are fully capable of developing alcoholism as adults in their 30s, 40s, 50s, and beyond, regardless of their social environment, because of having experienced other key risk factors. This was the case for my mom.

Childhood Trauma. Childhood trauma (which can have strong connections with social environment) refers to traumatic or stressful events happening to a child before age 18. As you read in Chapter 4, childhood trauma has a profound impact on how, or if, brain cells "talk" to one another. This impact is the result of what is now understood to be toxic stress. This is the type of stress that occurs when neural networks controlling the fight-or-flight stress response are repeatedly activated. These neural networks are also in the Limbic System.

The Center on the Developing Child at Harvard University explains that toxic stress *"can occur when a child experiences strong, frequent, and/or prolonged adversity – such as physical or emotional abuse, chronic neglect, caregiver substance abuse or mental illness, exposure to violence, and/or the accumulated burdens of family economic hardship – without adequate adult support."*[44]

Toxic stress can actually change the physical development and function of a child's brain (also referred to as brain architecture).[45] These brain changes affect how a child copes. In other words, how they express anger, fear, powerlessness; how they interpret and respond to other people's words and actions; how or if they trust; and how they learn, as examples. These brain changes, in turn, have a profound impact on whether that child's brain will seek drugs or alcohol for their brain-soothing qualities [chemicals working on the dopamine-reliant pleasure/reward neural networks, for example]. They will also impact how that child's brain will interact with the chemicals in alcohol or other drugs if they do drink or use because of the brain changes caused by the toxic stress. Toxic stress and its role in all of this is more fully explained in Part 4.

And about childhood trauma… Much of what we now understand about the role childhood trauma has on the developing brain; its influence as a key risk factor for developing alcoholism (or other drug addictions); and why treating childhood trauma is key to successfully treating alcoholism is the result of the CDC-Kaiser ACE Study. (ACE stands for Adverse Childhood Experiences.) This is such an important understanding that I have added a section on ACEs and the Childhood Trauma Connection below.

**Understanding Risk Factors Helps a Family Member
Recognize Where Their Loved One's Drinking Pattern Might
Be on the Line: Alcohol Use → Alcohol Abuse → Alcoholism**

We often get so caught up in how many drinks or how often a loved one drinks or the excuses for why a loved one got so drunk that we lose sight of the real problem – drinking behaviors.

If you think your loved one's drinking is a problem based on one of the assessments you did in Chapter 3 or the information you've read so far, ask yourself if your loved one has experienced any of these key risk factors: genetics, childhood trauma, early use, mental illness, and social environment. If you answer, "Yes," that can be a first step in recognizing the extent of your loved one's alcohol use disorder. The more risk factors, the more likely their drinking has crossed the line from alcohol abuse to alcoholism. To get an official diagnosis, it's important to seek the advice and medical evaluation of a professional trained in the science of addiction. Chapter 7 provides a great deal of important information about all of this. And of course, a person can always self-diagnose themselves as having alcoholism.

Adverse Childhood Experiences (ACEs) and the Childhood Trauma Connection

I have added this section on ACEs (Adverse Childhood Experiences) because much of what we now know about ACEs (also known as childhood trauma) has been advanced since I wrote the first edition of this book. ACEs refer to traumatic or stressful events that happen to a child before age 18. Hence the connection with childhood trauma, one of the key risk factors for developing alcoholism described above.

Background

The concept of ACEs and their physical and emotional health consequences came out of a study conducted in the late 1990s by Kaiser Permanente, San Diego and the Centers for Disease Control (CDC).[46] It was a huge study involving 17,000 Kaiser patients. The study participants were mostly white, mostly middle to upper-middle class, all had health insurance, and all had jobs.

Participants were asked to fill out a 10-question questionnaire. Then, their answers were compared to their medical histories. The results showed that experiencing adverse childhood experiences were linked to a variety of physical and emotional health problems across a lifetime.[47]

These health problems included: depression, substance abuse or addiction to alcohol or other drugs, obesity, diabetes, suicide attempts, heart disease, cancer, STDs, broken bones, smoking, and having a stroke. The more ACEs a person had, the more likely they were to have or develop one or more of these health problems.

10 Types of Adverse Childhood Experiences Measured in the ACE Study Questionnaire

Of the 10 questions asked:

Five were personal, meaning it was something done to the child. These five included:

1. physical abuse
2. verbal abuse
3. sexual abuse
4. physical neglect
5. emotional neglect.

Five were related to other family members' behaviors that affected the child. These five included:

1. a parent who abused alcohol or other drugs or was addicted to alcohol or other drugs

2. a mother (or step-mother) who was a victim of domestic violence

3. a family member in jail

4. a family member diagnosed with a mental illness

5. the disappearance of a parent through divorce, death, or abandonment.

The study found that almost two-thirds of the 17,000 participants had experienced at least one ACE. Of those with one ACE, 87% had two or more. The more ACEs the person experienced, the more likely they were to have developed an alcohol (or other drug) use disorder, marry someone with an alcohol (or other drug) use disorder, have depression,[48] or any of the other health problems listed above.

This was certainly true for my mom who had five ACEs (sexual abuse and the disappearance of a parent were two of her five). A person with five ACEs, for example, has an eight times greater chance of being an alcoholic, and a person with four or more ACEs has twice the risk of cancer.[49] My mom had breast cancer and developed alcoholism. Similarly, I had four ACEs and developed eating disorders (anorexia for a year and bulimia for 11); it could have just as easily been alcoholism given my risk factors. This same pattern was true of my other loved ones with alcohol use disorders. One had five, another four, a third six, and others had fewer or more.

Since that original CDC-Kaiser ACE Study, many other kinds of adverse childhood experiences have been identified. These other ACEs include poverty, racism, bullying, watching a sibling being abused, losing a caregiver (grandmother, step-mother, grandfather, etc.), homelessness, surviving and recovering from a severe accident, living in a war zone, witnessing a grandmother abusing a parent, involvement with the foster care system, and involvement with the juvenile justice system, as examples.

Resilience Trumps ACEs

Now, just because a child experiences ACEs does not mean that child will develop the toxic stress consequences I've described and will cover more fully in Chapter 9. Nor does it mean they won't live a great life. And that's thanks to resilience. Resilience refers to a child or an adult's ability to bounce back in spite of experiencing adversity, like ACEs. Basically, resilience is the result of what are called *protective factors*.[50] These protective factors can include having at least one stable, safe, nurturing relationship with a parent, teacher, grandparent, coach, youth leader, or similar adult in a child's life. It can be living in a supportive community or family or the biological and developmental characteristics a person is born with.

The interesting thing about people who experience ACEs is that many have high levels of resilience, which is how they survived, and even thrived, in spite of their ACEs. Not only this, but for *some*, the source of their resilience is also the person most responsible for some of their ACEs. I'm afraid the "why" of this is beyond the scope of this book, however.

Why Experiencing ACEs is So Harmful to One's Health

It took until roughly 2009 before the CDC-Kaiser ACE Study started getting the notoriety it deserved. Additionally, other research was being conducted following the study's release that identified what it is about experiencing ACEs that causes health problems across a lifetime. This research showed the connection is toxic stress, which is the subject of Chapter 9.

Why Am I Explaining So Much About ACEs/Childhood Trauma

There are five key reasons to know about ACEs:

1. ACEs/childhood trauma is/are a significant risk factor for developing a severe alcohol use disorder (or other substance use disorder).

2. 1 in 4 children lives in a family with a parent addicted to alcohol or other drugs.[51] Children growing up in a home with parental alcohol (or other drug) abuse or addiction are experiencing at least 1 ACE (namely, a parent who abuses or is addicted to alcohol or other drugs). As a result of coping with a parent's drinking or alcoholism-related behaviors, the child likely experiences several more ACEs, such as verbal abuse or emotional neglect.

3. ACEs related to a parent's alcohol and/or drug use disorder set up a child to have several of the key risk factors for developing an alcohol use disorder themselves (social environment and childhood trauma, for example, and of course, genetics).

4. Successfully treating alcoholism requires treating ACEs/childhood trauma because the brain created maps of alcohol (or other drugs) as the "answer" to their trauma-related triggers.

5. ACEs-related toxic stress consequences experienced as a child stay with that child as an adult unless mitigated or treated. If left untreated or mitigated, and the adult becomes a parent, they may find themselves unknowingly "parenting with ACEs." For more on this concept, please check out ACEs Connection – *Parenting With ACEs* online.

To learn more about ACEs and the 10-Question ACEs Questionnaire, I suggest you watch the five-minute video by KPJR Films, *ACEs Primer*.

You'll also want to visit *ACEs Science 101,* on the website, ACEs Too High, and check out *Got Your ACE, Resilience Scores?* on the website, ACEs Connection. To learn more about the toxic stress consequences of trauma/ACEs on children, I suggest you visit the *Center on the Developing Child at Harvard University* website and/or watch Dr. Nadine Burke Harris, California Surgeon General's, TED talk, *How Childhood Trauma Affects Health Across a Lifetime,* also found online.

You've now learned about brain wiring and mapping and the characteristics and risk factors that can cause a person to develop the disease of alcoholism – and I hope you have gained some insights about your own loved one's drinking. At this stage, you may also have a better understanding of why alcoholism is a brain disease. You may recall this chapter began with the discussion about mistaken notions surrounding this whole concept of alcoholism being a disease. Now, before we leave this chapter, I want to talk about two other misconceptions surrounding the topics of alcoholism and alcoholics: *choice* and *forgiveness.*

About the Idea of Choice

One of the more destructive myths about alcoholism is that it's a choice or worse, yet, a lack of willpower. It wasn't until my work in this field that I learned just how many, many, many alcoholics try mightily to exert their willpower over how much they drink. And time and again they fail to do so, adding new layers to their self-loathing and shame.

This belief about alcoholism being a choice, a lack of willpower, drives the alcoholic and their loved ones to continue making one Herculean attempt after another to battle the disease in isolation. And it drives the alcohol abuser and their loved ones to find ways to excuse the abuse for fear it might be labeled "alcoholism."

So let me explain the facts about choice.

Choice is involved with the first decision to drink, and it is involved in all the decisions to continue drinking up to and until the drinking crosses the line from alcohol abuse to alcoholism.

Once a person has this brain disease, they still have choice, but it is not about choosing how much or when to drink or deciding to hold off for a few months and then just having one or two a week. At that point, it is about choosing to do whatever it takes to *not* drink because if they drink, they kick-start all the brain mapping around their triggers, risk factors, and the characteristics of this disease.

Bottom line: a person with a severe alcohol use disorder is incapable of predictably controlling how much, when, or if they drink, and therefore their drinking and alcoholism-related behaviors, as long as they drink ANY amount.

If you are interested in learning more about the research explaining the science of the brain disease of addiction (whether it is to alcohol or other drugs), check out these resources that can be found online: *The Surgeon General's Report on Alcohol, Drugs, and Health (2016)*; the National Institute on Alcohol Abuse and Alcoholism (NIAAA)'s *Alcoholism Treatment Navigator*; the National Institute on Drug Abuse (NIDA)'s *Drugs, Brains, and Behaviors: the Science of Addiction*; and the American Society of Addiction Medicine (ASAM)'s *Definition of Addiction*.

Why Forgiveness Is Eventually Possible

One of the most life-changing outcomes of learning what I have explained in this chapter has been forgiveness – forgiveness of my mom, forgiveness of the Alexes in my life, and forgiveness of myself. Someone once suggested I look at forgiveness as letting go of wanting a different outcome. It's not about erasing or excusing or pretending all of the hurt was not soul crushing. Rather, it is about letting go of the idea that any of us could have done anything differently with what we knew about all of this at the time – which was a big fat zero!

Understanding this information also helped my mom forgive herself the way I'd already forgiven her. Finally, she knew in her heart of hearts that she wasn't a bad person or a bad mom or a mom who didn't love me enough to stop. Rather, she'd developed this disease over time as her drinking moved from use to abuse to alcoholism. She developed this disease, in large part, because she had three of the key risk factors: genetics, social environment, and childhood trauma (which consisted of five ACEs measured in the ACE Study). She developed this disease because the science and medical protocols needed to prevent, diagnose, and treat it had yet to be discovered. And it was these understandings that resulted in my mom telling me during one of our phone calls, "Lisa – *please – please* use my story – our story – to help others."

Gaining a better understanding of how alcohol hijacks the brain and how a person's drinking moves up the line from use to abuse to alcoholism is one thing. But beyond that, your next burning question is likely the one I had at this point: "Is there a cure? That's the question we'll explore in the next chapter.

Chapter 7
Is There a Cure?

Almost 16 million Americans struggle with alcohol use disorders. Yet, only 10% of those with alcoholism get the help they need.

Compare this with 15.5 million Americans who are living with all forms of cancer,[52] meaning they got the diagnosis and treatment they needed to survive. And that's because cancer is diagnosed and treated like the medical condition it is.

This disparity in the treatment of alcoholism vs. cancer is one of the biggest reasons I wrote this 10th Anniversary Edition. I wanted loved ones to know there have been dramatic changes in the diagnosing and treatment of alcoholism thanks to scientific research in the last 10-15 years.

Before I describe these research findings, it's important to understand the first step in treating alcoholism starts with a non-medical action step – namely stopping the denial.

Stopping the Denial

A person doesn't just wake up one day with alcoholism. It's a progressive, developmental disease and key to the progression of this disease is DENIAL.[53] Denial is a very human defense mechanism we all use at one time or another to protect ourselves from facing something we just don't want to face. It can be seen in the eyes of a guilty four-year old who denies breaking a vase for fear of being punished, or in the tears of a lover who doesn't want to admit the relationship is over, or in the dieter's pretending the size of a piece of birthday cake doesn't really matter.

But for the person whose drinking is moving from alcohol abuse to alcoholism, denial distorts reality, hurts other people, leads to years of destructive behaviors, breaks their family apart, or literally kills another person in a drunk driving accident. And yet the drinker still denies their *drinking* is a problem. Instead, they adopt an arsenal of offensive behaviors in order to protect their ability to drink – everything from flimsy excuses to devious lies, whether they "accidentally" hide a bottle in a gym bag or pretend it's an urgent matter to go out late at night because a "friend" needs help.

The old saying, "a good offense is a great defense," is an excellent description of what the alcoholic or alcohol abuser does in order to get their loved ones to join with them in the denial that makes their drinking somehow okay. That offense is built on enforcing the two most important "rules" in the alcoholic or alcohol abusing household:

Rule #1: Drinking is not the problem.

Rule #2: Do not talk to *anyone* (not family, not friends, and certainly not strangers) about the drinking or the behaviors related to the drinking. Above all, attack, minimize, or discredit any family member who does because drinking is not the problem. See Rule #1.

These two rules are keys to the "denial of reality,"[54] which allows the disease and/or the abuse to progress unchecked. As the alcoholic or alcohol abuser's denial-type thinking and drinking behaviors escalate, other, often arbitrary and unpredictable, rules are also adopted and/or changed in order to deal with any cracks in the family's denial.[55] For instance, the alcoholic or abusive drinker may demand the children be in bed by 7 p.m. one evening when they normally go to sleep at 9. Or else they may get everyone out of bed to clean up the kitchen when it's never mattered before.

Before we continue, I want to underscore the point I made in Chapter 2. I prefer the phrases: "person with a severe alcohol use disorder" or "person with a mild alcohol use disorder," or "person with an alcohol use disorder." But for simplicity's sake going forward, I will typically use the common terms: "alcoholic" when referring to a person with a "severe alcohol use disorder" and "alcohol abuser" when referring to a person with a mild or moderate alcohol use disorder.

A Good Defense is a Great Offense – Denial with a Capital "D"

The arsenal of offensive behaviors alcoholics and alcohol abusers use to defend their drinking[56] include, but are certainly not limited to, those listed below. As you read through this list, you may see some that are similar to those exhibited by your loved one. It helps to know that the cause of these behaviors is the brain wiring and mapping around alcohol's hijacking of their brain described in Chapters 5 and 6. It is not you, their job, your parents, their boss, your children, or another family member.

Anger. Alcoholics and alcohol abusers are often, but not always, filled with anger – anger with themselves for not being able to control their drinking and anger at others for their attempts to stop them. They use their anger in a variety of ways. It can be outright yelling or throwing things, it can be sarcasm or mean-spirited "joking," it can be a look or a tone of voice, or it can be cutting words said through clenched teeth and a forced smile.

Minimizing. Alcoholics and alcohol abusers are masters at downplaying or minimizing the significance of what they've done and expecting others to go along with their version of events, instead. Maybe you've heard one of these versions of minimizing: "It was no big deal; everyone was doing shots last night. Quit nagging me!" "I wasn't driving *that* fast. Why are you getting upset?" "So, I forgot to mail the rent check again. I'm only human. Can't a person make an honest mistake sometime?!?"

Rationalizing. This is when the alcoholic or alcohol abuser offers a credible but vague explanation for their drinking behavior, something like, "They served dinner so late. I hadn't eaten all day, and the alcohol just went to my head."

Judging. One way to make themselves feel better is to make others out to be less worthy than they are with comments such as, "Well, at least I come home every night, not like that guy your sister is married to." "I may have a few drinks now and then, but you can't even wash the dishes right!"

Blaming (not taking responsibility for their actions). Alcoholics and alcohol abusers often excuse their drinking or destructive behaviors as due to something or someone else – a bad boss, a no-good friend, an unsympathetic spouse, or a bad day at the office.

Lying, Deceiving, and Deflecting. Alcoholics lie, withhold, break promises, cover up, and deceive in order to protect their drinking. In time, the lying becomes second nature, and they can lie with absolute ease on so many fronts and act crushed when you don't believe or trust them. This lying and deceiving is typically subconscious, by the way. To their hijacked brain, alcohol is critical to their survival so whatever it needs to do to get it, it does. They also become very good at deflecting a direct answer to your question or accusation with some kind of attack of you. For example, you ask, "Did you stop at the bar on the way home?" and instead of "Yes" or "No," they answer, "What is this, 20 questions? And why are the kids still up?" It was this constant lying, deceiving, and deflecting – this slicing and dicing and mincing of words – that really fueled my anger and frustration.

Family Members and Friends Have Their Own Denial, As Well
Denial is what allows the family member or friend to excuse or rationalize or defend themselves against the drinking behaviors. For example: telling themselves things like, "everyone drinks too much now

and again;" "lots of people drink and drive – he just got caught"…Or striving to be all things to all people so their loved one won't drink…Or working hard to get good grades and stay out of trouble so their mom/dad won't have one more thing to deal with. Denial is what causes family members and friends to adopt stress reactions, traits, and coping behaviors in order to "survive" (explained in Part 4).

As I've said before, family members and friends often subconsciously engage in this denying to avoid labeling their loved one as someone with a drinking problem they cannot control or worse yet, of being an alcoholic. They often do this because they, too, accept society's belief that alcoholism is a moral weakness, a character flaw, a lack of willpower, a choice. But they also do this out of fear their loved one doesn't love them enough to stop. And they do this out of fear that to leave would put their children in more danger than if they stay.

In reading later chapters, family members and friends will better understand what they can do to stop their own denial.

For now, the key take away is that unless the person with alcoholism and their family members and friends break through their denial, the consequences of a loved one's drinking will continue to spiral, and together, they will "all fall down." It only gets worse. It cannot/will not get better until the denial ends.

There Is No Logic

One wife said, "It wasn't until he tried to strangle me in front of the kids that I left him. Yet the verbal and emotional abuse I took from him for years and the insane arguments we'd get into when he was drunk left me a wreck for days. But I would always try to make it okay in my mind, telling myself things like, 'This time it'll be different,' or 'I can't leave – who would protect my kids when they're with him?' For some reason, being physically attacked finally made it 'okay' to leave. Oh! And get a load of this. He said he'd be willing to take me back if I'd apologize for making him mad enough to attack me. And to think I used to try to make sense of that kind of logic!"

So, Is There a Cure?

I'm going to give two answers to the question of whether or not there is a cure:

- The answer is "Yes" for those who abuse alcohol.
- The answer is "No" for those with alcoholism.

Now, those are only short, simple answers, but as you may no doubt realize by now, the complex issues you and your loved one face require more than a simple "Yes" or "No" response. In this section and the rest of the chapter, I'll explain more about what you need to know in order to find the answers you are seeking for your loved one and for yourself.

For Alcohol Abuse

The "cure" for alcohol abuse is to stop drinking or to change one's drinking to fall within "low-risk" drinking limits. (As you know from reading earlier chapters, alcohol abuse is an outcome of excessive drinking that includes repeated binge drinking and/or routine heavy drinking, and it is classified as a mild/moderate alcohol use disorder. Refer to Chapter 2 for the details on "low-risk" drinking levels.) Another way alcohol abuse can be viewed as "cured" is for the drinker to register a score under 8 on the AUDIT, the World Health Organization's (WHO) Alcohol Use Disorders Identification Test (see Chapter 3).

It is very important this change in alcohol intake be done honestly. That means the, "I only had two drinks" version of changing one's alcohol abuse will not work when each drink was double or triple the size of a standard drink. Neither will the, "It was a bunch of us from the office – everyone got plastered." …Or the, "What's the big deal? I only drink a couple of six-packs on Fridays and Saturdays," versions.

Inviting your loved ones to read this book might help them appreciate the importance of getting their drinking under control, now. You may also invite them to visit NIAAA's *Rethinking Drinking* website to find suggestions for stopping or cutting down.

For Alcoholism

There is no cure for alcoholism in the sense that "cured" would mean a person could someday drink "normally." (Again, from earlier reading, you recognize that alcoholism is also referred to as alcohol dependence, addiction to alcohol, brain disease, brain disorder, and it is classified as a severe alcohol use disorder.) The good news, however, is that alcoholism can definitely be *treated*. That treatment can lead to complete remission for people with this disease. Remission means they never drink alcohol again and enjoy living their lives in recovery. The really good news is it's never too to start.

❖ *By the time I was 18 years old, I was drinking all the time and looking at doing prison time. I'd never gotten past eighth grade, doctors had labeled me with all sorts of illnesses that said I could never learn, and society had washed their hands of me. But I overcame and today I have a Ph.D. in clinical psychology and work at the largest trauma research center in the nation. I want other teenage girls to know that no matter what kind of a beginning they've had, they can have an amazing finish.*

What *You* Need to Know About Alcoholism Treatment and Recovery

As you've gathered, developing the disease of alcoholism is "personal" and so is treating it. There is no right- or one-size-fits-all way to treat alcoholism (or other drug addictions). However, there are common objectives:

- Stopping all alcohol use.

- Improving brain health.

- Getting help for underlying risk factors and alcoholism-related behaviors and one's cues/triggers to drink (in other words, rewiring, remapping their brain for healthier thoughts, feelings, and behaviors).

- Maintaining ongoing recovery.

Achieving these objectives will take a lot of time, of course. But the following points will help you understand what it generally takes for a loved one to successfully treat and recover from alcoholism. And remember – there is no one single or right way to do this.

They Don't Have to Hit Bottom

"Hit bottom" is an expression used to describe the point at which a person with alcoholism may have finally run out of money, friends, family, their home – or illusions of control – and at long last admit they have a problem controlling their drinking. This old notion that a person has to hit bottom before they can be helped is wrong, wrong, wrong. In fact, the earlier the progression of the disease is interrupted – treated – the better.

Think of it this way, if your loved one had ANY other socially "acceptable" disease, like cancer, you would be researching every treatment option you could find, leaving no stone unturned. And it's likely they would too. You would probably be talking and working together to identify and evaluate treatment options. And you would no doubt be talking to your close friends and family members, as well, and maybe even telling your boss why you're under stress. Heck, your friends and neighbors might be bringing you dinners, picking up your children after school while you and your loved one meet with treatment providers, and taking your children for a Saturday afternoon so you could take a nap and regroup. That's what they'd be doing if your loved one had cancer. Unfortunately, it's the nature of alcoholism and the secrecy and shame that surrounds it that makes it difficult to bring your loved one and others who can help into the discussion about diagnosis and treatment.

Having said all this, the decision to seek treatment is still your loved one's. You can't make them. At the same time, trying to blame or shame a person into treatment doesn't work either.

One of the best ways to help your loved one "raise their bottom," however, is to get help for yourself in order to take that all important first step, stopping the denial. You'll understand why and how as you continue reading this chapter and those that follow. Now, to continue, here are some other suggestions that can help you sort this out.

Be Solid in Your Understanding of the Disease

Only when you are grounded in the facts about this disease can you be certain there is no amount of alcohol they can drink. There are no deals to be made for drinking only on holidays or Friday nights. Any amount of drinking kick-starts the alcoholism-related brain maps. Again, only when you're grounded in these facts will you be strong enough to set boundaries and get the help *you* need (which is, as I've said, a topic that will be explained in later chapters).

Accept That You – and They – Are Powerless Over Alcohol

You may have heard the expression that someone is "powerless over alcohol." If you are a person who doesn't have a problem controlling how much you drink, this makes no sense. But if you think of it this way, it might make more sense: They are powerless over their *brain*; therefore, they are powerless over their *behaviors*, if they drink *any* amount of alcohol, period. And, if they are powerless over their brain if they drink, then you are certainly powerless over it too. Therefore, you are also powerless over their behaviors when they drink. I know this idea may be hard for you to accept right now, however you will save yourself a lot of struggle and grief if you try to accept the truth of it.

Focus on the Drinking Behaviors Not the Person

Instead of zeroing in on, "You're an alcoholic," stick with talking about their *behaviors* – how they act and what happens when they drink. As importantly, don't try to talk about their drinking behaviors when they are actively drinking because you are not talking to a brain that can "reason." Here are a couple suggestions for how to start the conversation when they are sober:

- I don't know if you're aware how much your behaviors change when you drink, but last night, for example _____. I've been doing some research as to why this happens and have found resources that explain so much. I'd really appreciate if you'd read _____ so we can talk about it. I'm not sure what to do next, but I do know your drinking behaviors are not going away if you continue to drink.

- I've been doing some searches online trying to figure out if I should say anything about how you behave when you drink too much and found this great website, NIAAA's Rethinking Drinking. I'd really like you to do their anonymous, online assessment and take a look at the other information on the site and then let's talk about it.

Pay Particular Attention to Trauma I ACEs (Adverse Childhood Experiences)

Time and again when I speak before audiences or talk one-on-one with individuals or engage in conversations with therapists and other medical professionals, I ask, "Have you heard of the CDC-Kaiser ACE

Study?" Time and time again, the answer I receive is "No." This lack of awareness continues to shock and sadden me because the ACE Study was conducted in the late 1990s. Yet, using this study's findings and treating a person's ACEs as part of their treatment plan can have a profound impact on their recovery success – because childhood trauma is one of the key risk factors for developing alcoholism. This is why I included that separate section on ACEs and the ACE Study in Chapter 6.

❖ *It was hearing Lisa's presentation on the neurobiology of addiction – especially the part about Adverse Childhood Experiences – that I practically jumped out of my seat screaming, "YES!" – that's me! It's a much longer story, but basically, I got the right kind of therapeutic help for my ACEs and that paved the way for me finally being able to succeed in doing the other things that also helped me succeed in my recovery.*

Know It Must Be Treated Like Any Other Chronic Disease

As previously explained, disease by its simplest definition is something that changes cells in a negative way. When cells change in a body organ, the health and functioning of that organ changes. In the case of lung cancer, for example, cancer cells in the lungs change the health and functioning of the lungs. Alcohol addiction – alcoholism – changes cells in the brain, which in turn changes the health and functioning of the brain.

But it *is* a disease, and like other chronic diseases, **it *is* treatable**. And like other chronic diseases, treatment requires the 3-stage disease management approach:[57]

- Stage 1: detox/stabilization

- Stage 2: acute care/rehab

- Stage 3: long-term continuing care.

Again, putting it in terms of other diseases, consider heart disease. If someone presents with a heart attack in the emergency room, Stage 1 – detox/stabilization – is implemented immediately – no questions. The intervention at this stage is all about getting the heart pumping and stabilizing all vital signs while the next course of action is determined. These next steps could be running tests, getting MRIs, etc., and of course taking a complete medical history.

When a course of care is decided, Stage 2 – acute care/rehab – begins. With this stage, the person may have surgery – a triple bypass, for example (acute care). This acute care is followed by rehab. In this case, rehab would be a stay in the hospital. During this rehab period, the patient's body accepts the surgical changes and the person gains knowledge and tools for living with what's happened and information about what they need to change in order to protect their heart health.

Stage 3 – long-term continuing care – is also fully expected and accepted when treating heart disease. This involves a long-term continuing care plan, which may include diet changes, medications, heart health improving exercises, stress-reducing practices, therapy to cope with what happened and how to get over the fear of it happening again. All of these would be offered in increments to coincide with the healing of the heart. AND, it would include regular follow-ups with the medical team to be sure all was going as planned. If it weren't, changes to care would be implemented. Most importantly, at no point along the way is the person who presented with a heart attack blamed or shamed if they have another heart attack!

Sadly, understanding the importance of Stage 3 for the success of alcoholism treatment and recovery is sorely missing.[58]

Note: The above example of the treatment for a chronic condition like heart disease is not to suggest there are specific timeframes for each stage, nor that every person needs to go through all three stages separately when treating alcoholism. In other words, when dealing with alcoholism, a 30-day residential treatment program might also provide detox, thereby addressing stages 1 and 2.

Know What Is Needed to Treat This Disease

As you just read, we must accept that this disease cannot be completely treated in 30 days any more than we would dream it is possible to completely treat cancer in 30 days. (Check out the American Cancer Society's treatment timeline for cancer for comparison.) It is going to take time. It took time to wire and map the brain to develop the disease, thus it will take time to unwire, remap, and heal the brain of this disease.

Unlike the story I shared in Chapter 1 of my mom's success with her speedy breast cancer diagnosis and treatment after finding a lump, it is rare that you can just take your loved one to the doctor to talk about alcohol use disorder symptoms and/or request a referral for a more in-depth evaluation. Nor can you simply go to the doctor yourself to get that information or referrals for your loved one. Again, this is changing, but in the meantime, I'm sharing some suggestions about what is needed to treat this disease – whether treatment involves a residential, inpatient, or intensive outpatient program, or a self-directed program.

These suggestions are taken from two excellent, online resources created by the National Institute on Drug Abuse (NIDA). One is for adults, titled: *Principles of Drug* [and Alcohol] *Addiction Treatment: A Research Based Guide (Third Edition).* The other is for adolescents, titled: *Principles of Adolescent Substance Use Disorder Treatment.* A third online resource is also used. It is created by the National Institute on Alcohol Abuse and Alcoholism (NIAAA) and is titled: *NIAAA Alcohol Treatment Navigator.*

Please understand the following list of suggestions about treatment is not meant to overwhelm you. Rather it's to share the complexity of issues involved in treating this disease for some people. Take time to consider these recommendations and determine the ones that apply in your loved one's situation. That can greatly help a person find the right treatment for *them* and thereby succeed in *their* recovery.

- No single treatment is appropriate for everyone, nor must it be a residential treatment program. Treatment varies depending on the specific factors that contributed to an individual developing alcoholism (or other drug addictions) and/or the level of their commitment to do whatever it takes.

- Effective treatment attends to multiple needs of the individual, not just their alcohol use disorder, such as any associated medical, psychological, social, vocational, and legal problems that could be triggers to drink during the treatment and recovery process.

- Remaining in treatment for an adequate period of time is critical. In other words, that adequate period of time must incorporate long-term continuing care in the treatment/recovery process. The appropriate duration for an individual depends on the type and degree of their problems and needs. As with other chronic illnesses, relapse can occur and should signal a need for treatment to be reinstated or modified, NOT as a sign the person didn't want recovery badly enough. We certainly don't look at a person whose breast cancer returns as not wanting to be breast cancer free badly enough.

- Behavioral therapies—including individual, family, or group counseling—are commonly used forms of treatment. Behavioral therapies vary in their focus and may involve addressing a patient's motivation to change; providing incentives for abstinence; building skills to resist drinking; replacing drinking-involved activities with constructive and rewarding activities; improving problem-solving skills; and facilitating better interpersonal relationships.

- Anti-craving medications can be an important element of treatment for many with alcoholism, especially when combined with counseling and other behavioral therapies. Acamprosate, disulfiram, and naltrexone are medications approved for treating alcohol cravings, which helps people stabilize their lives. In other words, these medications enable them to live through the craving and carry on with their efforts to wire new, healthy, alcohol-free coping skills. Think of these medications as bridges between neurons until the brain re-establishes its natural neurotransmitter/receptor connections. Note: If a person uses anti-craving medications, they should also be involved in counseling and other behavioral therapies. This is known as Medically-Assisted Treatment (MAT).

- Many individuals with alcoholism also have other mental disorders (also referred to as mental illnesses). Because alcoholism often co-occurs with other mental illnesses, patients presenting with one condition should be assessed for the other(s). And when these problems co-occur, treatment should address both at the same time.

- If the person is an adolescent, treatment is different. This is due to the brain developmental processes under way during adolescence (explained in Chapters 4 and 6). If this is the case, check out the National Institute on Drug Abuse (NIDA)'s *Principles of Adolescent Substance Use Disorder Treatment: A Research-Based Guide.* You can find this online.

- Some people seek a diagnosis or help from a physician who is certified in addiction medicine by the American Board of Addiction Medicine (ABAM). These physicians cross a range of specialties, including psychiatry, family medicine,

pediatrics, and emergency medicine. The ABAM
certification is to assure the American public that the
physician has the knowledge and skills to prevent, recognize,
and treat addiction. Visit their website at ABAM.net to learn
more or to find a physician with an ABAM certification.

Use the information contained in these resources, so you/your loved
one can make a list of the questions you/they will ask a treatment
provider (if you are looking for outpatient or residential treatment or
behavioral therapy options, for example). Getting answers to those
questions will help confirm whether the provider can meet your loved
one's treatment needs. The Substance Abuse and Mental Health Services
Administration (SAMHSA) has a free, anonymous, online treatment
provider search tool you can also use. It can be found by searching this
phrase, FindTreatment.SAMHSA.gov.

It's possible your loved one may structure their own
treatment/recovery based on this information, as well. Again, it doesn't
have to be a residential treatment program. For example, your loved one
may elect to have naltrexone injections for cravings; participate in
SMART Recovery for peer support; engage in cognitive behavioral
therapy with a therapist specializing in addiction and childhood trauma;
practice yoga for mindfulness; incorporate diet changes to add more
nutrient-rich foods to repair neurotransmitter damage; or commit to daily
running for aerobic exercise. They might also get physical therapy to
improve nerve pain – for example if they had problems in their shoulder
caused by an old injury (for which they found drinking helped ease the
pain). In other words, there are many ways to do this. The point is for
your loved one to find ways that work for them, and if one way doesn't
work, then to try another.

Like Any Other Disease – Successful Treatment Depends on Commitment

It is helpful to understand that, like other diseases, treatment for alcoholism depends on the patient's commitment.

Type 2 diabetes, for example, is typically treated with diet, exercise, and oral drugs. If a patient forgets to take their drugs or chooses to follow an unhealthy diet or decides to only exercise on Sundays, that person will likely suffer the consequences of worsening their Type 2 diabetes. Those consequences include damage to the heart, eyes, kidneys, and circulatory system. Treating the disease of alcoholism is no different.

Additionally, just as we talk openly about other, more "traditional" diseases, such as Type 2 diabetes, cancer, or heart disease, we must do the same with alcoholism (and other drug addictions), in my opinion. No one would choose to be an alcoholic, just as no one would choose to have cancer. Yet, society's continued presumption that alcoholism is caused by a lack of willpower and a complete selfish disregard for loved ones perpetuates the shame and denial that keeps alcoholics from getting the treatment they need. There is an equally negative consequence to family members by this failure to talk openly about this disease.

When you think about it, we don't expect our loved ones to recover from cancer or Type 2 diabetes in anonymity, shrouded in secrecy, misinformation, stigma, and shame. Why should recovery from alcoholism or living with someone who abuses alcohol be any different?

Appreciate What it Takes to Bolster Brain Health

Little did we know until this new brain research that taking steps to support our physical health was also good for our brain health. Below you'll see very brief descriptions of what several powerful brain healers/brain changers can do. Think of them as infrastructure repairs for the brain, just as repaving, filling potholes, and re-striping are infrastructure repairs for our highways.

Nutrition. Here is one small example of why nutrition is important for brain health. It has to do with neurotransmitters, the all-important chemical messengers. Neurotransmitters are made up of vitamins, minerals, and amino acids. We can find those in nutrient-rich foods. In addition to helping neurotransmitters, nutrient-rich foods help rebuild receptor sites and maintain steady levels of glucose in the brain. (Remember, the brain must have glucose for energy to function.) This is not to say you have to go on a particular diet or cut out certain foods. Rather it does mean the more whole, unprocessed, nutrient-rich foods you eat, the better your brain works.

Exercise. Aerobic exercise in its many forms (walking, swimming, climbing, dancing, kick-boxing, anything that moves the body and increases heart rate) also works to improve brain health. It helps stimulate and balance neurotransmitter levels. It increases production of endorphins (think "runner's high"). It helps control levels of cortisol (one of the key stress hormones). And it boosts levels of BDNF (something that helps with forming new neural networks and protecting the ones you have). Strength training exercise also provides brain health benefits.

Sleep. Most of us think of sleep as a time the brain rests. You will likely have guessed by now, nothing could be further from the truth. It is now understood that sleep allows neurotransmitters to balance out. It lets the brain do its work to process the information we took in that day and store it in memory. It also helps break down excess stress hormones. As for why it is part of this section on recovery options? When you are caught up in alcoholism, you do not get the kind of sleep you need for brain health. Meaning, you don't get that restful, 7-8 hours of sleep that is NOT "helped" by any number of sleep aides on the market.

Mindfulness. This recommendation does not necessarily refer only to yoga or meditation, although those are certainly terrific mindfulness practices. Rather it is basically about doing something that helps you pay attention to the present moment, instead of worrying about the future or fretting about the past. It is also the idea of doing something differently in order to change neural network patterns and therefore brain maps. It turns out the expression, "Change a Thought, Change a Behavior" – a slogan sometimes used in therapy and recovery circles – is true, although it's often much easier said than done.

Understand Relapse

Like other chronic diseases – cancer or heart disease, as examples – relapse (returning to drinking for a day or two or for an extended period of time) is a 'hallmark" of this disease,[59] as well. And, like other chronic diseases, when a person relapses it doesn't mean they didn't want their recovery badly enough. [I mean, seriously, a person treating their cancer learning their cancer is back is not what that person *wants*.] It simply means their treatment plan needs to be adjusted, changed. In other words, don't forget the all-important Stage 3 for treating chronic diseases. If one thing isn't working, try another and another and another.

The current research for people treating their substance use disorders, like alcoholism, shows that more than 60 percent experience relapse within the first year.[60] At one to three years *in treatment*, relapse rates drop to about 34 percent. And at five+ years *in treatment*, relapse rates drop to less than 15 percent.[61] And remember, "*in treatment*" refers to any one or more of the suggestions listed above or any other programs or practices your loved one has found helpful.

I know these numbers may sound depressing, but they are very similar to relapse rates of other chronic diseases, like cancer, for example.

The key takeaway, here, is that along the way, your loved one's brain is changing, rewiring, remapping, and healing. This means your loved one's brain health, thoughts, feelings, and behaviors are absolutely changing for the better – a better, healthier, happier life – as recovery progresses. And if relapse does occur, they can adjust their treatment and try again.

❖ *He relapsed eight times – eight! Three residential rehabs, three attempts at "controlled" drinking, and two using a 12-step program only. It wasn't until he finally got the right diagnosis – co-occurring disorders – that he finally got the right kind of help for both his alcoholism AND his PTSD, anxiety, and depression that things changed. Happy to say, he's doing great, and it's been 18 months!*

For a Short Video on The Science of Relapse

Check out the video clip, "The Science of Relapse," produced by HBO for its documentary, "Addiction." This documentary was a collaboration between HBO, the National Institute on Drug Abuse (NIDA), the National Institute on Alcohol Abuse and Alcoholism (NIAAA), and the Robert Wood Johnson Foundation. It can be found on YouTube, *HBO The Science of Addiction.*

Understand the Difference Between Abstinence and Recovery

To be effective, treatment must deal with BOTH abstaining from drinking *and* addressing the physical, social, and/or psychological conditions that contributed to the person developing alcoholism in the first place. This combination of abstinence *plus* the work on underlying issues is referred to as being *in recovery.*[62] Being in recovery is an extremely important concept to understand.

People with alcoholism who are in *recovery* tend to have been or still are involved in one or more of the programs or practices described above *while* they also abstain from drinking. People with alcoholism who attempt sobriety by *abstinence only* are generally not as successful as those who go through "recovery."

Those not in recovery are sometimes referred to as "dry drunks" because they generally continue the offensive behaviors they exhibited while drinking though they are not actually consuming any alcohol. The offensive behaviors continue because they are not dealing with their underlying contributing risk factors and cues and triggers for drinking in order to rewire, remap their brain for healthier thoughts, feelings, and behaviors. This, in turn, may also cause them to substitute drinking alcohol with other equally destructive compulsive behaviors or addictions, such as shopping, Internet porn, opioids, sex, eating disorders, or gambling.

Keep in mind, however, that an alcoholic's recovery program may change over time. What might have been necessary in the beginning (several 12-step meetings a day or in a week, for example) may not be necessary as recovery progresses. Above all, the recovery path a person with alcoholism takes must be left entirely to them to decide. Just as you could not control their drinking, you will not be able to control their recovery.

There Is A Difference!

Abstinence = not drinking.

Recovery = abstinence combined with an effort to deal with the physical, social, and psychological issues that led to their development of the severe alcohol use disorder.

If you love someone who has a problem with drinking, this all might sound terribly overwhelming, even hopeless. If you are feeling at all like

I did at this stage, the next question screaming in your head is, "So, now what!?!" The short answer – "Help yourself!" It will likely be impossible for you to believe, right now, that helping yourself is the only way you can help your loved one. But it's true.

Likely, it is also impossible to believe that you may even need help or that it's 100% okay to want and insist on getting help solely for yourself. That was certainly the case for me – for years and then decades! But I encourage you to continue reading. You may recognize parts of your situation in the remaining chapters, which may prompt you to try something different – entirely for *yourself.*

PART 4

The Family Member's Experience
...and the Concept of Secondhand Drinking

Chapter 8
Now What?

At this point, you may be receptive to the idea that alcohol abuse can be "curable," but alcoholism cannot – because it's a chronic brain disease that can be *treated* but not cured. You've learned what happens when alcohol "hijacks" the brain of your loved one. And you may accept that within the brain of a person with alcoholism, the craving for alcohol can over-ride even the basic human drive for survival needs like food or sex – which means there's very little you can do to stand in the way of such a force.

All of this newfound knowledge, however, can leave you with one big question: "Now what?"

Do you keep putting up with your loved one's drinking behaviors? Do you work harder than ever to keep everything together now that you understand what's going on? Do you pack your bags and leave? What *are* your choices?

Just as there is no one-size-fits-all approach to treating alcoholism, so too is there no one correct answer to these questions. Some people stay, some people leave. Let me give you two examples from the hundreds of people who have contacted me through my blog, email, or speaking engagements to show how even people in very similar circumstances can make very different choices:

❖ *So, I guess until he gets a few DUIs, I can't leave my abusive alcoholic husband. It really is hopeless. But I love my kids more than I love myself, so I will stay. Even though the emotional abuse he puts us all through, especially my two oldest boys, 8 and 6, is enough to require therapy for the rest of their lives. He's damaging them so badly...but I'd rather them have emotional problems and be alive than leave him and they die in his care. It's absolutely heartbreaking.*

❖ *The constant worry gets you down but leaving and now protecting my kids is the best thing I have done. I don't hate her – only what she has done to the kids... passing out drunk, etc. It's just a shame – when she's sober, she's one of the nicest women you could meet. But the constant lies, the drinking, the verbal and physical abuse took its toll, making me miserable and unhappy. I had to leave.*

Both of these examples may sound like grim options. But I want you to know that these stories do not have to end on a sad note. There is help and hope for you and your loved ones to recover and live healthier and happier lives, as you'll learn in this chapter and those forthcoming in the rest of the book.

Right now, however, you may just be sorting out what to do in the immediate future.

In some situations, family members are able to confront their loved one on their own, telling them about the high cost everyone else is paying for that person's drinking.

Some families choose to set up a meeting called an intervention. An intervention is basically a carefully planned group meeting, best led by an intervention specialist. During this meeting, family members and very close friends tell the loved one how their drinking behaviors have created problems in the lives of those gathered at the intervention. Treatment options are generally identified some time before the intervention begins, and the loved one is encouraged to select one.

Other individuals and/or families have used CRAFT (Community Reinforcement and Family Training). It can be done at home. It teaches family members strategies on how to help their loved one and how to help themselves. There are two versions: one for if the loved one is a spouse, and one for if the loved one is a child. To learn more about the CRAFT program, search online for: "What is CRAFT? – The Center for Motivation and Change."

Since I did not participate in an intervention or know of the CRAFT program prior to 2003, I cannot really speak to either from personal experience. Nor did my loved ones choose to get help after any of the *hundreds* of confrontations I'd had with them in which I shared the high cost I and others were paying for their drinking behaviors.

Rather, for me, answering "Now what?" began when Alex checked himself into a residential treatment center to help mitigate the legal consequences of multiple DUIs. As I shared in Chapter 2, when Alex finally got to rehab, I had a brief giddy feeling because finally, I was proven right and could declare: "I knew it! I knew he had a problem!" Of course, at that time, I also clung to the gravely mistaken notion that he would get treatment, stop drinking, and everything would go back to normal – as if he were just going into surgery for a broken leg and once the cast was off, he and the rest of the family would be good as new. So, before I make suggestions about how you might answer the question, "Now what?," let me tell you a little of what I went through. It might help you make decisions about your own next steps.

Family Members, Friends, and Others

Throughout the remainder of this book, I'll be using the words, "family members," but of course this information applies to and is intended for friends and others who are closely involved with or affected by someone who drinks too much.

The Turning Point for Me

By the time Alex admitted himself into the residential treatment program, I was so angry, bitter, and frustrated that I could hardly see straight. My world had been reduced to rigid absolutes: good or bad, black or white, truth or a lie, you're with me or you're not. I looked forward to our weekly family group meetings at the center. Those meetings were the first time I got to really let Alex have it and express my anger and anguish about what life had been like with him when he'd been drinking. I was able to say what I had to say without his being able to interrupt me, or even more frustrating, to flip the exchange so it was somehow *my* fault. The whole purpose of those family group meetings was to give a voice to the family members of the alcoholics and addicts (the term used to identify people with other drug addictions) who were also enrolled in the program.

It was comforting and validating to hear the stories of other families – stories very similar to my own. I listened to the children – those brave enough to speak up – and vigorously nodded my head in agreement, for their stories were my children's stories.

And so, for weeks, Alex and I gathered with those assigned to our Wednesday night family group session. I ranted and railed and commiserated with the other spouses and parents of the alcoholics/addicts. I told Alex how truly rotten it felt to be manipulated and lied to and what it was like to suffer through one broken promise after another. And, when he'd throw in a "yeah but…" or a "but, you…" at me, a group member or the family therapist would say, "Let her speak."

But I soon realized Alex wasn't actually "hearing" me, and that infuriated me even more. He gave lip service to "getting it," after listening to all he'd put me through. But I'd heard and trusted those kinds of words many times before. In fact, his lip service about "getting it" was one of the reasons we were still so stuck. So, I would look to someone from the treatment team to tell him for me, believing that if *they* told him, then he'd listen. It was crucial to me for Alex to understand and own what he'd done. But nothing worked and my anger festered.

So, you can imagine my reaction when the family program therapist suggested *I* get help. "Me? Why me? *He's* the alcoholic!" I'd argue. She explained that my getting help would not only help me, but it would also help him. While I wanted to help him, I didn't have time, I argued. I was already juggling life "outside" while he was in residential treatment. The last thing I wanted or *needed* was to have to do one more thing to help him. I'd been doing that for years, I complained.

I continued to resist her gentle suggestions for weeks. Desperate, I finally took her advice. As I shared in Chapter 1, I started attending Al-Anon meetings, (a free, 12-step program for family members and friends of someone with a drinking problem). I doubled my weekly individual counseling sessions with my therapist and forced myself to find time to attend additional family group sessions at the treatment center. And, as a writer and researcher, I buried myself in books, conversations with others in my situation, and websites addressing alcoholism, alcohol abuse, addiction, and help for the family (though there were very few, at that time). It was during this research I learned why family members were referred to by terms you may have heard yourself: *codependents* and *enablers*.

About the Terms: Codependent, Enabler, and Codependency

It would be one thing if alcoholism or alcohol abuse just struck one day, like waking up with the flu, but it doesn't. It ekes and creeps and slowly crawls forward.

In order to accommodate and survive the progression of the alcoholic's disease or a loved one's alcohol abuse, the family members who love them have had to adapt and change their thinking and behaviors and join in the denial protecting it. In other words, they've had to adopt their own version of denial as explained in Chapter 7. Some describe this progression (this process of slow-building denial) as being similar to what occurs when a frog is placed in a pot of water, which is then brought to a slow boil. The frog doesn't jump out of the pot when it reaches the boil because it's adapted to the warming water temperature along the way.

Through all of this adapting and accommodating of the alcoholic and/or alcohol abuser's drinking behaviors, family members unconsciously collude to make the unacceptable acceptable.[63] Just as the alcoholic or alcohol abuser is focused (dependent) on alcohol, the family members' lives are focused (dependent) on the alcoholic/alcohol abuser's use of alcohol – they are "co" "dependent" with the alcoholic/alcohol abuser on their alcoholism or their abusive drinking. This is why alcoholism is often referred to as a "family disease"[64] and why codependents are also referred to as "enablers." It is also why a codependent's denial-type behaviors are often called "enabling" – meaning they enable the alcoholic/alcohol abuser to continue the denial that protects their drinking.

The term, "codependency," became known in popular culture when Melody Beattie introduced it in her book, *Codependent No More,* first published in the mid-1980s and selling millions of copies worldwide since. Melody had her own experiences with alcohol and other drug addictions and with childhood trauma (what would have been referred to as adverse childhood experiences if that term had been identified back then). She was also the spouse of an alcoholic who presented himself as in recovery but whom she'd later learn had been drinking and lying about it all along. It was "during her work with the spouses of addicts at a treatment center, she realized the problems that had led to her alcoholism were still there."[65] In other words, she understood what it's like to love and/or be in relationship with someone who drinks too much and to have experienced active addiction, herself.

To be clear, however, codependency is *not* a disease. You cannot die of codependency, and the potential for death is one of the components in the definition of a disease. Rather, codependency is a "learned emotional and behavioral condition that can be passed down from one generation to the next."[66]

Broadening the Term Codependent to Include Living in a Dysfunctional Family

Subsequent study of the issue of codependency found that people living with a chronically physically or mentally ill person also developed similar kinds of emotional responses and behaviors. In other words, codependency was not confined strictly to those living with an alcohol abuser or alcoholic (or a person with a drug use disorder). Thus, the term codependent was broadened to describe a person who grew up and/or lives in a dysfunctional family.[67]

A dysfunctional family is defined as one where one or more of the following underlying problems existed (or exists):

- An addiction by a family member to drugs, alcohol, relationships, work, food, sex, or gambling.

- The existence of physical, emotional, or sexual abuse.

- The presence of a family member suffering from a chronic mental or physical illness.[68]

Interestingly, these underlying problems are also adverse childhood experiences as measured in the ACE Study.

It is important to understand that the mere presence of one or more of the underlying problems listed above is not what makes a family dysfunctional. What makes it dysfunctional is when a family member's confusion, sadness, fear, anger, pain, or shame over the underlying problem is ignored, ridiculed, minimized, or denied.[69] This is an important distinction to understand. For when a family does not openly and honestly acknowledge a problem exists, they most certainly don't talk about it or confront it. Sure, they may yell and scream and rant and rave about and around it – like I certainly did – but not in a way that leads to change.

Specific to this book's focus on a loved one's drinking as the underlying problem, the dysfunction occurs when each family member is left to do one or more of the following:

- interpret what they think is going on

- obey, at all costs, the two primary family rules explained in Chapter 7:

  Rule #1 – Drinking is not the problem

  Rule #2 – Do not talk to *anyone* (not family, not friends, and certainly not strangers) about the drinking. Above all, attack, minimize or discredit any family member who does because drinking is not the problem. See Rule #1

- develop toxic stress and stress reactions, adaptive traits, and coping behaviors common to family members that helps them suppress their emotions, so they don't spill over and break one of the family rules (which in time multiply and are ever changing)

- assume their needs and wants are not worthy of attention since everyone's focus must be on the needs and demands of the family member who is abusing or dependent on alcohol and that to ask for or expect attention is selfish or petty.

The Consequences of Living in a Dysfunctional Family With a Loved One Who Drinks Too Much

Because there is no open, honest recognition and/or statement of the problem, one family member may try to reason with the alcoholic or alcohol abuser. Another may learn to "read" their behavior in order to assess what's about to happen – constantly wondering "How bad is it going to be?" That family member may then modify their own behavior or try to manipulate another family member's behavior in order to pacify the alcoholic or alcohol abuser to defuse the situation. A third family member may take it upon themselves to pick up the pieces and cover up after the alcoholic or alcohol abuser's drinking binge, while another may try to convince their loved one to stop drinking entirely. One may plead, scream, yell, cry, or perfect the silent treatment. Another may work as the peacekeeper between the alcoholic/alcohol abuser and the other family members. And, still another may decide it's all too crazy and leave altogether, either physically and/or emotionally.

In such a family, mom may change jobs and get a position where she can work from home to keep the children safe from the outbursts of an alcoholic father. The eldest daughter might cover for her alcoholic mom and become overly responsible for cooking, cleaning, and household chores. Meanwhile, the younger children might find as many ways as possible to avoid being home, either by spending excessive amounts of time with other friends or throwing themselves into after-school activities.

The following examples, drawn from readers of my books and blog, illustrate the realities of what living in a dysfunctional family with a loved one who drinks too much does to a person:

❖ *"I'm having an impossible time trying to 'do it all' – work full time, drop off and pick up the kids, never leave them alone with her – but if I don't stay with my kids 24/7 when they're not in school, I'm afraid she might get drunk and think she's safe to drive or start her crazy talk, which they don't understand and then she gets mad at them for that. What do I do?"*

❖ *My wife has a drinking problem (and an eating disorder btw). She drinks 4-5 bottles of wine a week at home but also drinks during the day at work (we own a business). At least 3-4 nights a week she passes out on the couch. Unfortunately, she will drive with our daughters (8 and 10 yrs. old) when she's been drinking. I have had to stop traveling for work because I can't trust her alone with the kids. If there were to be an emergency, she wouldn't be able to take care of it. We are headed for divorce, but I am terrified for my girls. In this state, it is very hard to take custody away from the mother and even harder to prove her drinking problem because she's never had a DUI or any legal issues. I am worrying myself to death over this.... I just want my girls to be safe.*

❖ *Why can't you stop? Why can't you think of me? Why can't I win your heart and mind and fill the hole in your heart that is lacking the passion a father feels for his child — his daughter?*
I miss you, and I will never stop loving you. ...I need to feel the love of a father. Experience the adoration that I have never had. I wish I only knew what it was like because it seems so good. Why don't you love me? Why don't you care enough to care?
I miss you forever because I don't know what it's like to have you.
I love you.
And I hate you.

❖ *I have been with my husband for many years, hoping on many occasions that he would just die and get it over with. I am still fairly young and pray that I can have someone who doesn't smell like liquor when they go to bed at night.*

Sixteen years ago, I separated from him and told the courts about his drinking and the abuse that came along with it. The mediator said no one could wake up drinking and go to bed drinking – but they didn't know him. Needless to say, they gave him visitation with my young son. I was scared to death. Soon after, he received three DUI's and lost his license. A few years after that he received a felony. By that time, we were back together. The judicial system failed me and I was in fear of something happening to my child. My family thinks I'm crazy to be with this man but I know that I've done the right thing for

MY family. I've done what the legal system refused to do – protect my child!

Reframing Codependency as Secondhand Drinking

All of what I've just shared about codependency, codependents, enablers, dysfunctional families, and the family rules was incredibly enlightening at the time I published the first edition of this book in 2009. But I was still conflicted with the idea of calling myself a codependent or an enabler. I found the terms were equally difficult for many of the people with whom I was working to grasp. Or at least, it was difficult for them to accept this terminology in a way that could lead to wanting to make changes themselves. A common reaction was, "What? Me? Codependent? An enabler? That's like blaming the victim for a problem I did not cause!" And like me, so many would give lip service to seeking some kind of help *after* their loved one got "fixed." Of course, that logic was followed by some version of, "But, really, why do *I* need help? This isn't *my* problem!"

At the same time, the dramatically expanding body of brain research and the neurobiology of addiction and toxic stress research I'd been studying since my first book's publication, pushed me to ask a key question: "Why not a new way of understanding codependency?"

As usual, I dug deeper to answer that question. And it was in that research, I found the CDC-Kaiser ACE Study particularly helpful, as well as the research on toxic stress that I introduced in Chapter 6.

Against the backdrop of this new science, I believed it was possible to reframe the concepts behind codependency and enabling in a way that allows those affected to better understand what has happened to them. In my view, we needed to recognize that just as excessive drinking affects the brains of our loved ones, so does the toxic stress caused by repeatedly coping with their drinking behaviors affect our brains, too. (Note: you'll get more details on toxic stress and what happens to our brains in the next chapter.)

So, after my years of research, personal recovery work, giving presentations, and consulting with individuals, families, professionals, treatment centers, and the like, I coined a new term to reframe the concepts behind codependency and enabling.

That term is **Secondhand Drinking**.

I coined this term in 2009 to draw the connection with secondhand smoking in order to shed a very bright light on the fact that people who love / live with someone who drinks too much experience very real physical and emotional health and quality of life consequences. These consequences can last a lifetime or pass to the next generation if not treated or mitigated.

Secondhand Drinking Explained

Secondhand drinking refers to the negative impacts of a person's drinking behaviors on others. Those negative impacts can include anything from sleepless nights spent worrying about whether a loved one is in a car wreck to lost wages because of having to stay home to help an alcoholic sober up enough to function. It can include toxic stress consequences, such as migraines, stomach ailments, sleep problems, anxiety, skin conditions, heart disease, and depression.

These negative impacts can also extend to those maimed or killed by drunk drivers, as well as to anyone affected by alcohol-involved sexual assault, domestic violence, suicide, or homicide. They can even extend to those who are worried about and trying to help someone experiencing secondhand drinking, such as the mother of a daughter who is married to an alcoholic.

So, what is it actually like to experience secondhand drinking?

Below you'll read a few examples readers and consulting clients have shared with me. As you'll see, these experiences are similar to the examples used to illustrate the realities of living in a dysfunctional family with a loved one who drinks too much. Some may sound very familiar to you.

❖ *I lost my job because of his drinking. I was constantly distracted at work worrying about all the things there were to worry about. I was under constant stress trying to stay in front of all the things he did when drinking that I made some major mistakes on two big client portfolios.*

❖ *It is worse on the weekends. During the week, he is very functioning, and it doesn't bother me. He works, helps with our son, pays the bills, seems fairly normal...But without fail, every single weekend there is an episode. I hate weekends. Hate them. We no longer do ANYTHING on the weekends – we can't! He's so belligerent and obnoxious and can barely stand up if he hasn't passed out. I just can't put my family and friends through spending time with him. Besides, they've basically quit inviting us. I don't blame them.*

❖ *He drinks and drives all the time. He's going to get in a wreck and likely kill or seriously injure someone, which is horrible enough. But I'm also scared to death of what this would do to me and my children financially. We'd lose everything.*

❖ *We lost our apartment because he didn't take the rent check to the landlord for three months even though he always told me he did.*

❖ *I want him to leave because his staying is killing me! But if I tell him to leave, is he going to fall apart? He always apologizes profusely (when he's sober), he cries, says he needs me...I feel like my body is split. I need to stay strong to take care of my kids, but I feel like he's grinding me to the ground.*

Important to Know About Drinking Behaviors and Alcoholism-Related Drinking Behaviors

The drinking behaviors a family member copes with get far worse as their loved one's drinking progresses from alcohol abuse to alcoholism.

This is due to the brain wiring and mapping that occurs around their loved one's triggers, risk factors, and the characteristics of this brain disease.

In other words, when a loved one's drinking crosses the line from alcohol abuse to alcoholism, it's not just the negative impacts of a person's *drinking behaviors* on others. It's the negative impacts of a person's *alcoholism-related drinking behaviors* on others, as well. Alcoholism-related drinking behaviors are those mapped around the risk factors and characteristics of the disease – cravings and loss of control, as examples.

For simplicity's sake, however, I'll continue to just use the term, *drinking behaviors*, but know that when alcoholism is involved, drinking behaviors also includes alcoholism-related drinking behaviors.

Why Draw a Connection Between Secondhand Drinking and Secondhand Smoking?

When we, as a society, took the focus off the cigarette smoker and instead focused on the new science that explained what a person's cigarette smoke did to the health of others in its proximity, we had a sea change. Finally, people could understand that someone else's cigarette smoke was the reason for their severe asthma attacks, respiratory infections, ear infections, heart disease, or lung cancer.

Service workers' labor unions brought attention to the impact of customers' smoking on the wait staffs in restaurants. Gradually smoking was banned in countless eating establishments around the country – even in bars!

As this understanding grew, more people gained the information and the confidence they needed to take a stand against a person's cigarette smoke – *not* the smoker – and to do what they needed to do to protect and repair their own health, regardless of whether the smoker stopped smoking.

Eventually, cigarette smoking was banned in other public spaces (buses, trains, airports, hotel rooms, airplanes, workplaces, etc.). Individuals and families took similar stands in private spaces, banning smoking in their homes and cars.

And just as the phrase "fasten your seat belt" became a normal part of our conversations, so too, did "secondhand smoking" enter our everyday vocabularies.

New science is now available that can do similar things for people coping with a loved one's drinking behaviors.

When we, as a society, take the focus off the drinker and instead focus on the new science that explains what coping with their drinking behaviors does to others – we can create another sea change.

Finally, people will understand that repeatedly coping with a person's drinking behaviors is the likely cause of their migraines, anxiety, depression, sleep difficulties, stomach ailments, skin problems, heart disease, and similar health concerns. As you'll soon learn in the next chapter, these conditions are the consequences of toxic stress.

With this understanding people can get the information and the confidence they need to take a stand against drinking behaviors – *not* the drinker – and to do what they need to do to protect and repair their own health, regardless of whether the drinker changes their drinking pattern and/or treats their alcoholism.

This is not to suggest drinking alcohol be banned in public spaces. Absolutely not! Rather it's about raising awareness of secondhand drinking and some of the concepts I've covered so far, such as "low-risk" drinking limits, standard drink sizes, how the body processes alcohol, and how alcohol hijacks the brain. It's about raising awareness about the simple screening question introduced in Chapter 6: "Do you have a loved one whose behaviors change when they drink?" The answer to that question can open the door to conversations for sharing the concepts about what brain science is teaching us about alcoholism and alcohol abuse.

Imagine if some version or portion of this information was included on restaurant and bar menus, on workplace staff room posters, and in school instruction materials. Making this information available in everyday settings would educate and embolden people to take a stand against drinking behaviors – *not* the drinker – but their drinking behaviors.

For instance, if employees have just watched a co-worker drink several cocktails at the company party, for example, they'll know there's no point in trying to have a "meaningful" conversation with that person. Similarly, educating students about secondhand drinking and sending those educational materials home would help educate the parents. Then everyone in the family would know the same facts as everyone else. That means the dysfunctional family rules could be broken. This educational effort could work much in the same way as sending secondhand smoking educational materials home with students spread that health information into homes and families.

Not acknowledging and talking about secondhand drinking allows so many people to continue to suffer in silence and shame, such as the family member in this example who sent me an email after she'd attended one of my workshops:

❖ *My family fit the definition of dysfunctional. Sometimes things were calm, "normal" and other times things weaved in and out of alcohol-fueled name-calling, random threats, pity-party talk, blubbering accusations...even an alcohol-involved suicide attempt. But no one dared TALK ABOUT IT – instead our family "communicated" through the silent treatment, insane arguments, physical threats, blaming, shaming...but no two-way, rational conversations about*

"IT." And to the outside world, we were the perfect family. I walked on eggshells and became super nice, always pleasing, always assuming I wasn't good enough, lovable enough, always doing whatever seemed to be the thing I should do for others in order to keep things calm. It was crazy making! If only your idea of secondhand drinking had been understood and talked about back then.

My hope for reframing codependency as secondhand drinking is that eventually, we'll talk about secondhand drinking in the same way we talk about secondhand smoking. It's time. The health and quality of life of nearly 80 million Americans depends on it.

How Reframing Codependency as Secondhand Drinking Can Work

Below you'll see what others have had to say about this idea of reframing of codependency as secondhand drinking.

❖ *I love the reframing as secondhand drinking!! The term "codependent" can be difficult for people to grasp and accept. I know when I was first learning about codependence, I was very resistant to the idea because it conjured up very "weak" images for me and was very inconsistent with how I viewed myself. Looking at how secondhand drinking has affected me makes more sense."*

❖ *I have spent some time on your website in the last couple of days. I LOVE LOVE LOVE your term Secondhand Drinking. I so wish I had found you 12-15 years ago when I was so desperate for a voice, validation and direction.*

❖ *It took me almost 6 months to start seeing the light after I found your books and website. I knew I had to figure out how I had changed due to the years of secondhand drinking I've experienced. Although I still live with an active alcoholic, I am starting to change and I feel a lightness I haven't felt in years. I didn't realize I was carrying around this 'wet blanket' all this time and through the perspective I gained from your books, website, etc. the corners of that blanket are lifting. I did not realize the weight of secondhand drinking had on my well-being... Thank you for all the work you have done on this very painful family disease... Your work is helping to change one family 'one day at a time'.*

So, Where Do You Go From Here?

At the beginning of this chapter, you were asked to think about what you might do now that you've learned more about the brain research on alcohol use disorders. Perhaps you will continue the relationship with your loved one. Or perhaps you won't. You may participate in an intervention or try the Community Reinforcement and Family Training (CRAFT) process. You may try to have another conversation with your loved one to explain that your health has been seriously compromised. You may have to make other decisions if your loved one is your child or your parent. All of your choices will depend on your individual situation. I offer information and suggestions for doing this in Part 5.

But first, it's important to understand what it is about secondhand drinking that is so harmful to family members. As you'd likely expect, it has to do with the brain.

Chapter 9
How Toxic Stress "Hijacks" the Brain

Stress. We hear a lot about stress, and we experience a lot of stress – stress at work, at school, at home, in relationships…. It seems stress is just another part of life. And it's true. It is.

But there are different kinds of stress, and they all involve triggering of the flight-or-flight stress response. As you'll recall from Chapter 4, the fight-or-flight stress response originates in the Limbic System, the reactionary part of our brain that is responsible for survival functions. This triggering sets in motion automatic reactions centered around "fight, flight, freeze, or appease." [Shenandoah Chefalo, author of the book, *Garbage Bag Suitcase: A Memoir*, added that fourth reaction, "appease," based on her research and work. I agree with her and have incorporated it into my descriptions of the fight-or-flight stress response reactions, as well.]

To understand what happens to the brain of someone who lives with or loves a person who drinks too much, it's helpful to recognize there are three kinds of stress. They are positive, tolerable, and toxic.[70]

- Positive stress is the kind that gets us out of the way of an oncoming car. It happens in an instant and then our bodies settle down once the stressful event passes.

- Tolerable is the kind of stress that lasts a couple of weeks, such as when you face a looming work deadline or have to prepare your annual tax returns. This type of stress is tolerable because you know there's an end in sight, and generally, you're not alone in getting through the stressful period.

- And then there's <u>toxic</u> stress. This is the kind that happens over and over and over with no let-up, no resolution, no ending in sight. It's chronic, meaning it's ongoing, constant. It's the kind of stress a person experiences when repeatedly coping with a loved one's drinking behaviors. And it is this kind of stress that can have a profound effect on a family member's physical and emotional health and the very quality of their lives.

Toxic stress is the type of stress that most concerns us when we are looking at the family member's experience. To understand why toxic stress matters so much, I first need to explain how the fight-or-flight stress response works.

How the Fight-or-Flight Stress Response Works in GENERAL Terms

When a person's brain receives a cue that signals danger or a threat of some kind that cue triggers the release of key stress hormones: adrenaline, norepinephrine, and cortisol. These stress hormones cause a number of things to happen primarily to prepare the body to run (take flight) or to fight – such as tensing muscles (like those in the shoulders and back) to protect the body against injury or pain.[71]

These surges of stress hormones cause blood vessels under the skin to constrict to prevent blood loss in case of injury; endorphins to kick in to blunt pain; and the digestive system to shut down in order to conserve glucose for the energy needed to run or fight.[72] These stress hormones also cause the bronchial tubes of the lungs to dilate in order to carry more oxygen to the muscles; the blockage of insulin receptors at the nonessential tissues and organ sites in order to increase the flow of glucose to areas needed for fighting or running,[73] and an increase in heart rate and blood flow to the large muscles so as to enable a person to "run faster, jump higher."

It's impressive what our bodies can do in such a short time without "thinking" about it! Recall the light switch comparison. Our fight-or-flight stress response system can activate as fast as flipping on a light switch. That is, it's as fast as the brief moment it takes to carry the electrical current from the switch on the wall to the light bulb on the ceiling – which is why/how we can jump out of the way of an oncoming car.

All of these bodily reactions occur because the instinctual hardwiring of our fight-or-flight stress response was "built in" to be triggered by cues that signal physical danger in order to keep humans safe. This response was a vital instinct for early humans whose primary danger was physical. "Run or fight but don't just stand there – that's a gigantic woolly mammoth coming at you!"

This fight-or-flight stress response system is also "designed" to shut down access to important areas of the Cerebral Cortex – namely the prefrontal cortex – so the person doesn't take time to ponder the situation. They simply react. If you step off the curb when the "walk" sign comes on and look up as a careening car is barreling down on you, you don't stand there wondering why the driver is not stopping. You jump back to the curb. This instantaneous reaction is thanks to the stress response shut-down of access to important areas in the Cerebral Cortex.

But as you'll recall from Chapter 4, it is these important areas in the Cerebral Cortex where neural networks and brain maps involved with reasoning, judgment, perception, hindsight, and memory are located. These are what allow a person to "decide" whether the presenting stress trigger is actually a real threat or danger, which is an important function when the "danger" is not necessarily life threatening. Basically, we can think of these areas as the shut-off valve on the stress response.

For early man, however, with a much shorter, 25-year average life span and a very simple lifestyle (basically eat, stay safe, and reproduce), this fight-or-flight stress response system working the way it does was critical to the survival of the human species. And, it still is!

How Toxic Stress Hijacks the Brain

Today, however, with our longer life spans and more complex lifestyles, the fight-or-flight stress response is triggered more often than not by emotions, like anger, fear, frustration, and worry, over "things" or "situations" *other than* actual physical danger.[74]

The neural networks involved with emotions are also centered in the Limbic System. Because emotions are what "drive" the actions of our brains, they profoundly affect our decision-making and judgment – or lack thereof – when the fight-or-flight stress response system is being repeatedly activated.

Thus all of the physiological changes occurring when emotions, rather than actual physical danger, trigger the fight-or-flight system – the increased glucose, heart rate, and blood flow, for example – still occur. But, for the most part, a person does not engage in the physical activity (the fighting or running) that expends the energy these physiological changes are meant to support. Instead, all of that "stuff" just "sits" and "marinates" in various body organs and tissues, like the heart, brain, muscles, and stomach. It is generally not reabsorbed or expended like it is with positive or tolerable stress. *In this manner, stress becomes toxic.*

The physical and/or emotional health consequences of toxic stress, of all that "stuff" just "sitting" in various body organs and tissues, are many, as I've stated previously. They include headaches, stomach ailments, skin rashes, hair loss, racing heartbeat, back pain, muscle aches, anxiety, depression, migraines, difficulty concentrating, vertigo, and the like. *These are the symptoms* of toxic stress. And you can appreciate why these symptoms occur. If the digestive system is being shut down repeatedly to conserve glucose for energy to fight or run, that can cause stomach problems. If the blood vessels to the skin are repeatedly constricted to prevent blood loss in case of injury, it's no wonder a person can develop skin problems, as well as headaches and migraines. If shoulder and back muscles repeatedly tense to protect the body in case of injury or pain, it's no wonder so many of us complain of tightness and pain in these areas.

Given a family member routinely experiencing secondhand drinking is constantly on high alert, their fight-or-flight stress-response system is constantly reacting in "fight, flight, freeze, or appease" mode. When a drunken person starts calling you names and comes raging towards you, for example, fear triggers your fight-or-flight stress response and you react. You may try to get out of the way. You may start yelling. You may leave the house. But, in general, you don't just stand there.

Understanding basically how the fight-or-flight stress response works helps us appreciate that repeatedly activating it – which is what occurs when repeatedly reacting to a loved one's drinking behaviors – can move a person's stress from positive to toxic.

Stress Reactions Common to Family Members

As stated earlier, the fight-or-flight stress response reactions are centered around "fight, flight, freeze, or appease." These reactions would include the things you typically think, feel, say, and/or do when confronted with your loved one's drinking behaviors. Here are some examples of stress reactions common to family members living in a dysfunctional home with a loved one who drinks too much:

- Yelling, crying, physically lashing out (examples of "Fight").

- Shutting down emotionally when in conflict or facing an angry person (examples of "Flight" or "Freeze").

If You Loved Me, You'd Stop!

- Trying to make it stop by going along with the unhealthy behavior so as not to confront the person or make them angry or thinking it's the best alternative to keep you or your children safe (examples of "Freeze" and "Appease").

- Periods of rage, defensiveness, aggressiveness, and/or argumentativeness (examples of "Fight").

- Working hard to please everyone, being hyper aware of how others feel in an attempt to keep things going smoothly (examples of "Appease").

- Withdrawing from family and friends or enjoyable activities in order to devote time to fixing what's wrong or out of embarrassment over the drinking behaviors (examples of "Appease," "Freeze," and "Flight").

- Verbally lashing out in anger, blaming others or something else for how one feels, trying to manipulate others into doing what we think is necessary to keep the peace (examples of "Fight" and "Freeze").

- Searching for hidden bottles of alcohol and either emptying or hiding them thinking that will make them stop drinking or cut back (example of "Fight").

- Drinking to relieve the stress. It seems to work (at least for a while) because of the way alcohol works on the brain's pleasure/reward neural networks (example of "Freeze").

Of course, there are many, many other examples of fight, flight, freeze, or appease stress reactions when coping with a loved one's drinking behaviors, as we see in these examples:

❖ *I fix his favorite dinners. I have the kids done with homework and ready for bed. I make sure not to nag or ask him questions about his*

*day. I've tried just about anything and everything and walk on pins
and needles most of the time. But no matter what I do, he drinks.*

❖ *I remember being 14 or 15 years old, standing over the bathroom
sink, watching the beer glunk, glunk, glunk out of the tall cans at a
snail's pace. I remember wishing the beer would come out faster so I
could run back into my room and then lock the door before my
alcoholic loved one could come charging into the room – screaming
at me, throwing stuff at me, or worse, grabbing, shaking me, hitting
me. Over the course of my life, I probably spent collective whole
days searching for "the stash" of cans and bottles – and dumping
them out. I thought I was helping my alcoholic loved one by getting
rid of the "poison." I thought eventually this person would get
exhausted by the hiding and my dumping them out – and give it all
up. When I found those cans and bottles, I felt the satisfaction of a
detective with a solved mystery. I didn't understand until well into
my twenties, that I was 100% hurting myself and the alcoholic by
doing this.*

❖ *I just curl up in a ball when she starts her drunken tirades, until she
finally gets tired of yelling at me or turns her wrath on one of my
siblings. I just shut down. I'm numb all the time.*

Not All Family Members Have the Same Reactions to Stress

As with knowing there are a number of variables that can influence
how much is too much when it comes to drinking alcohol, so, too, is this
the case with reactions to stress – with whether or not it becomes toxic.
This is because there are many influences that affect how one person
copes with stress as compared to another. Here are a few of those
influences.

Not Understanding Some of the Complexities of Stress

Several Factors Affect If and How a Person "Reacts" or "Responds" to Stress. These factors include: emotions, genetic make-up, social environment, protective factors, health of the neural networks, and stage of brain development when the toxic stress began (especially brain development in areas of the Cerebral Cortex that influence how we think, perceive, remember, filter, judge, etc.).

Two additional factors contribute to the mix of how/why a person reacts or responds the way they do: moods and personalities. Moods are what occur if the emotion-driven brain state continues, whether it's for hours or days or longer in the case of some mental illnesses.[75] Personality (that is, being pessimistic, happy-go-lucky, etc.) is the label assigned to the "mind habits," the patterns of neural network activity a person wires as a result of their typical thoughts, feelings, and behaviors. Our personalities are greatly influenced by learned behaviors. For example, behaviors learned by mimicking a parent or sibling.[76] [This is an example, by the way, of the influence of social environment on a person's brain wiring and mapping.]

It's Not Just Drinking Behaviors. Clearly, we're not just triggered by a loved one's drinking behaviors. Stress triggers come in many forms, including anger, frustration, fear, and anxiety related to one's job, school experiences, friends, relationships, finances, traffic, homework, caring for a parent with dementia, a two-hour commute, and children. Yet, most often, the stress reactions a family member develops when repeatedly coping with a loved one's drinking behaviors get bound up with these other kinds of stressors. How? They are all triggered by the same kinds of emotions (anger, fear, frustration, worry...). This results in a family member's fight-or-flight stress response being hammered throughout their day, over and over and over! And it's not just by a loved one's drinking behaviors.

The ACEs – Toxic Stress Connection. The fact that the fight-or-flight stress response is one of the instinctually hardwired systems in place at birth is what explains why childhood trauma – adverse childhood experiences (ACEs) [and not just those measured in the ACE Study] – has/have such an influence on how a child's brain wires and maps. It also explains why experiencing secondhand drinking and other ACEs can cause a child to develop toxic stress and reactionary survival skills early in their young lives during the time in which their brains do not have the verbal and reasoning skills needed to express the "why" behind their behaviors. Those behaviors can get a child in trouble with friends, family, and at school. Thus, it's important to understand that a child's inappropriate behaviors are likely the outcome of their untreated ACEs. To help a child get to the root cause, the question asked should not be, "Why did you do that?" or "What were you thinking?" The question should be, "What happened to you?

For these reasons, it's important that a child or an adult treats/gets help for any impacts of their ACEs, in order to rewire, heal, change – "delete" – these ACEs-related toxic stress impacts.

This connection between ACEs and toxic stress also helps us appreciate why parents, like myself and my mom, for example, must do whatever we can to heal our brains and learn better ways of coping with a loved one's drinking behaviors. When we do, we are then better able to protect our children from experiencing secondhand drinking and secondhand drinking-related ACEs. Or, as in my case, to help them understand what happened and take necessary steps to heal their own brains. [The beauty of our brains is they are incredibly "plastic," meaning they can be repaired, healed, and rewired – even when one doesn't start the process until age 50 like me.]

If You Loved Me, You'd Stop!

Misdiagnosis of the "Real" Problem

Often people seek medical help for physical and emotional health ailments, not understanding the underlying cause is toxic stress. I know I did. At one point, I was diagnosed with situational depression and prescribed Zoloft and then Prozac. Neither drug did anything other than dull my sensations. It didn't fix the source of my situational depression, namely coping with a loved one's drinking behaviors. Had this research been known back in the day, my doctor could have asked a more relevant question, *"Do you have a loved one whose behaviors change when they drink?"* And had this research been known back then, my doctor would have directed me to resources that could have helped *me* get the help *I* needed.

As an aside, for several years after publishing the first edition of this book, I was a guest lecturer for the Eating Disorders and Addiction Rotation taught by Dr. Stanley Fischman at Stanford Medical School. After explaining what I have been sharing here, I encouraged his students to ask that question when their patients presented with the physical and emotional health ailments (the symptoms) of toxic stress. With millions of Americans repeatedly coping with a loved one's drinking behaviors, the likelihood their patient's symptoms were caused by secondhand drinking-related toxic stress was extremely high.

The ACEs / Secondhand Drinking / Risk Factors for Developing Alcoholism Connection

Many alcoholics and alcohol abusers were also affected by secondhand drinking. They also grew up in a dysfunctional family with a parent who abused or was dependent on alcohol. And that one Adverse Childhood Experience (ACE) can result in a child experiencing up to seven of the 10 ACEs measured in the ACE Study. These seven include having:

- experienced emotional abuse

- experienced physical abuse

- experienced emotional neglect

- experienced physical neglect

- witnessed mother being treated violently (alcohol-involved domestic violence)

- lost a parent due to separation or divorce (secondhand drinking- and alcohol-involved discord between the parents)

- had a household member who was in prison (alcohol-involved crime).

This helps explain why a person with alcoholism who experienced secondhand drinking may find it helpful to participate in both Alcoholics Anonymous and Al-Anon meetings or other kinds of dual recovery work programs and practices, like therapy. By taking this dual approach, they can address both issues: alcoholism and secondhand drinking. These are two separate brain changers. One involves the fight-or-flight stress response and the other involves the pleasure-reward neural networks. Both originate and are mapped in the Limbic System, the "reactionary," survival part of our brain.

Not Knowing Your Brain History

Looking at your own brain history can help you understand how your brain wired and mapped as you developed and aged. It also sheds light on the influences on that wiring and mapping. This can help you pinpoint areas where you may need help. It can also help family members appreciate the fact that they really can change their brains and therefore their lives. Because science now shows us that if we can *wire* "it" in, then we can likely *unwire* it. Or as my friend and founder of The Best Brain Possible, Debbie Hampton, said:

Good News / Bad News

The good news is your brain makes physical changes based on the repetitive things you do and experiences you have.

The bad news is your brain makes physical changes based on the repetitive things you do and experiences you have.

—Debbie Hampton, thebestbrainpossible.com

The science of the brain's ability to heal, rewire, and repair itself is referred to as "neuroplasticity."

And by the way, this idea of <u>likely</u> being able to unwire "it" if we can wire it in applies to the person with an alcohol use disorder, as well.

So I invite you to do the following inventory of your brain history. As you ask yourself the questions listed, try to dig down a bit to include your thoughts, emotions, reactions, coping behaviors, etc. You may wish to use a notebook or tablet for doing this.

WARNING. If at any time you feel uncomfortable, anxious, or triggered – STOP. You do not have to proceed. Skip this section. You may wish to talk to your doctor or with another mental health professional, instead, if something comes up for you while examining your brain history.

Trauma | Adverse Childhood Experiences (ACEs)

- Did you experience secondhand drinking as a child, teen, or young adult?

- Did you experience the kinds ACEs named in the ACE Study or other kinds of trauma not named in the study as a child, such as: bullying, being teased for having a learning difference, had a sibling with an alcohol or other drug use disorder, grew up in foster care…?

- Did you experience trauma as an adult, such as: sexual assault, deployment in war, work in law enforcement or as a fire fighter, had a loved one die by suicide, survived a horrific car accident and months of pain and recovery...?

- Other

Genetics

- Is there a history of alcohol abuse or alcoholism (or other drug abuse or addiction) in your family?
- Is there a history of mental health problems (also referred to as mental illness) in your family, such as anxiety, depression, OCD, PTSD, bipolar...?
- Other

Social Environment

- What were your home, school, and neighborhood environments like – calm, safe, nurturing or chaotic, unsafe, scary?
- Did you grow up food deprived or without adequate medical care or stable housing?
- Did you have adults or trusted others help you build protective factors (described in the "Resilience Trumps ACEs" section of Chapter 6).
- Did you feel welcomed and accepted by your friend group or have at least one close friend during your school years to whom you could turn for friendship and support and could trust to have your back?
- What was your college experience (if you went to college) like?
- What is your workplace like? Are there stress producing

components with it – boss, co-worker, workload, company culture...?

- Other

Early Use

- Did you drink or use other drugs during your tween, teen, or young adult years? Do you still – if so, what's your drinking pattern?

- Did you (or do you) have other behavioral disorders that helped you "cope," such as overeating, bulimia, anorexia, cutting, or other self-harm practices?

- Other

Mental Illness (Mental Disorder)

- Do you have a clinically diagnosed mental illness? Are you getting help?

- Do you have bouts of depression or anxiety or other undiagnosed, sad, unsettled kinds of feelings?

- Other

Stress

- Do you have sources of stress unrelated to your loved one's drinking, such as your job, commute, children, marriage, finances, or a co-worker's drinking, etc.?

- Do you have a close friend or significant other whose behaviors change when they drink (or use other drugs)?

- Other

<u>Other</u>

- How is your physical and emotional health? Are you anxious, depressed, or tired all the time, angry? Do you suffer frequent headaches, migraines, or stomach problems?

- Jot down anything else that comes to mind that wasn't mentioned above.

The benefit of taking a look at your brain history is to gather insights into the experiences that have influenced the countless numbers of thoughts, feelings, and behaviors your brain has mapped over the course of your life.

Looking at your brain history may also help you better appreciate why you've coped with and tolerated your loved one's drinking behaviors the way you have thus far. It may also help you recognize that there are some things you want to change or need help with to change in order to fully reclaim your life. Suggestions for how to change are found in the remaining chapters.

Looking at My Own ACEs and Getting Help for One in Particular Really Set Me Free

It was several years into my secondhand drinking recovery during my 50's when the full-on, in-your-face, heart-breaking, gut-wrenching reality of having been sexually assaulted as a teen came crashing in while I was in a therapy session. I'd been able to give lip service to it happening for many, many years, but with about as much emotion as saying, "I went to the grocery store, today."

It wasn't until I let the details of what happened break through and out, as if in repeated flashbacks, that I started the journey that really set me free. Details like the sounds, textures, leering sneer, flaring nostrils, heavy breathing, clammy skin, beads of perspiration, words, carpet, wallpaper, fumbling of clothes... SHAME, FEAR, confusion, and frozen shock.

And it wasn't just the details of the assault. It was the details of the cover-up I was asked to take part in and to which I agreed. I recited an apology scripted for me, saying, "I am sorry if I did something that made you think I wanted you to do that." And there were other details around that cover-up that are still too yucky for me to share publicly. Suffice it to say, this was the beginning of the stripping away of "Lisa."

It took several therapy sessions and then several years after my therapy ended to process all of this. Sometimes, waves of anguish would wash through me and out of my mouth and eyes through wailing and tears and out of my body through convulsive spasms. Sometimes, I would pound on my bed and rage and yell and stomp and jump hard from a place so deep, I had no idea it was even in there, nor that I could make those sounds and pounds with such volume and strength. In somatic therapy teachings/beliefs/practices, it would be said that I was finally breaking the mind (brain)/body connection that had locked in around the stress reactions I experienced back then – and that had stayed locked in during the years that followed.

I share this story because I'd already been dealing with my secondhand-drinking related ACEs using tools I'll be sharing in the remaining chapters. And I'd made huge progress, for sure. But it was coming to terms with this one particular ACE that really set me free. And sure – the memory never goes away; it just gets softer. But now, I can embrace the fact that it wasn't my fault or something of my doing. I finally let go of the guilt and the shame. As importantly, I finally let go of the fear. For as it turned out, fear became one of my most frequent stress-triggering emotions ever since that awful day.

Letting go of all of it became the key to living *my* life – to finding and then fully coming back into "Lisa."

Chapter 10
Finding Your Own Recovery

So far in this part of the book, you've learned about the family member's experience, including codependency, dysfunctional family rules, secondhand drinking, and toxic stress. You've also had the opportunity to think about your own brain history. And you may have given some thought as to whether you have any stress reactions common to family members.

At this point, you may be considering the idea of recovery for yourself. But what does it mean for family members who've been experiencing secondhand drinking to find their own recovery – their secondhand drinking recovery? After all, in the eyes of society, you and others close to the loved one who drinks too much, haven't done anything "wrong" – unlike the person with the alcohol use disorder, whose lying and deceptions may have destroyed a career, a credit rating, or a family.

As far as most family members are concerned, everything they've been doing has been done with all the best intentions to help the alcoholic or alcohol abuser to stop or get a grip on their drinking.

So then, what is there to "recover" from?

Obviously, family members have to deal with the issue of toxic stress that results from repeated exposure to secondhand drinking. But who isn't stressed nowadays? And who else is going to do what you've been doing? And seriously, who has time for this? And so what if you change – that still leaves your loved one's drinking problem untouched!

To answer these questions, I'd like you to use your imagination here:

- Imagine you and your children carry on with your plans to go to a movie even if your husband doesn't show up on time, hasn't called or texted, and you suspect he's stopped for a drink?

- Imagine letting go of an argument you're having with your wife who's been drinking most of the evening and making a statement along the lines of, "It seems we see this differently," and then walking away and truly NOT caring whether she agrees?

- Imagine making a statement like this to your loved one – and know that you mean it when you say it: "You know I love you, but the way I've been coping with your drinking has affected my life, my physical and emotional health. So, I need you to understand that if you continue drinking, you will need to find somewhere else to live." And suppose that before you take this step, you've thought through what it will actually mean for you, for them, and for the likelihood they'll actually leave.

- Imagine believing in your heart of hearts that your loved one won't drink or relapse or pass out just because you go out with a friend for the evening.

- Imagine telling your childhood friend you will no longer loan her money, make excuses about why she doesn't show up at events or work, or lie to her husband when he calls looking for her – and then calmly stick by your decisions even if your friend pleads and begs.

It's entirely possible to turn these imagined situations into your new realities. And that's what recovery for the family member or friend is all about.

Obviously it will take work on your part. After all, you'll be rewiring and healing your brain. But you can live a life that is far beyond what you might imagine right now when you make the kinds of changes presented in this chapter and the ones that follow.

Here's an example of what one reader shared about one aspect of her secondhand drinking recovery:

❖ *I practiced this idea with my therapist and will never forget the first time I told my mom, "I've got to hang up, now. We'll talk more later." And then I actually hung up! It was apparent she'd been and was still drinking. It was after dinner and she usually started drinking mid-afternoon. I could hear the pause while she sipped from her glass of wine and then continued her drunk talk. It was never a "conversation." Typically, she'd go on about some old slight or grievance – pause, sip – or some new self-pitying discovery – pause, sip. If I tried to interject something, she'd just find a way to take what I'd said and use it to launch into some other convoluted story. I resented her for it and more often than not felt angry, frustrated, and sad after one of these calls. But that day, it was such a relief to know – and to really believe – what I'd been realizing through therapy was true and okay and not selfish. Namely that I don't have to talk to her when she's been drinking! I can hang up or not answer. Instead, I'll talk to her before mid-afternoon, or not at all!*

An Overview of What Recovery for the Family Member Looks Like

Recovery for the family member is about changing *where* you think – moving from automatic reactions to thoughtful decisions, moving from the "reactionary" part of brain to the "thinking" part. This switch from the Limbic System to and within the Cerebral Cortex is what allows a family member to stop the denial and start doing what's necessary for their *own* brain health and wellness, regardless of whether their loved one stops drinking, gets treatment, or changes their drinking pattern.

In other words, it's not about changing *what* you think but *where* you think. You cannot help having your initial reaction to an emotional trigger, but you can engage your rational decision-making processes to stop the reaction and replace it with a more reasoned, productive response.

Making this switch involves:

- Understanding the disease of alcoholism and the condition of alcohol abuse so that you're confident you know what you're *really* dealing with. Obviously, you're NOT in a position to diagnose your loved one; however, you can develop a layperson's general understanding of the issues. You've likely completed this step by having read this far.

- Stopping your denial. Suggestions for how to do this are a part of setting boundaries and adopting some of the other suggestions shared in Part 5.

- Looking at your brain history (done in Chapter 9) for "things" with which you may want help.

- Identifying your stress reactions, which you also did in Chapter 9, and your traits and coping behaviors common to family members, which you'll do in this chapter.

- Taking steps to re-wire/re-map your brain, which are the practical tools and tips you'll be learning as you read Part 5.

Knowing Where You've Been Sheds Light On Where You Want to Go

Explained in the introduction to this section, recovery for the family member is about changing *where* they think. In other words, it's about moving from automatic reactions to thoughtful decisions, moving from the "reactionary" part of brain (Limbic System) to the "thinking" part

(Cerebral Cortex). In order to do this, it's helpful to learn about adaptive traits and coping behaviors that are common to family members.

Adaptive Traits Common to Family Members

If you moved to a frozen climate and lived there for many years, it's likely you'd become accustomed to the cold and could withstand low temperatures better than someone who suddenly arrived for a visit from the equator. Or, if you made your home in a city like Denver, it would probably be easier for you to breathe in the high-altitude air compared to someone from a low-lying state like Florida. Both of these examples illustrate how we humans adapt to our surrounding environments in order to survive.

Similarly, we also adapt when living with or interacting with a loved one who drinks too much or who has developed alcoholism. We develop traits that enable us to survive the onslaught of stress – stress that has become toxic – stress that is caused by repeatedly coping with drinking behaviors.

At this point, you may want to complete this short assessment to see if you have developed some of the adaptive traits common to family members of loved ones who drink too much (or have other drug use disorders). It probably won't surprise you. I scored a whopping 31.5 out of a possible 36 back in 2003. [When I did this, it was referred to as an assessment of codependency traits, and you may still hear it referred to as such.]

Identifying Adaptive Traits

Answer each question with your first reaction and write down whether your response is: (Y) yes or (N) no or (S) sometimes. (You'll see how to score your assessment at the end of the list of questions.)

1. Is your attention focused on protecting or pleasing others?
2. Are you highly critical of yourself?
3. Does it upset you when people are critical of you?

4. Are you more aware of how others feel than of how you feel?

5. Do you have difficulty saying, "No," when someone asks for your help (even if saying "yes" causes you to overextend yourself)?

6. Does what others think of you affect how you feel about yourself?

7. Do you keep silent to keep the peace and/or avoid arguments?

8. Is it hard for you to express your feelings when someone hurts your feelings?

9. Do you feel guilty when you stand up for yourself instead of giving in to others?

10. Do you or did you live with someone who abused/was addicted to alcohol or drugs or was chronically ill (physically or mentally)?

11. Do you tend not to express your emotions or reactions spontaneously, instead taking your cues for how to express them from others or the situation?

12. Do you try to solve the problems and relieve the pain of those you love and worry their lives would go downhill without your constant efforts?

13. Do you hold onto relationships that aren't working believing there is something you can or should be doing to make it work?

14. Do you have stress related illnesses (headaches, depression, skin rashes)?

15. Do you work or eat or exercise compulsively?

16. Do you fail to recognize your accomplishments or minimize them when someone else does?

17. Do you fail to give much thought to what you like or where you want to go or what you want to do with your life?

18. Does fear of rejection or criticism affect what you say or do?

19. Do you feel more alive when handling, worrying about, and/or doing things for others?

20. Do you take care of others easily yet find it difficult to do something just for yourself?

21. Have you slowly withdrawn from extended family, friends, and/or your regular activities over the years?

22. Do you spend a lot of time worrying or anticipating and planning for every possible eventuality of a perceived problem?

23. Do you shut down emotionally when you are in conflict or facing an angry person?

24. Do you often mistrust your own feelings and fret about whether they're acceptable or justified before you express them?

25. Do you try to "read" the words of others in order to determine their "true" feelings instead of taking what they say at face value?

26. Does your life feel chaotic or out of control?

27. Do you feel a need to argue over differences of opinion until the other person sees and/or agrees with your view and feel angry or wrong or sad if they don't?

28. Do you find yourself feeling angry often?

29. Have you lived with someone who belittles or withholds "normal" demonstrations of love and affection?

30. Do you rarely set aside time to do things you want to do, things that are not "productive" or accomplishing something for someone else?

31. Do you have a hard time doing a "good enough" job, or do you keep at it until you think it's just about perfect?

32. Do you have trouble asking for help or for what you need, or do you have trouble with even knowing you need help or

want something?

33. Do you find yourself trying to do something productive, even juggling several things at once, most of the time?

34. Do you procrastinate?

35. Do you feel humiliation or that you've somehow failed if your child, spouse, or significant other makes a mistake or gets into trouble?

36. Are you most comfortable (not necessarily happy, but comfortable) when things are kind of crazy or chaotic or there is a lot to do?

Okay. Now's it's time to tally your score. Each "yes" counts as 1, and each "sometimes" counts as 1/2. If you scored:

- 1 – 5 you are probably doing just fine

- 6 – 12 you may be somewhat affected by secondhand drinking

- 13 – 22 you probably are highly affected by secondhand drinking

- 23 – 36 it's really a good thing you're reading this book!

If you scored like I did, you're likely having a reaction similar to mine – "So??? What's wrong with being kind, caring, wanting to make things work out for everyone, deferring to others…?" And, the simple answer is, "Nothing."

Those of us who love someone with an alcohol use disorder (and consequently are experiencing secondhand drinking) are some of the nicest, most empathetic, "give the shirt off their back," kinds of people. And, there's nothing wrong with that. It's just that when these gestures are always *outwardly* directed – like attempting to get your loved one to cut down or stop drinking, for example – then your personal satisfaction slowly becomes contingent on your loved one's reaction to your gestures. For example, when your husband doesn't cut down or stop drinking or your child doesn't thank you enough for something you've done, you may convince yourself there is something more you can do, so you re-double your efforts to get *them* to change. You may get angry or sad. Or you may feel like a failure or victim – "No matter what I do, it's not good enough."

The objective, now, is to learn how to re-direct some of this caring and concern towards *yourself* – and to let others take care of themselves, including your loved one with the alcohol use disorder. Suggestions for how to do this are shared in the remaining chapters.

Before moving on to those chapters, it may be very useful for you to take a look at the coping behaviors common to family members of loved ones who drink too much, as well.

Coping Behaviors Common to Family Members

You may see the progression now of what happens when someone is dealing with a loved one's drinking behaviors. First, there is the *repeated triggering* of the fight-or-flight stress response system by *emotions*. Then this triggering causes the family member to *react* from a place of "fight, flight, freeze, or appease," and in time develop *stress reactions* common to family members.

From there, the family member develops *adaptive traits* to counter the offensive drinking behaviors. By their very nature, these stress reactions and adaptive traits give rise to a number of *coping behaviors* also common to family members.

Here is the opportunity to identify those kinds of coping behaviors for yourself. Take some time to read through the following list and descriptions. Then go back and jot down those that may apply to you.

And please do not feel attacked or judged or somehow wrong or bad if any of these do describe some of your coping behaviors. They are

100% normal when you live with a person who abuses alcohol or is an actively drinking alcoholic – especially when you don't understand the disease or the condition of alcohol abuse. They are how you survive. But stopping or changing these coping behaviors will be how you thrive!

Obsessing. Obsessing over the alcohol abuser or alcoholic's drinking and going to great lengths to prevent or stop it, such as searching the house for hidden stashes of liquor and removing them when found, pouring drinks down the drain, listening for the sound of opening beer cans. In time, obsessing over what everyone else in the family is doing or not doing, as well.

Enabling/Denying. Ignoring, denying, rationalizing, minimizing, making excuses for and/or actively hiding the alcoholic's or alcohol abuser's drinking and drinking behaviors; pretending the problem is not as bad as it really is in order to comply with the family rules in dysfunctional families. It's important to recognize, however, that the family member's denial is not so much a result of putting their head in the sand as it is a lack of knowledge about the disease of alcoholism and the condition of alcohol abuse. In time, enabling/denying can morph into other kinds of unacceptable behaviors (rudeness, selfishness, verbal abuse…) from other family members, work associates, and friends.

Controlling and Manipulating. A compelling need to be in control of the people you care about – wanting desperately for them to either stop drinking (the alcoholic or alcohol abuser); to stay safe and be on a better path (the children); or to have everyone see the situation the same way (drinking is not *really* the problem; everything will be fine if we just all obey the "rules"). Methods of controlling include little white lies and omissions, deceiving, and/or manipulating. Methods of manipulating include: nagging, pleading, crying, criticizing, and/or offering constant suggestions in the attempt to get others to do what you think is best – all designed to avoid an outright request, fearing a clear, truthful statement might trigger a tirade or drinking binge or break a family rule. Often, family members of loved ones who drink too much believe what they are doing is not controlling; it's just "helping," just making sure everyone is getting or doing what's best for them, which often leads to the next coping behavior, defensiveness.

Defensiveness. Stems from the constant fear or worry that others don't understand or agree with you. For instance, you may try to explain, defend, or argue until others do understand or agree (which they often don't) and that lack of understanding/agreement then increases your defensiveness. It's a vicious cycle. You or other family members usually can't handle any questioning or criticism because it feels like a personal attack on motives, objectives, or plans – which, after all, are only meant to keep *everyone* happy or, at a minimum, safe.

Inability to Know What You Feel or Want. Difficulty identifying and expressing your own feelings as you spend so much time trying to anticipate and accommodate those of the alcoholic/alcohol abuser and the other family members. This evolves into caring deeply about what others think of you and believing that if others don't approve, then you must be wrong or bad (because that's how it works under the family rules). Often, this results in basing your words and actions on the fear of what you think another's feelings or reactions might be – or freezing up when yelled at or barraged with another person's emotional outburst (and then physically or mentally retreating from the situation).

Argumentative. Allowing yourself to be drawn into arguments, often over minute and insignificant points, believing that to forgo the point is to admit the other person is right and believing that if the other person is right, then you are wrong. This stems from the constant arguments with the alcohol abuser or alcoholic about what constitutes "normal" drinking, broken promises, and the like, and always being wrong because they're adamant they're not the problem – you are the problem or something else is.

Worrying. Worrying about everything – finances, the alcohol abuser or alcoholic's job, the children, what others think, what will happen if _____? Or worrying if what you've said or done is not good enough or is wrong and therefore spending inordinate amounts of time trying to make sure others understand what you've done or said and why. The latter makes sense because most of the family member's efforts to keep things under control don't work, so you assume personal responsibility for those failures, believing somehow it is/was your fault.

Dependent. Staying in an unhealthy relationship because you can't get the other person to acknowledge their part in why the relationship doesn't work. You need that person to admit they, too, have a part in why the relationship is unhealthy and believe that person's acknowledgement or approval is necessary before you can leave or end it.

Resentful/Angry. Sometimes feelings of deep-seated rage caused by the resentments built as a result of the alcoholic or alcohol abuser's repeated lies, deceptions, and broken promises and your own inability to control what's going on. In time, resentments build towards others in the family who may have a better rapport with the alcoholic or alcohol abuser and are not supportive of your view of things.

People Pleasing. Your attention is focused on pleasing or protecting others; feeling deeply wounded and/or becoming anxious when others speak critically of you; feeling responsible for solving the problems and relieving the pain of those you love or care about; being more aware of how others feel than how you feel; feeling miserable because of someone else's behavior; experiencing great difficulty saying, "No." This stems from trying to keep the peace and obey the dysfunctional/alcoholic/alcohol abuse family rules in order to be accepted by the family and/or keep it intact.

Martyrdom. It was a real shocker to me to learn I was a martyr extraordinaire. I mean I had it down! It's the idea of doing something for others expecting something in return, instead of just doing it because I wanted to do it with no strings attached. It stemmed from my believing that giving, giving, giving; accommodating, accommodating, accommodating; fixing, fixing, fixing; suffering, suffering, suffering made me a good person. But it turned into the attitude of, "After all I've done for you, the least you can do is _____ (stop drinking, clean up your room, do the laundry, jump to it when you know I'm upset even though I haven't told you why I'm upset, tell me you love me, make my birthday special because I sure go out of my way to make yours special...)." Over time, my suffering brought me a lot of attention and pity, but it certainly didn't bring me joy. Frankly I'm shocked I still have close friends from those days given how much of my "conversation" was a "rinse and repeat" of the same old "poor me, this is what I'm going through" list I'd reported the time before.

Inability to Trust. Especially of the unknown, given life with an alcoholic/alcohol abuser is fraught with unknowns, inconsistent behaviors, manipulations, lying, and deceit. It's like living with a person with multiple personalities, which keep splitting again and again and can never be confronted, as that would break the family rules that enforce denial. Each broken promise, lie, deception, or manipulation is somehow masked, excused, or ignored. This absolutely crushes your ability to trust and that inability subsequently fuels your fear(s) – all of which spills over into everyday life.

Taking on Too Much. One of the ways a family member "stays safe" is to keep doing any number of things – whether it's volunteering at the children's school, organizing the book sale, cleaning (seriously cleaning) the house, running errands, helping others, mowing the lawn, managing the many aspects of their child's life in today's world of sports, academics, volunteer work, jobs, tutoring, homework, multitasking (like making breakfast, giving a child a spelling test, emptying the dishwasher, and prepping dinner while breakfast is cooking), eating at your desk while working….you get the picture. But this level of doing is stressful, really stressful. And we know what stress does to the brain (and body).

Deferring. Experiencing a sense of guilt when asserting yourself; not giving much thought to your own self-care but always being there to care for others are all hallmarks of deferring.

Blaming, Shaming, or Feeling Like a Victim. Believing that all problems stem from the alcoholic/alcohol abuser's drinking and trying to shame the alcoholic/alcohol abuser for their behaviors in an attempt to get them to stop drinking and then feeling like a victim when they don't. In time blaming, shaming, or feeling like a victim in your other relationships (friends, bosses, co-workers…), as well.

If it's any consolation, I'd developed just about all of these coping behaviors over the course of my 40+ years coping with the Alexes in my life. And don't forget, I scored a whopping 31.5 out of a possible 36 on the adaptive traits assessment.

Today, I'm far, far better, but I can still get triggered and fall into one of these old maps when I'm under stress. Now, I know how to stop the reaction – usually right away or within minutes – and move into the "thinking" part of my brain sooner rather than later by using one of the many recovery tools I'll be sharing in the next two chapters.

To conclude Part 4, all of a family member's stress reactions, adaptive traits, and coping behaviors are developed for a reason. They're so they can uphold the family rules in a dysfunctional home where drinking is the problem. But when you focus "over there," you lose track of what's "over here" – *you*! So, what you've done in these last two chapters is start a road map for what you may want to change for the sake of your own brain health. And believe me, I completely understand if the very thought of all this makes you want to slam this book shut. I was there, myself.

If you do decide to start your secondhand drinking recovery, however, I suggest you take some time to go back through once you've finished reading this book and choose the stress reactions, traits, or coping behaviors you want to change, first. It's critical you start small. Trying to do too many all at once will only trigger your fight-or-flight stress response system, and we all know where that goes.

But know that every step in a different direction is a step towards building new brain maps. Really. I've had more than 16 years of practice, now, and listened to the stories of *hundreds* of family members who embraced the idea they needed help, got it, and found it radically changed their lives.

I'll leave you with one last story. It's what I call, "The Dance." Let's face it, that's what living with a loved one who drinks too much is – a dance. But all it takes to change a dance or start a new one is for ONE partner to learn new dance steps. After you read this story, I invite you to take the next steps in reclaiming your life…changing *your* dance.

The Dance

I'd told Alex about my fears concerning what might happen if he insisted on coming home once his time in rehab ended, instead of following the treatment center's recommendation and going to one of their SLEs (sober living environments). Yet, there he was doing that "thing" he did and me doing that "thing" I did. He with that "I'm so sorry" expression, pressing me to let him come to our home instead of the treatment center's SLE, to let him do what *he* wanted – playing on the notion that if I loved him, I would. And there *I* was acting on my feeling that I needed to somehow make it okay for him because if I loved him, I should. After all, he'd stopped drinking, gone into rehab – what more could I want or expect him to do?

It was *us* doing the "dance" we'd done a thousand times before. That day, I was furious to find myself even considering doing it, again. I erupted!

I erupted from a place so deep – a place where years of broken promises, lies, disappointments, and deceit had festered, until this one…more…*tiny*…little request proved to be the last straw. I erupted because I simply didn't know how to feel, let alone say, "NO! This isn't right for me. I don't care if it's right for you or the man in the moon. It isn't right for me!"

Instead, I was getting it all mixed up in my love for him and my ingrained belief that I had to do what *he* wanted as a demonstration of that love. I was getting it all mixed up in my belief that not doing so would be selfish on my part and in my world, being selfish was bad, bad, bad. Suddenly, it all came crashing in, and my fury poured out as we engaged one more time in the dance of manipulation we both did so well – a dance choreographed by years of fear, anger, and love.

If You Loved Me, You'd Stop!

PART 5

Reclaiming Your Life

Chapter 11
Practical Tools and Tips to Help With Reclaiming Your Life

Chapters 11 and 12 are all about giving you practical tools and tips for changing *where* you think – for switching from automatic reactions to thoughtful responses.

I've organized a number of practical tools and suggestions for making this switch into six general categories as follows:

- Jar Your Thinking

- Change Your Perspective

- Improve Communication

- Anticipate Your Own Slips and Relapses

- Reach Out to Others for Help

- Take Care of Your Brain Health

The first two categories are included in this chapter, and the remaining four will be covered in Chapter 12.

Remember:
the only brain you can change is your own.

Jar Your Thinking

These suggestions center around the ways in which you have the power to do something – anything – to take your hand off the "light switch" (the trigger) or to turn it off (the reaction) if you've already flipped it.

If You Loved Me, You'd Stop!

For example, if your loved one comes home drunk, rather than reacting with anger or any one of the coping behaviors explained in the last chapter, just stop for a moment instead. Then ask yourself these questions: "Has yelling ever worked before?" "Wouldn't he/she be shocked if I just said, 'hello,' and then announced, 'I'm headed out to the movies?'"

But to get from that split second, deeply mapped reaction of anger (given the years of practice you've had activating it), try one of the suggestions that follow to jar your thinking. In other words, use these suggestions to switch out of your reactionary Limbic System and into your thinking Cerebral Cortex. This process of switching from being reactionary to thinking doesn't eliminate your angry feelings. But it does allow you to *respond* – to change your old coping behaviors – in a manner that works for you. Simply put, it helps you hit the pause button on your fight-or-flight stress reaction.

Use Reaction Stoppers

"Reaction stoppers" are actions or other tactics that help you stop yourself as soon as you are aware of that surge of anxious, angry, sad, frustrated, or scared emotions that can erupt when dealing with your loved one or simply going through your day. The point is to find something that works for you and use the "reaction stopper" as soon as you feel your heart rate pick up; as soon as you find yourself falling into one of the stress reactions or coping behaviors described in Chapters 9 and 10. It will take time for your brain to map the new "thinking" responses, but reaction stoppers are a first step in that process.

HAALT. Hungry, Angry, Anxious, Lonely or Tired. HAALT is one of my favorite slogans. It's a play on the word "halt," and it's a strong reminder to just stop! I run through the letters of the acronym HAALT and first ask myself, "Am I hungry?" It's not uncommon to find you haven't eaten much when under stress, yet hunger is the brain's way of telling you it needs glucose – it needs its energy source. If you eat a nutrient rich meal or snack, you are giving the brain those important nutrients it needs to function at its best. Next, I ask, "Am I angry, anxious, or lonely?" These are common emotions we feel throughout our day. So, if we can identify the emotion, we can next decide if it's caused by our present situation or is it something that's lingering from before. If it's the latter, we can make the conscious choice to deal with it later and continue with what's at hand. Lastly, I ask myself, "Am I tired?" You learned in Chapter 7 that sleep is critical to brain functioning. If you are tired you know it's your brain telling you, take a nap or go to bed early tonight.

Generally, I've found that when I HAALT at the first sense of that unsettled feeling (emotion), I can get to the real source of my angst, which very often is not what I thought it was. Then, I can deal with the source issue appropriately, such as: stopping to eat, calling a friend, taking a nap, or figuring out exactly what I'm angry or anxious about. If I don't, then I usually make things worse because I've done something like rush my daughter through something we'd planned together because my thoughts are consumed with being mad at Alex. Instead, I could have just eaten a nutrient-rich snack because my "real" problem was that I was hungry. After I've eaten, I calm down and can "reason things out." In so doing, I can decide to focus on enjoying my time with my daughter for now and know I'll figure out what to do about Alex, later.

All you're doing with HAALT, then, is taking a step back. You are not necessarily resolving anything. But if you recognize you're feeling lonely, for example, you accept that feeling (emotion) but don't act on it by calling your old boyfriend in order to stop the feeling.

Wear a Rubber Band, Bracelet, Necklace, or Carry a Coin. Keep something with you that you can snap, grab, or roll between your fingers to calm yourself before you do or say anything.

BREATHE. Someone once said to me, "The only thing we need to live from moment to moment is oxygen." When we are under stress we often don't breathe very deeply. When we remind ourselves to just BREATHE, we are jarring our thinking and bringing our brain one of the most important things it needs to survive, oxygen.

Make a Fist. Hold up your hand, fingers spread wide. Bend your thumb over your palm. Now close your fingers over your thumb. Look at the side view of your fist. It resembles a brain. The part near your wrist is the cerebellum. The closed fingers are the Cerebral Cortex. Now open your fist and inside is your thumb, the Limbic System. Making a fist reminds you that you have the ability to control your Limbic System (thumb) with your Cerebral Cortex (fingers).

Flip the Light Switch. Picture the light switch example I've referred to frequently throughout this book to explain how quickly we can engage embedded brain maps when triggered. KNOW that you *do* have the ability to turn off the switch or not touch it. You just have to do whatever it takes to make that happen.

Make a List of Reaction Calmers. By this I mean to make a list of things that can take your mind off what triggered your reaction and buy yourself time to calm down. You'll want to make any necessary arrangements, as well, so you can just do one of the things on the list. These reaction calmers can include taking a short walk; going to a yoga class (for which you'll have on hand a yoga class schedule); listening to music (for which you'll have created a variety of playlists for just this sort of thing); or calling your coach, mentor, or 12-step program sponsor – whatever makes you smile or at least helps you return your heart rate to normal.

Take Stock of Your Common Emotions

Remember – emotions are generally the triggers of a person's stress reactions and coping behaviors. Spend some time thinking about yours. Are you often angry, afraid, frustrated, worried...? These could be the same emotions you feel in various situations throughout your day – and not just because you're dealing with a loved one who drinks too much. Make a list. What better way to stop the reaction and coping behavior than noticing and dealing with the emotion from the start, right? Of course, that's much easier said than done when you're just starting your recovery journey. In the beginning – simply learning the importance of recognizing and/or being aware of your common emotions is a huge step.

Do a Body Check

Given the emotional and/or physical health consequences of toxic stress – muscle aches, anxiety, depression, stomach problems, racing heartbeat, and migraines, as examples – doing a body check is another way to jar your thinking. Is your jaw tense? Does your neck or back ache? Do you feel a migraine coming on? Getting in touch with what's going on in your body can be a clue to take stock of what's going on in your brain.

Get in Touch With How You REALLY Feel

"Tell us 'How do you feel?' and 'What did you do for yourself this week?'" These were the first two questions we all had to answer during "check in" at our family group meetings at the residential treatment center to which Alex admitted himself. At first, I thought it was *really* dumb. I had one feeling – anger – and as for doing something for myself, I didn't have time! I was too busy keeping the home front going while he was in residence at the center. And, before that, I was too busy keeping everyone squared away while I battled his drinking (a battle I'd been engaged in for decades with my mom and the other Alexes in my life). Besides, doing something for myself sounded – well – selfish.

Our family group's therapist kept at it, however, week after week. She didn't allow answers like, "fine," "good," or "okay," either. Giving an "acceptable" answer was difficult for most of us, and our therapist was often greeted with a look that said, "So what's wrong with "good," "fine," or "okay"?" We'd eventually learn to appreciate that those answers were vague and intentionally evasive, as we began to understand the reason for her effort.

Our family therapist was helping us unlearn one of a family member's primary coping skills – that of "not feeling." This pre-meeting "check-in," as it was called, forced us to think about ourselves, about how *we* felt and not about how someone else felt. In time, we could describe our feelings with words like, "frustrated," "anxious," "betrayed," "used," "stressed," even "hopeful," "happy," and "content." Knowing how you *really* feels breaks through your belief that you're FINE.

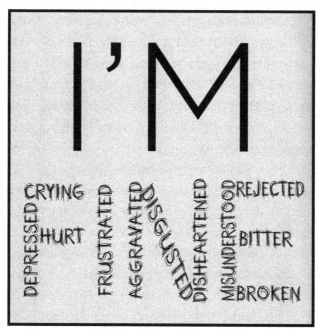

Image 11.1 Get In Touch With How You REALLY Feel –
Using One of These Words Instead of, "I'm Fine"

As for, "What did you do for yourself this week?" it could be something like taking a walk, getting a manicure, watching a football game, not reacting to our loved one when they came home drunk. It could be as simple as going out for ice cream with the children. But, initially, most of us couldn't answer this question either. We'd offer reasons, like: "I was swamped at work." "I had to finish my tax return." "I had to take care of my mother-in-law." "My friend's mother was ill, so I had to watch her kids." These all seemed like reasonable reasons, but our family therapist would just nod and say she understood (and you believed her because she really did). Then she'd gently encourage us to try to do something for ourselves the following week.

Believe it or not, eventually we got that, too. Some got so bold as to do something on a daily basis (like exercising) and others actually did something way out of the ordinary, like taking a weekend trip with a friend. Being able to do something "selfish" was hugely satisfying and (dare I say) "Fun!" It was also freeing because we could see that taking the focus off the alcoholic/alcohol abuser or another family member did not cause our world to fall apart. For most of us, it was also the first time, in a long time, we'd thought about what might (or did) make us happy, and not what we thought would make someone *else* happy. Doing something solely for yourself is one way to start changing your coping behaviors common to family members, such as people pleasing, martyrdom, or being continuously resentful/angry.

So, I would suggest you try this exercise periodically throughout the day. Ask yourself how you're feeling without answering "good," "fine," or "okay," and then ask yourself what you would like to do for yourself and do it! Learning how you feel and what you want will eventually free you to do something for yourself on a more regular basis. (And, what *you* want may be to do something for someone else. That's okay! It's what *you* want to do.) As importantly, it helps you get comfortable with setting boundaries that are healthy for you! (How to set boundaries is covered in Chapter 13.)

Use Some of the Sayings and Slogans

The sayings and slogans you'll read below generally help with your longer-term goals vs. stopping an immediate reaction, although I and others certainly use them both ways. Many come from 12-step programs, like Al-Anon, or they're words of wisdom passed down through the ages.

In the early days of my secondhand drinking recovery, I'd write these phrases on Post-it notes and stick them on my mirror in the bathroom. Or else I'd stick them on a cupboard door or on the dash of my car to remind me there's an alternative to my "crazy" reacting/coping behaviors.

<u>One Day at a Time</u>. You've probably heard this saying or seen it displayed on posters because it is often used in recovery circles. It's a simple reminder to us all to slow down and just take things one day at a time – instead of imagining and trying to control what happens in the next month or year. And sometimes, for me, this idea boils down to the "next 3 to 5 minutes at a time." It's the idea that no matter how bad it may be, you just have to get through this one day (or the next few minutes) and somehow that makes it seem achievable.

<u>"I have been through some terrible things in my life, some of which actually happened."</u> – Mark Twain. This one speaks to the futility of worrying about what may or may not happen.

<u>Anger is one letter away from (D)anger</u>. I've had a heck of a lot of it and now use this slogan, or simply picture a <u>D</u>anger sign, to pull me back from the insanity that overwhelms me when I give in to being angry.

<u>Fear is the darkroom where negatives are developed</u>. I use this statement to keep me from giving into the panic caused by the unknown. I used to have an intense fear of the unknown and could not take action because I didn't have all the answers or know all of the possible

If You Loved Me, You'd Stop!   183

outcomes. "What if . . ." was my common refrain. Now, I don't let fear dictate what I do or don't do. This is not to say I never feel fear, but now I know how to face the emotion and stare it down.

If you don't like what you feel, change what you think. Yes, we really do have absolute power over what we think. We can think whatever we want to think, thus we can feel however we want to feel. One of the things I do when I keep getting the same negative thought(s) over and over [especially when I'm dealing with a problem that takes time to correct, for example] is to literally say, "Stop." And when the thought pops in again (and again), I jar my thinking with another of my thought stoppers, which can be just saying the word, "STOP." Then I replace the problem-related thoughts with ones about something good in my life, or I'll force myself to notice beauty in my surroundings and focus on that. This only works, of course, if I've taken time to think through the problem and know I'm doing what I can do about it at that particular time. If I'm really wound up, I set aside time to look at my "worry list." (Yup, I made a "worry list" – a list of concerns, to-do's, what-if's to handle, things to "fix"..., with timeframes and action notes for each one, so that I could get them out of my head and down on paper and know I had my worries covered. That way I was free not to stress about those worries.)

Patience. Just as it likely took you a long time to get to this point, it will take time to change your stress reactions and coping behaviors. Be patient with yourself and count every time you do it differently as a success – even if you slip again tomorrow. This is how you wire new brain maps.

Second Half of the Serenity Prayer. The first half of the prayer is most familiar. It reads: God, Grant me the *Serenity* to accept the things I cannot change, *Courage* to change the things I can, and the *Wisdom* to know the difference.

I really like the second half, as well: Grant me *Patience* for the things that take time, *Appreciation* for all that I have, *Tolerance* for others with different struggles, and the *Strength* to get up and try again, one day at a time.

"Every accomplishment begins with a decision to try." — Edward T. Kelly. In other words, don't wait until you have all the answers or an assured outcome before you start.

Let It Go. I had no idea how to do this in the beginning. I would talk about something that was really upsetting and do what I needed to do to come to terms with it, but then it was like a kite on a string. I'd let it go, but it'd be still be up "there" floating. Maybe it was not as much on my mind as before, but it was still there. Finally, I started to think of "letting go" as using a scissors to cut the string and watch the kite fly away. And when the upsetting something popped back into my head (as it typically did for a while after), I'd immediately say to myself, "Snipped," as a gentle reminder that I'd thought it through and made my decision. There was no point re-thinking it because it had been dealt with.

Don't Just Do Something, Sit There. I actually have a placard with this expression on it and would smile whenever I saw it. It was a reminder that I don't have to clean the whole house just because there's dust on a table – especially if the whole reason I'd gone to sit at that table was to read a book. Reading a book for 10 minutes or so, settled my mind far more than dusting ever did!

Fear is a Big One

Fear is one of the most common emotions experienced by family members of someone with an alcohol use disorder, and generally it starts with, "What if _____?" What if he drinks? What if she tries to pick up the kids when she's drunk? What if he gets in an accident because he's drunk? What if she gets loud and obnoxious at mom's birthday party? What if my daughters say anything about last night to their friends? What if treatment doesn't work?"

Entire afternoons can feel like one long, "What if?" because "What if?" leads to still another and that leads to still another. All of these "what ifs" running a steady stream through a family member's mind results in worrying, one of the most common coping behaviors family members develop when living with or loving someone who drinks too much.

So the next time you hear your inner voice saying, "What if _____?" stop yourself for a minute and try to register your heartbeat (is it racing?), your facial expression (is your brow furrowed, are your lips pursed?), your jaw position (is it clenched?), and your thoughts (are they bouncing over a number of "what if" options?). Any one of these is your signal to stop. But then what?

Consider using one or more of the tips and tools shared in Chapters 11 and 12. And for the really tough ones, consider something like the approach I used to tackle fear.

How I Tackled Fear

Fear had ruled my life for decades. But several years into my recovery, I kept noticing how fear was triggered in so many ways beyond having a loved one with an alcohol use disorder. By that time, I'd set firm boundaries with just about everybody in my life, and yet, I was still triggered by fear.

I was sick and tired of fear sending me down the rabbit hole, so I took drastic measures. Those drastic measures included taking up rock climbing, to prove my fear of heights was just a reaction to the emotion of fear, not any "real" danger. I took up scuba diving to prove my claustrophobia – my fear of enclosed, tight spaces that I can't easily escape – was just a reaction to the emotion of fear, not any "real" danger.

And to do both, I worked with qualified instructors in those fields and my highly trained and experienced daughter – people I *trusted* (something I also had to work on because my decades of coping with loved ones' drinking behaviors had shattered my ability to trust).

Working with people I trusted allowed me to practice new behaviors when fear struck, teaching me it was okay to trust myself. Those experiences helped me believe that I just needed to calm myself enough to "think" through the cause of the fear and know that if I'd been able to conquer my fear of heights and enclosed, tight spaces, I could certainly conquer whatever new one popped up. In other words, I could recognize fear is an emotion signaling danger or threat (a good thing for jumping out of the way of oncoming cars). But I could also take a moment to pause when it isn't a life or death situation to ask myself, "What is the "real" issue here?" And from there, know that I have the power to take action (respond). I don't have to give into fear.

Change Your Perspective

The Cambridge online dictionary defines perspective as "a particular way of viewing things that depends on one's experience and personality." Here are some suggestions for changing yours.

Full-Stop the Denial

Denial was discussed in Chapter 7 as one of the defense mechanisms needed by a family member (and their loved one) to support the two key rules that allowed the drinking to go unchecked. Generally, by the time a family starts to deal with their loved one's alcoholism or alcohol abuse, the denial that's in place is pervasive because the drinking behaviors have been going on for so long. We say things to ourselves and to each other, like: "It's not that bad." "He still works." "She only drinks on the week-ends." "She's stopped for two weeks so of course she can control it." "All adults drink." We act like nothing's wrong and jump on anyone who suggests otherwise. But it's denial that makes it possible for everyone concerned – both the loved one who drinks too much as well as you and others in the family – to continue accepting unacceptable behaviors.

Stopping the denial does not mean you have to confront your loved one in an attempt to get them to agree that they have a drinking problem. Nor does it mean the alcoholic/ alcohol abuser has to stop drinking before you can stop *your* denial. Rather, it simply means to stop telling yourself and the other family members that your loved one's drinking or their behaviors before, during, or after drinking are not an issue.

When you talk about any aspect of the situation with one another or with the alcoholic/alcohol abuser (when they have NOT been drinking) in a calm, respectful tone, it allows you and the other family members to risk trusting that what you *are* seeing and experiencing *is*, in fact, real. It allows you to learn how to trust yourself – to trust your gut feelings – and other people in a manner that's healthy for you. Stopping the denial is what allows you to come to grips with some of the stress reactions, traits, and coping behaviors you may have developed and would now like to change.

Know There Really Isn't a Score Card

It took a long time for me to understand I didn't need to get other people to agree that I was right or to see our "difference" the way I saw it. I'd spent YEARS of my life arguing, believing I had to win any argument – and "winning" meant the other person said I was right or that they understood my point. I needed that agreement or understanding in order for my opinion to be right or okay. Being right was critical to my self-image of myself as a good person.

I am happy to say this is no longer the case. And my gosh, it's amazing how much time I've gained in my life to do other things now that I'm not engaging in arguments (including the imaginary ones I'd hold in my head to practice for the real thing).

Change the Dial on Self-Talk Radio

What? Have you ever had these kinds of one-sided conversations with yourself? "There you go, again." "You're so stupid." "Why'd you say that?" "I should have finished that and would have if I wasn't so disorganized." "Who do I think I am?" Now, ask yourself, "Would you ever talk to a friend like that?" Of course not. It is important to stop being so hard on yourself. When you change the channel on self-talk radio, you can begin to see your many great qualities, and in time you can accept that you are a person with feelings that deserves the respect of others.

Banish Absolutes – All Good / All Bad,
All Right / All Wrong

Generally, people and situations are not all good or all bad, neither all right nor all wrong. This is especially important to remember when you love an actively drinking alcoholic or someone who abuses alcohol. Stopping yourself from reacting to your loved one's rotten drinking behaviors and thus reacting to him/her as if ALL of their behaviors are rotten will help you separate their good qualities from their drinking behaviors. When you do, you can love them with all your heart (well, actually your brain). You can accept that at their core, they're good people with a disease or a drinking problem – a disease or condition that's changed much of their thinking and many of their behaviors. [Note: This is not to say you have to look for or accept the good qualities in everyone and ignore the rest. There are some people whose truly rotten qualities make it impossible to live with them. There are some good people with wonderful qualities that are just not a good match for you. And, there are some alcoholics or abusive drinkers whose drinking behaviors are absolutely intolerable.]

Try Cognitive Restructuring Using Grammatical [Polar] Opposites

One of the key issues for family members is to stop seeing life in absolutes as discussed just above. When you view things as all good/all bad or all right/all wrong –a distortion occurs simply by virtue of the grammatical opposites expressed in these all-or-nothing absolutes. When you replace an absolute with a realistic thought, the distortion goes away. Once the distortion clears, it allows you to think of a response that will work for you.

The following exercise is a form of Cognitive Behavioral Therapy (CBT), which is designed to give you the opportunity to move from your typical reactionary behavior to a more reasoned response. I've adapted it a bit to use some of what worked for me in the beginning – namely, to think of the polar (grammatical) opposite to my first reaction or thought. Then, I look at them both, which makes it easier to see the "appropriate" response. If you're like me, as you get solid in your recovery, you'll find the more reasoned response is usually somewhere between the two opposites. In time, you can use this practice with others in your life – your children, your boss, and your friends.

In this example, the trigger is a phone call to a mother from her alcoholic daughter:

1. Identify the upsetting event.
    (My daughter called and talked on and on about how she was really broke and had her rent due and needed gas money.)

2. Identify your feelings (emotions).
    (Mad, sad, anxious, guilty.)

3. Identify your first reaction.
    (I've got to fix this! I think I can spare $200. I can't let her lose her apartment. Where would she live?)

4. What is the grammatical [polar] opposite of your first reaction?

   (No way am I going to send her money. She's an adult. If she'd stop drinking, she could hang onto a job and have plenty of money.)

5. Then, ask yourself, "How do I feel?"

   (Calmer but still sad her drinking gets in her way of keeping a job. I love her so much; it breaks my heart to see her like this but giving her money hasn't worked, either.)

6. Now, ask yourself, "How do I want to respond?"

   (I'm not going to comment when she talks about being broke – just listen without judgment. I've told her before what I think, but I can't keep rescuing her, either.)

For more information about this idea (and the "official way" it's used), you may want to read David D. Burns, M.D., *The Feeling Good Handbook.* Take this concept a step further and read *Mind Set* by Carol S. Dweck, Ph.D.

Buy One of the Al-Anon Books

Even if you never step foot in an Al-Anon meeting, I urge you to buy one of their books, *Courage to Change, One Day at a Time,* and *Hope for Today.* Each one has 365 short messages on 4 x 6 pages. These messages are indexed by subject: anger, asking for help, boundaries, change…. This way you can look up how you're feeling at any given moment and read several messages that will help calm you down and put things in perspective, again. My copies have worn spines and dog-eared pages, and I still use them from time-to-time.

Know It Could Be Better!

One of the ways family members (myself included) keep ourselves so stuck is by accepting unacceptable behavior and justifying it by telling ourselves, "It could be worse." Then we list all the things that could be worse: "My daughter could have cancer." "I could be paralyzed." "My husband could beat me."

One day, when I was doing one of those "It could be worse" lists, a friend interrupted me and said, "Yes, but it could be better!" "Wow," I thought, "she's right."

It took a while, but in time, I'd reminded myself of that (right after I'd counted my blessings, of course!), and it's made a huge difference. Instead of living in craziness (because it could be worse), I look for ways to make positive changes when I feel someone's behavior or some situation is unacceptable – because, it could be better!

Chapter 12
More Tools and Tips

In addition to learning to "jar your thinking" and "change your perspective" as explained in the previous chapter, you'll now discover more tools for developing healthier ways to deal with life when a loved one drinks too much. The four general categories of tools and tips covered in this chapter are:

- Improve Communication

- Anticipate Your Own Slips and Relapses

- Reach Out to Others for Help

- Take Care of Your Brain Health.

Improve Communication

Typically, communication is in shambles when families are coping with loved ones who drink too much. But what if a family like yours could develop the kind of communication where everyone is free and encouraged to break the silence and denial – which of course means everyone is free to speak their truth, be respectfully listened to, and not demeaned by someone on the offensive? What if everyone could accept that differences of opinion are okay – not as something to fight about – just differences of opinion? Here are some suggestions for improving your part in the communication process.

Say What You Mean, Mean What You Say

Learning to speak up for yourself – sometimes called "speaking *your* truth" – produces amazing results (not only with the alcoholic or alcohol abuser, but with the other relationships you share, as well). It is often hard to do, however, or at least takes a lot of practice, given how long we've been accomodating the unacceptable.

For example, have you ever answered a question such as, "Do you mind if I go out?" with a reply like, "Well, okay if you *want* to go." When you think about it, however, what you're really saying (without verbalizing the words out loud) is, "Yes, I *do* mind if you go out." And, if the person asking the question took you at your word and left, you'd likely be mad at them because they didn't guess what you really wanted them to do. They didn't read your mind.

In this example, you likely don't trust that you have the right to ask someone to do something for you. Asking doesn't mean you'll get it, but at least you won't be mad about something that may or may not have happened. For example, if you'd answered the question, with, "I'd really like you to stay with me this evening," that's the truth of how you feel. It then gives the person doing the asking the opportunity to either say, "No problem. I'd love to stay here with you." Or "How about if we spend tomorrow evening together. I really would like to go out tonight." Speaking your truth gives you the opportunity to receive another's honest answer.

By the same token, you could be on the flip side of this exchange – the one being asked the question. In that scenario, you might "hear" the question, "Do you mind if I go out?" as "Please ask me to stay." For listening is the other side of direct communication and speaking your truth. Family members become experts at "hearing" their *own* feelings – the feelings *they* attach to another person's words; feelings that are not necessarily those of the person doing the speaking. In hearing *your* feelings to spoken words, you are reacting to something that may or may not be true. You are reacting to what you *think* is being said and then adjusting your truth and your responses to accommodate your interpretation, instead of simply taking others at their word. Taking people at their word and asking for clarification if you are not sure what they meant leaves any further explanation up to them to provide and not for you to second guess.

Another example of indirect communication (not speaking your truth), is when something is clearly bothering you – maybe you're slamming cupboards or have a scowl on your face – and someone asks, "What's wrong?" And then you reply, "Nothing." You've lied, and they know it. A better answer is to say, "There is something wrong, but I don't want to (or I don't know how to) talk about it right now. I'll get back to you when I can."

Now you can likely see that your indirect communication exchanges are the result, in part, of the years you've spent molding yourself to the needs of others in order to comply with the family rules that reinforce the alcoholic's or alcohol abuser's drinking. When a person is "forced" to deny the truth on so many fronts in order to survive, they eventually deny *their* truth – what they do/don't want, what they do/don't feel, what's good/not good for them. They become so enmeshed with the others in their life that their sense of self is deeply diminished. Instead, how another person feels is simply how *they* feel. What another person wants is what *they* want.

Additional Suggestions to Help With Direct Communication

The following suggestions will help with direct communication beyond the idea of saying what you mean and meaning what you say. By using some of these suggestions, you can begin to unlearn the coping behaviors centered around "not talking," "not trusting" and "not feeling"[77] in order to uphold the dysfunctional family rules.

Understand that conflict is simply a difference of opinion, and a difference of opinion does not have to mean a fight. You don't have to agree with my opinion, and I don't have to agree with yours. No one has to be "right." This is extremely hard for family members to do because they see unresolved conflict as a reflection on them – as if it's proof they are somehow the one at "fault." Therefore, they tend to argue until the other person agrees they are correct. But as time goes on, this need to argue turns you into a target for the alcoholic or alcohol abuser. [The "target" concept is described later in this chapter.]

Realize "No." is a complete sentence. You don't have to explain yourself unless *you* want to. If pressed to say more, you can say, "No, not now. Please give me some time to think about it." (Remember: you have a right to choose how and if you wish to respond.)

Walk away. If you don't want to talk at that moment because you don't know what to say or are too upset, and the other person is pressing you to keep going, walk away. You don't have to stay and fight or talk just because the other person insists on it. Instead, say something like, "I'll have to get back to you on that," and then walk away. It's best if you can give a timeframe on when that might be – even if it's just something like, "within the week." This was really hard for me. I viewed "walking away" as "saying" they were right.

Take people at their word. Try not to attach your thoughts and feelings to another person's words. Take their words at face value. If you really are wondering what they meant, then ask them – directly. "It sounds like you are unsure about whether you want me to go out. Am I hearing your question correctly?"

Say it only once. It is so easy to say something to a person and when that person doesn't respond the way we want them to, to then try to use a prodding question or offer a "suggestion," and then a similar, though slightly different suggestion, again, and again, and even a few days later – again. These kinds of efforts are actually attempts to manipulate and/or control another person's thinking so it matches our own. Manipulation is a huge part of "communicating" in the homes of alcoholics/alcoholic abusers because it's impossible to enforce the dysfunctional family rules if one person starts telling the truth. As for saying it only once (assuming your loved one hadn't been drinking when you said it), know that they hear you. Maybe you say it another time, but if you keep saying it after that, it's heard as nagging or manipulation, and there's no way they'll then do what you ask.

Know that NO ONE has to agree with your truth! Think about it – when there's an accident, there can be several witnesses and each one will see the same accident in a slightly different way. This is how we must think about speaking our truth. If it's our truth, then it's what we feel, we see, we want, we need. We do not have to get the other person's agreement or approval in order to make it true for us.

You Don't Have to "Take" Offense

This idea of not "taking" offense to what someone says or does was especially hard for me to grasp, let alone do. It was difficult for me to fully accept that what I thought or felt by what others said or did was entirely up to me, meaning: I can choose to "take" offense and then argue or feel hurt or lash out. OR, I can choose to not "take" offense, but ask for clarification or do a reality check, meaning "I know I can't be the reason for their reaction. I wasn't even there!" The choice is entirely mine. Here's an example.

Say you ask your husband for help with the children after school. He responds, "I'm working. Can't you do it!" Instead of getting defensive (taking offense) and saying something nasty, you can simply "detach" (not "take" offense) and say, "No, that's why I'm asking. Since you're busy, I'll ask someone else." In this manner, you've left his issues with him and taken what's yours to deal with – finding someone to help with the kids. In so doing, you haven't gotten yourself all worked up and angry by fighting about whose work or commitment is more important. You've "detached" from the emotions of the situation.

The Right Kind of an Apology Can Make YOU Feel Better

Because we interpret being "wrong" as somehow being bad, it's hard for many of us to say we're sorry. We often say something like, "I'm sorry your feelings got hurt, but I was just trying to help you." Do you see how this kind of an apology makes it the other person's responsibility to "unhurt" his or her own feelings and protect ours at the same time?

A true apology is when we honestly take responsibility for our part and leave the "but" out of it. Listen to this one, instead: "I'm sorry I interrupted your telling me about what you wanted to do this summer and instead jumped in asking how you thought you could possibly work and go to summer school at the same time. That must have made you feel like I didn't trust your judgment or your ability to think it through. I'm really sorry."

Now that's an apology. And, with this kind of an apology you free mind space for yourself, as well. You don't have to keep justifying to yourself in those hamster-wheel type thought processes about why you said what you said – because, after all, you were only trying to do what was best for them, so of course you were justified in your reaction.

Being honest with yourself about your part in the exchange and then sincerely apologizing for your part will make YOU feel SO much better. The added bonus is the person you've apologized to will feel like you truly understand the nature of your wrong-doing and that you really are sorry for what you did. Often that helps the other person acknowledge their part, if any, and/or realize it's okay to trust you.

❖ *I had an explosive temper. Before I started seeing a counselor, I would rage and yell and believed I had a "right" to express myself that way because things were so awful when he was drinking. In time, my temper explosions spilled over into how I dealt with my children – even for things like not picking up their clothes. The next day or sometime later – if I even did apologize – I'd say something like, "I'm sorry I blew up, but I'd asked you six times and you still hadn't picked up your clothes." My counselor helped me see that my behavior was as much a problem for my kids as was his drinking. It took work, for sure, but in time I learned to apologize without making it seem their behavior gave me a right to be so crazy mad. I also worked on doing things differently with my husband and his drinking so I didn't walk around angry all the time.*

Conflict vs Argument

A **conflict** is a **difference**. Therefore, a conflict is not "bad" because a conflict is simply a difference of opinion.

An **argument** (fight) is a conflict that is not managed effectively. Therefore, a conflict does not have to result in an argument (fight) if it is managed effectively. How? By direct communication using the suggestions just shared in the section above.

———————

Tell Me No Lies, by Ellyn Bader, Ph.D., Peter T. Pearson, Ph.D. and Judith D. Schwartz, explores these concepts in depth.

Anticipate Your Own Slips and Relapses, They're Part of Your Recovery

Be neither surprised or disheartened when you *relapse,* which means going full-tilt back to old stress reactions or coping behaviors. Remember these embedded brain maps can activate as quickly as the brief moment it takes for an electrical current to move from the light switch to the lamp.

Do not be surprised or disheartened when you *slip* – which is a little different from a relapse. With a slip, you revert to your old ways, but then catch yourself or change your behaviors sooner, rather than later. A *relapse* is when you get deep into your old coping behaviors and stay there for a while.

In fact, all of this work to reclaim your life generally feels and gets worse before it gets better – because you are trying to reverse, stop, or change stress reactions and coping behaviors around emotions you've been engaging in for years. And, if your loved one is in recovery (in the case of alcoholism) or working to change their alcohol use (in the case of alcohol abuse), their individual growth and recovery or change will impact you, as well. In addition, if you have children – suffice it to say that adds a whole other dimension. But don't get discouraged. It really is worth the effort. It just takes time.

So, use your slips and relapses as opportunities for learning, not as reasons to beat yourself up. Unlearning years of the repeatedly activated stress reactions and coping behaviors doesn't happen instantly. Knowing some of the signs[78] that a slip or a relapse may be lurking can help you take steps to avoid it or minimize its impact. Here are a few:

Taking on too much. For some family members, always doing something is how they keep the negative thoughts at bay. However, taking on more than you can physically and/or emotionally handle can leave you exhausted, which makes clear-headed thinking even more difficult, which makes automatically reacting and NOT rationally responding more likely. For some, taking on too much also leads to procrastination – feeling overwhelmed by having so much to do and not knowing where to start so you end up doing nothing or something else, instead.

White lies and other dishonest behaviors. When you feel the need to cover up or deny your feelings or values by telling yourself, "It's no big deal, it's just a little white lie," it's generally a sign an old, ineffective behavior is re-emerging.

Argumentativeness/Defensiveness. Picking at others and/or defending yourself for small (in the overall scheme of things) or ridiculous points or behaviors are signals that you are not dealing with a bigger, underlying issue.

Depression. You may not necessarily experience clinical depression but instead feel a sad malaise – the "just want to crawl in bed" kind of depression – that often occurs when you are trying to stuff your own feelings or desires in deference to another person's. That malaise can also arise because what's nagging you is "too big" to think through so it feels better not to think at all. Sometimes, though, your condition could actually be diagnosed as clinical depression. Recall that depression and anxiety are common mental health outcomes (symptoms) of toxic stress. If it persists, you should consult your physician or a qualified mental health professional.

Resentments. There is a saying, "An expectation is a resentment under construction." And resentments are poison for family members. They keep us stuck – whether we're feeling anger, disappointment, or self-pity. To avoid expectations that result in resentments, try to speak your truth. Tell the other person what you want or need or what you are feeling about a given situation. If the other person wants to change or do as you so desire, good for you. If they don't, they won't. But, if you don't tell them, they can't do anything one way or the other. It's the expectation they will do as we desire (or they'll "just know" what we want because we think they should if they really loved us) that creates the resentment when they don't do what we expected. That, in turn, sets us up to feel sorry for ourselves or to feel like a victim of the circumstances. I love what Brené Brown wrote about resentment and "co-dependence stuff" in her May 31, 2019 article, "What Being Sober Has Meant to Me," quoted here: *Turns out that resentment is a shitty but effective indicator light when I'm taking care of others in the wrong way. And, by wrong way I mean trying to control situations by looking generous but really trying to protect my own self-interest.*

Other signs include: Prolonged gossiping (which means your focus is on someone else's business and not your own), feelings of inordinate anger (likely because you don't know how to cope with the underlying problem), and "yeah, buts" – every time someone (or even you) offers a plausible suggestion to resolve an issue, you say, "Yeah, but...".

When you experience one of the signs that a slip or relapse may be lurking, STOP yourself and think more about what is really going on. You may want to call someone you trust to talk it through. Just know you don't have to react immediately or continue reacting. As you calm down and take the time to "reason things out," you'll likely figure out what the real issue is and be able to respond effectively.

Reach Out to Others for Help

I cannot stress enough the importance of getting outside help in order to learn how to stop the denial and some of the other stress reactions and coping behaviors you may have adopted over the years. When you keep going around and around with all of this inside your mind, you keep getting the same answers. If you've experienced trauma | Adverse Childhood Experiences or have a mental health disorder, like anxiety, depression, bipolar, or PTSD, it's just about impossible to "heal" yourself without the help of a professional who's been trained to help people with those conditions.

Not only that, but the conversations you've been having (or not) with yourself or others in your family are not working, nor is your loved one able to be there for you. Loved ones generally can't give the kind of apology you need to hear, for example, until they are further along in their own treatment/recovery or in their efforts to change an alcohol abuse drinking pattern. It can take months before they can face all they have done to hurt you. Additionally, they will not be able to listen to your feelings and respond in a manner that will help you until they have done what they need to do to heal and rewire their own brains.

This outside help can take many forms – several of which are described below. It can even be as simple as reaching out to someone like myself who studies and simplifies this research. As two people shared with me:

❖ *Thanks for taking my call and talking with me about what has been going on. There are a lot of us "out here." It hurts – but thanks for the thoughtful conversation. The alone feeling is the worst, and you can't tell others what is wrong. I thought it was hard when my husband had Stage 4 cancer, but it is very much worse seeing him now.*

❖ *I have to share with you that a huge weight has been lifted from my heart (or brain?) after reading through your website and reaching out to you. My daughter is on day one of a 28-day rehab program. Ordered your book about "...being in treatment, now what?" I had wondered what would happen after her 28 days are up. She has too. Also, it had never entered my mind about healing our family or that we even needed it. My mother, sisters and I have been involved with raising her young daughter (almost 2 years old), worrying about my daughter, worrying about my granddaughter's future - it really has impacted the family. We'll be working on that. But sitting here at my desk, I feel... for the first time in over a year...hopeful.*

Know that whatever you choose to do to change your situation and reclaim your life is what is right for you at that moment in time (and that could be choosing to do absolutely nothing!). You don't (and can't) do all of it at once, nor is there any checklist you have to follow in order to "do it right." The entire objective is to make changes that feel reasonable and right to *you*. See how those changes feel. If they help, keep at them and then move forward with another when *you're* ready.

Therapies

Many family members/friends try one or more types of therapies, including:

- Cognitive-behavioral therapy (CBT), which is aimed at changing the family member/friend's thoughts about and reactions to relapse-provoking situations. For example: identify the stress reactions and coping behavior, the triggering emotions, and the circumstances in which the relapse-provoking situation occurred. Then identify changes you can make and practice them to push the development of new neural networks. Repeatedly doing this will promote the creation of a new, healthier brain map that will be more resistant to relapses.

- Marital, family, and couples therapy, which often occurs several months after the loved one has been working on their recovery in order to give all concerned time to come to terms with what's gone on – and to start the process of changing their own brains.

- Individual therapy, which is working one-on-one with a therapist.

- Brief therapies, which are generally one to six sessions designed to promote recognition of the problem and a willingness to change.

- Other therapies – many have found Eye Movement Desensitization and Reprocessing (EMDR), Tapping (Emotional Freedom Technique), Somatic Therapy, and Exposure Therapy helpful, as well. I found EMDR and Tapping very helpful, in addition to my CBT therapy with my therapist, who was the one who introduced me to both.

Regardless of which therapy type is pursued, if any, it is critical to work with a therapist who understands addiction, trauma, and the family member's experience. Unfortunately, many therapists don't. Lucky for this person, their therapist did:

❖ *My dad was an alcoholic and a gambler. My mom was angry most of the time. I tried to keep to myself as much as I could, but their fighting was so mean and loud and constant that it was hard to get away from it. Eventually they were so focused on their fighting, it was easier to just "disappear," so I spent most of my time at a friend's house. I was in my early-30s when I finally started seeing a therapist because I was so anxious and depressed most of the time. She helped me understand that was a "natural" outcome of growing up in a family like mine, so I worked with her for several years to unravel what my family experiences had done to me. Happy to say my life is much better now.*

Group Counseling or Workshops

Meeting in groups with others whose relative or friend is an alcoholic or abuses alcohol is a huge aid, primarily because it helps you learn you're not alone and then because you can bounce ideas off one another. It's important, however, that the group be led by someone with extensive experience in understanding alcoholism, alcohol abuse, and the family member's experience. This kind of gathering is somewhat different than a 12-step program meeting which is described next because it allows what is called "cross-talk." Cross-talk is the ability to talk to another person in the group and/or comment on what they've said. In a 12-step program meeting, cross talk is not allowed.

12-step Programs

Often family members and friends attend one of the following 12-step programs: Al-Anon, Alateen, ACA (Adult Children of Alcoholics), and CoDA (Codependents Anonymous). Al-Anon, for example, is a 12-

step program for the family and friends of someone who has a problem with alcohol. Basically, Al-Anon meetings are about people sharing what works for them, with no judgment or expectation of what others should or should not be doing. Know there are Al-Anon meetings specifically for parents, for teens, for women or men, for spouses, and for other groups of people. I say, go and see what happens. If one meeting doesn't feel right, then try another. There's no timeline, no "right way" to do a 12-step program. And to find a meeting, do a little online research for meeting times and locations.

❖ *I don't think I walked into my first Al-Anon meeting. I think I crawled. I was just so sick and tired of being sick and tired, I was willing to go to whatever lengths it took to get better. Then I started to tell the truth. I made some real friends who didn't judge me or give me advice. WHAT a gift! They were there for me in such an unconditional, loving way that it shocked me. Since then I've been there for newcomers over the years and to 'pay it forward.'*

Other Peer Support Groups

12-step programs are not the only way. There are many other groups that can be equally helpful. Some people attend several different kinds of groups as they get a sense of what works for them. There is Smart Recovery for Families & Friends, for example, and the National Alliance on Mental Illness's Family-to-Family program offers help to those whose loved one has a co-occurring mental disorder.

Talking with a Spiritual Advisor and/or Following a Faith-based Program

Whatever type of spiritual advisor you seek or work with, it's important they have a thorough understanding of alcoholism as a brain disease and the family member's experience.

Mentor or Family Recovery Coach

These kinds of support options are relatively new when it comes to working specifically with the family. But they can be hugely helpful. Just as some people have personal trainers for physical fitness, so too can you have a professional family recovery coach or mentor to help you get back on your feet. They are generally not therapists, however. They are coaches/mentors there to help you find and succeed in your own recovery.

Meditative / Body Work / Creative Practices

Some of these practices include yoga, Pilates, dance, art, music, or meditation practice. Or, you could engage in physical therapy, acupuncture, deep body message, or somatic therapy. Sometimes using these in combination with any of those described above helps with unlocking the physical manifestation of the stress reaction. In other words, unlocking (rewiring) the emotional trigger/reaction/physical manifestation brain map. Remember: the stress response is designed to prepare the body to fight or run. Just working on the physical manifestation doesn't "fix" the emotional trigger/reaction sequence. Or more simply stated: a combination of both can help with healing the brain/body connection.

Take Care of Your Brain Health

The following provides an additional overview of the suggestions first presented in Chapter 7. These were listed as "things" that can help bolster the brain health of a loved one in recovery from alcoholism. They also apply to family members recovering from toxic stress.

Nutrition, Aerobic Exercise, Sleep, and Mindfulness Activities for Brain Health and Functioning.

As has been stated throughout this book, a person can change their thoughts, feelings, and behaviors by rewiring their brain. One key, but often overlooked, part of rewiring the brain is improving the health of the neural networks, themselves. To that end, this new brain research is helping us understand that four key activities we've long understood to be good for the physical body are also good for the brain. They are nutrition, sleep, aerobic exercise, and mindfulness activities. Pick one or part of one or two until you get it/them down and then add another. You don't want to be adding more stress to brains already burdened with toxic stress.

Nutrition. Unlike other body organs, the brain is incapable of making and storing glucose, which is its sole fuel source. No fuel, no brain activity. The brain requires a daily dose of about twenty percent of the body's glucose supply – a staggering amount given the brain is only two percent of the body's total weight. [79] The brain gets its glucose supply from the carbohydrates in the foods we eat, which are broken down and transported to the brain via the bloodstream. For optimum brain health, however, it can't be any old carbohydrates, like those in candy or sugar-packed soft drinks. The brain needs complex carbohydrates, such as those found in whole grains, fruits, and vegetables.

Protein, available in lean meats, poultry, fish, beans, eggs, and milk products, are also vitally important.

Another important outcome of eating nutrient-rich foods is their help with neurotransmitters, those chemical messengers that convert and carry the electrical signal from one neuron to the next. These are made up of vitamins, minerals, and amino acids. Thus, eating nutrient-rich foods can help with repairing and building neurotransmitters and thereby improving the electro-chemical signaling processes damaged by toxic stress.

Healthy fats, like omega-3 fatty acids found in tuna and salmon, are important for building the neuron's cell membrane. And it goes on and on from there. Suffice it to say, nutrient-rich foods are astoundingly important to brain health – something better understood as a result of this new brain research. But if you are not inclined to learn the nitty-gritty about nutrition, and let's face it, who has the time when grappling with a loved one's alcoholism/alcohol abuse and/or treatment, consider following the U.S.D.A.'s *Choose My Plate.gov* guidelines. Just know you don't have to follow any particular diet or eating plan, nor completely give up the "good stuff" – ice cream, cookies, or sour dough bread with lots of butter. Just indulge in those foods occasionally.

Think of nutrition as "food" for "thought."
The more nutrient-rich the food, the "better" the thought.

Aerobic Exercise. Using a hiking metaphor: In order to change the brain and therefore a person's thoughts, feelings, and behaviors, they have to let the old, well-worn neural network pathways grow over while they slash and tread a whole new series of neural network pathways. Or, to use a traffic metaphor, a person has to take a different highway to detour around a road closure.

For the family member or friend experiencing toxic stress consequences (or the person with an alcohol use disorder or anyone else wishing to improve their brain health), aerobic exercise can be a brain-saver. It increases levels of serotonin, norepinephrine, and dopamine (those all-important neurotransmitters) and rebuilds the connections between the billions of neurons in the brain.[80] It increases levels of an important neurotrophine, BDNF, which nourishes our brain cells "like fertilizer" and allows "new information to stick as a memory."[81]

Aerobic exercise pumps blood and oxygen to the brain at a faster than normal rate. (Remember: oxygen and glucose are the two things the brain needs to survive.) Aerobic exercise helps the brain and body get rid of all that unexpended "stuff" triggered by the fight-or-flight /stress response system but never used to run or fight.

The further benefits of aerobic exercise are equally interesting, but in the hopes of not overwhelming you, suffice it to say, it is critical to brain health. How much does it take? An average of 30 minutes/day of moderate-intensity aerobic exercise, five days a week, is a baseline. It needs to be aerobic, however – meaning any kind of exercise that gets your heart rate up. My favorite kind of exercise is dancing – and it doesn't take a drive to the gym. I have several play lists for all kinds of moods but with a beat that gets me up and dancing around my house. Other aerobic exercise activities include brisk walking, running, riding a bike, and swimming – whatever makes *your* blood pump faster.

Additional types of exercise are also important to pursue. Strength training, for example, helps with muscle, balance, and ease of movement.

Remember:
Exercise is as important for our brains as it is for our bodies.

Sleep. Sleep provides a third kind of critical support for brain health. And, generally all concerned get very little of what is known as "good sleep." This is the kind that's not routinely aided by sleep aids or routinely interrupted by anxiety and worry over all of this.

It takes about 6.5 to 8 hours of uninterrupted, peaceful sleep to give the brain what it needs, namely "down time," not to be confused with idle time. Believe it or not, the brain remains incredibly active during sleep. Sleep allows the brain to repair neurons, re-balance neurotransmitter levels, and sort, process, and log into memory that day's activities.

Mindfulness Activities. By the time a loved one enters (or is seriously contemplating) treatment, all concerned – family members, friends, the person with a serious alcohol use disorder – are consumed 24/7 with thoughts related to the alcoholism and/or secondhand drinking impacts. Mindfulness can help you settle your mind long enough to register what you're trying to do differently or to stop yourself once you've gone down the reactionary path laid out by old brain maps. As you can imagine, mindfulness activities must start out in very small increments. To not think about anything related to all of the problems related to your loved one's drinking for an hour is impossible at first. To not think about the situation for three to five minutes is doable. And actually, taking three to five minutes to engage in a thought-calming process helps people understand that they can let go a little. This "letting go" helps a person see that when they stop putting their focus on their loved one's alcoholism/alcohol abuse and its effects, it does not lead to the worst-case scenario(s) they've imagined would happen.

As you become comfortable with three to five minutes of engaging in mindfulness, you can move it to 10 and then 20 minutes and however long you want to go after that. Mindfulness activities include just about anything that requires your focused attention, such as doing yoga, exercising (and keeping your thoughts focused on the physical activity and not on texting or talking on the phone), or a walk (and making yourself notice the colors and sounds around you). Mindfulness activities could also involve meditating, engaging in spiritual practices, having fun, or learning something entirely new. Mindfulness is about forging a new neural pathway to give your brain a different place from which to think, feel, say, and do.

Mindfulness takes practice, but as mentioned above, you can start with just three to five minute increments at a time. One of my absolute favorite all-time videos to explain a simple mindfulness practice (works for kids and adults) is *Just Breathe* by Julie Bayer Salzman & Josh Salzman.

❖ *I was told meditation was all about not thinking. It was about letting thoughts come and go. It wasn't about trying to not have thoughts. Rather, the point was trying to not latch onto them – just let them float in and then out. To do my meditation this way, I was told to get in a comfortable place and a comfortable seated position. And lastly, I was told to breathe in deeply and breathe out fully – and focus on breathing while letting my thoughts float by. I was game to try because there's so much talk about how important meditation is.*

I set a timer for 3 minutes because otherwise I kept checking my cell phone time. It was HARD – really hard – not to jump up and write a note about a thought or just text someone what my thought told me I needed to do. But I kept at it for many weeks until I got the hang of it and increased my time to 5 minutes. The best part of this whole effort is that it taught me I don't have to act on a thought just because I have it. And it taught me to just BREATHE when I'd get a feeling that set my heart racing and remind myself – I don't have to act, just BREATHE.

Remember:
Mindfulness activities help you with responding (from Cerebral Cortex) vs. reacting (from Limbic System).

Oh…and don't forget to drink water. Lots of water. I'll spare you the science. Just know it's good for the brain!

I urge you to use some of the tools and suggestions I've shared, but only when you're ready. Take your time. Reclaiming your life takes time. Often what is needed in the beginning of your secondhand drinking recovery changes or lessens as you become more confident and comfortable with your *real* self. And, as you incorporate some of the tools and tips that you find work for *you* – and as they become your new way of coping with your loved one and others in your family – those new coping behaviors will spill over into all of your other interpersonal relationships, as well. They will become your new, rational "thinking" behaviors as opposed to your old "reacting" behaviors.

Best of all, they will free you to enjoy *your* life.

Chapter 13
Changing Your Relationship with Your Loved One

This chapter will help you build on the suggestions offered in Chapters 11 and 12 in order to change the relationship you have with your loved one.

Remember Who You Are Talking To So You Don't Take What You Hear Personally

You would not be reading this book if you didn't know the frustration of trying to convince your loved one their drinking is a problem. You would not be reading this book if you didn't know what it's like to talk to an alcoholic or alcohol abuser at night – and then find them the next morning with no recollection of what they'd said, let alone done or agreed to do.

Now that you understand you've been talking to someone who's altered the neural networks in their brain – and therefore altered their ability to "think straight," especially when drinking – you can understand that you have not been talking to the loved one you once knew. They are no longer the person they were before the onset of their alcoholism or alcohol abuse.

You may also have believed it was *you* they were talking to, criticizing, blaming, or raging at. Now, you can see *you* were not the person they were attacking. And it wasn't your loved one doing the attacking...not really. Instead, the attacks came from a person "blinded by alcohol" who was lashing out inappropriately.

To give yourself a visual picture of what I mean here, consider this example used in recovery groups:

Place a bottle of alcohol in front of you. Stare at it. Talk to it. Tell it to do something. Ask it why it's just sitting there. Heck, yell at it. Does the bottle respond the way you want it to? Now, if you were to pour the contents of that same bottle into your loved one, you would have the same kind of control and/or influence over his or her behaviors – None![82]

So, the next time the alcoholic or alcohol abuser in your life tries to talk or blame or engage in any number of negative, demeaning ways towards you while they are drinking or hung over, try to keep your cool and your reactivity low. Instead, give yourself the opportunity to thoughtfully respond instead of automatically reacting. Walk away, nod politely, or use one of your new tools or tips instead of wasting your time talking to someone who's drunk or hung over. Just picture the bottle of alcohol and know that it is the "person" to whom you are speaking – someone who is not there at all.

Understanding this helps you to not take personally what your loved one says or how they behave towards you. This is similar to the earlier suggestion, "You don't have to 'take' offense." This will help you with the next suggestion, "Get Rid of the Target," but first – The Three C's.

The Three "C's"

There is a helpful saying in family recovery circles called, "The 3 C's," and it stands for:

You didn't **C**ause it (their drinking)

You can't **C**ontrol it

You can't **C**ure it.

This makes a wonderful mantra to chant when you're tempted to take personally the words or behaviors the alcoholic or alcohol abuser exhibits towards you when they've been drinking.

Get Rid of the Target

The offensive moves the alcoholic or alcohol abuser uses gives them power WHEN YOU REACT. When YOU go on the defensive and employ the stress reactions and coping behaviors you've developed, you give up your leverage.

What Is Meant by the Target?

When you react to the alcoholic's or alcohol abuser's anger with anger…or to their denial with accusations…or to their broken promises with pleading or a tirade about how rotten they are, you give them a target. For when *you* get defensive, *your* stress reactions and coping behaviors become *their* target. In this way, the alcoholic or alcohol abuser doesn't have to take responsibility for what they've done or wonder what you're thinking or feel the shame of having let themselves (and you) down, one more time. Instead, they can lay it all on you. They can tell themselves things like, "Why bother, nothing I do is good enough?" "Who wouldn't drink if you had someone nagging you all the time?" "And they say *I* have a problem with anger – ha!"

Other behaviors that may turn you into a target include lecturing, moralizing, scolding, blaming, threatening, arguing, pouring out drinks, yelling, trying to fix things, losing your temper, manipulating, speaking for them, or uttering the words, "If you loved me, you'd stop." You've likely gathered by now, "targets" are those stress reactions and coping behaviors you've adopted to survive. So be aware of yours and then use one or more of the suggestions in this and the previous two chapter to help you "remove" them.

Perhaps this visual helps. Picture yourself as a door. As long as the door is closed, the alcoholic or alcohol abuser has a target – the door – to pound on and slam into. But, if you open the door (and you step aside), there is nothing there for them to strike. They're stuck yelling or pounding at the air. YOU are out of the way.

Suggestions for Removing Yourself as the Target

So how are you going to quit being their target, to stop giving them a "door" to batter?

Here is one of the best pieces of advice I received to get me started when I was beginning my efforts to reclaim my life. I was told to think of my first reaction and then do the opposite because my way of "thinking" was what had gotten me so stuck.

For example, if you normally quietly and stealthily checkup to see if your loved one is sneaking a drink so you can catch them in the act and then call them on it – don't. Don't give them the target of your confrontational words, which they can then deflect with lines like: "What? Don't you trust me?" or "Jeez can't a guy have a drink once in a while?" Instead, do the opposite. Go for a walk, run an errand, pick weeds. If you normally read the riot act to your loved one in the morning following a binge – don't. Don't become the target of verbal put-downs such as: "You are such a nag!" or "Who put you in charge?" Instead, do the opposite. Greet your loved one with respect and then go about your morning without confronting them at all. If you want to confront them later that day when they're less hungover, or the next day when they haven't been drinking, then say something like, "I'd like to talk about your drinking behaviors last night. Is now a good time? If not, then let's agree on a time to talk."

If you normally use the looks-that-could-kill silent treatment to let your loved one know they hurt your feelings when drunk last night – don't. Try, instead, to wait until they're sober and then tell them with words, using a respectful, matter-of-fact, tone, your thoughts and feelings. But do not expect to be "heard" (remember they are more likely to deflect and defend their offensive behaviors than to truly listen to you). Express yourself for your benefit, not theirs. Let me repeat: express yourself for *your* benefit. You do not need to be caught up in whether they "hear" you or agree with you – that's the old dance; that's the target you're removing.

Doing the opposite of what you would normally do will likely be extremely difficult at first. But just remember, doing it your way hasn't worked either so you might as well give it a try.

Caution: As you progress in your recovery, you will want to move away from this kind of "opposite" thinking, however. Why? Most things aren't just an "either-or" situation, as in all good or all bad. And as you read in Chapter 12, in the Section, Improve Communication, one of the suggestions is, "Banish Absolutes." But, in the beginning doing the opposite helps to dislodge your grooved, coping behaviors so you can be open to more effective ways of responding.

Bottom line: NOTHING you do can make your alcoholic or alcohol abusing loved one stop drinking. They must do it for themselves. But, if you remove yourself as a target, you give them the opportunity to truly feel the consequences of their own guilt, shame, remorse, frustration, and self-loathing. When you remove the target, they are left to come to terms with their own behavior, and you don't have to suffer the consequences. Best of all, you're free to do other enjoyable things because you're not wasting your emotional and physical energy in an exchange that will get you nowhere.

Just Like Algebra

In a way, the steps you take to reclaim your life from the effects of having a loved one who drinks too much can be likened to an algebra equation. While this comparison may not seem like a comforting thought – depending how you feel about Algebra ☺ – consider this:

If the algebra equation is $x + y = z$, then changing x or y will change the value of z. For example, if $x = 6$ and $y = 7$, then z (the answer) = 13. Now, if you change x to 7 and leave y as 7, then z changes to 14 because $7 + 7 = 14$.

In terms of the families of persons with alcohol use disorders, if _you_ change x (and you're x), even though nothing changes with y (your loved one), then z (your relationship) still changes. It cannot possibly stay the same.

This is not to say it will be as cut and dried as algebra with a single solution answer, but the concept is the same. *Change yourself and your relationships will definitely change – including the one you have with you!*

Setting Boundaries

There is a somewhat darkly comic saying in recovery circles that goes something like this, "when the family member has a near death experience, it is not their own life but rather the lives of their loved ones that flash before their eyes." This is because family members who love those who drink too much are generally living everybody else's lives because they don't know how to set boundaries. Instead, their lives become enmeshed with those of others. Thus, learning to set boundaries can be one of the MOST HELPFUL recovery tools you can develop.

To help you better understand this concept, take a moment to think about how much time you spend worrying about your loved one, thinking about what they should or should not do, of what they've promised to do but haven't done, and replaying various scenarios in your mind based on what would happen if they did thus and such instead of this and that. Think about how you do this same thing with others in your life, as well – your children, friends, co-workers, or parents. And then think about all the many variations of those scenarios that arose once your loved one(s) actually took an action that was not in line with all of your thinking.

Exhausting, isn't it? Now, ask yourself, "Was it worth the emotional and physical time it took from me, from my day?" Sure, it's important to have your thoughts and suggestions and to make them known, but it's equally important to let go of the outcomes.

So, **boundaries are the limits we set on ourselves and on others** (and not just on the alcoholic or alcohol abuser – it can be with anyone – a boss, child, friend, or an in-law).

Boundaries allow us to take care of ourselves and at the same time, let go of trying to control others. They help us to reclaim "I."

The following can help you set boundaries that work for you, including how to set them.

Know What a Boundary Is

A boundary is the "line" that establishes where you and your business leave off and where other people and their business begins, leaving everyone to mind their own business.

Minding your own business, then, is about letting other people (including your children) take care of anything and everything that is within their power to do. It's about letting them live *their* lives while you live yours. It's okay to offer a gentle reminder or be willing to help. But it is not okay to butt in, or to manipulate through asking endless variations of the same question in order to get the answer or behavior *you* want, or to nag until other people do what you think is best for them. That means not cleaning up the empty cans left on the kitchen counter and or the liquor bottle and glass left on the coffee table when your loved one stumbled to bed last night. It means not picking up your child's dirty clothes from their bedroom floor and washing them. It means closing the bedroom door, instead (so you don't have to be triggered every time you walk by the open door) and letting them do their own laundry. [This assumes they're 10+ years and have been shown how to handle laundry. If you haven't, that's another boundary – show them how and tell them the new plan.] You'll find other examples of setting boundaries later in this section.

Setting boundaries is about minding your own business and allowing others to mind theirs.

It's about not making another person's problem yours or trying to smooth the way for other people so they do not "suffer."

Take a Look at Your Existing "Boundaries"

The examples listed below are often referred to as "enabling" behaviors [I know, I *really* dislike that label, too, but reviewing these examples can nevertheless be a useful exercise for you]. They are some of what the family member has been doing in order to make the drinking and/or alcoholism-related behaviors somehow okay or something a "good" mom, dad, husband, wife, brother, sister, child, or friend would do if they *really* loved their loved one who drinks too much.

These behaviors are what allows the "denial" and dysfunction in the family to continue. They are what cause family members to react to emotions (like anger or fear) as if they were fact, triggering the fight-or-flight stress reaction. They are what contribute to how/why a family member tolerates the progression of "awfulness," a level of awfulness they could never have imagined in the beginning. They are examples of unhealthy boundaries.

- Beginning with the statement, "I allow my loved one to_____" (fill in the blank by checking those that apply)
    - ☐ verbally, emotionally, or physically abuse me or my children or other family members
    - ☐ slide by at work while I cover for them
    - ☐ come and go at all hours
    - ☐ not spend time with the children or me
    - ☐ not keep appointments or follow-through with plans

- ☐ not repay debts
- ☐ be bailed out of jail
- ☐ live rent free
- ☐ drink too much while in my home
- ☐ borrow money
- ☐ have meals prepared or laundry done by me when they are fully capable of helping and/or doing so
- ☐ use my car
- ☐ other

- Beginning with the word, "I _____" (fill in the blank by checking those that apply)
  - ☐ protect my loved one from others or protect others from my loved one
  - ☐ make excuses for my loved one's behaviors
  - ☐ minimize my loved one's actions, lies, and excuses
  - ☐ don't confront my loved one because of their possible reactions
  - ☐ lie about what is really going on – to myself and others
  - ☐ don't confront (at least in a productive manner) my loved one when they've broken a promise to me
  - ☐ accept my loved one's explanations and reasons for their behaviors as something other than drinking too much
  - ☐ lend money when I know they haven't stopped drinking
  - ☐ pretend to the children that nothing is wrong, that it's not as bad as it seems, or that it's something else
  - ☐ other

Suggestion: In both the examples above, inserting the word, "don't," after the word, "I," (I *don't* allow my loved one to_____, and I *don't* _____) gives you the foundation of a healthy boundary. Go back to those statements and try it out. Notice how it feels when you say, "I *don't* _____."

Examples of Healthy Boundaries

Below are various examples of healthy boundaries that you may decide to create for yourself.

- Do not talk about anything important with your loved one when they are drinking or hung over. Just don't. And especially don't engage in nagging or trying to shame your loved one about their drinking in hopes that *this* time they'll do something about it. And to remind yourself why to keep this boundary: ask yourself, has it done any good so far?

- Do not drive with your loved one (they're good at hiding how much they've had to drink – see the text box below this section). An alternative to this is to install a breathalyzer interlock device, which requires a person to blow into the device. If alcohol is detected, the car won't start. This may seem drastic, and obviously you'd have to use it to start the car when you drive, but if drinking and driving is an issue, then you need to protect yourself and your children and all of the other drivers on the road.

- Do not answer your loved one's phone calls after a certain hour, for example, 4 p.m., if that's the time when they typically start drinking and changing behaviors.

- Do cut back your volunteer hours in your child's classroom (or elsewhere) to just one afternoon a week instead of two or three to leave time for you to do something you want to do.

- Do not join in the slicing and dicing and mincing of words. If you "know" they're not being truthful, you know. Let go of trying to get them to tell the truth and agree with you. They won't; they can't. Their brains have been hijacked by alcohol. Just remember – there isn't a score card.

- Do not have alcohol at every family get-together, especially ones that are to celebrate the children's birthday or some other child-centric gathering (if the alcoholic or alcohol abuser does not want to come, that's their decision).

- Do get help for yourself.

- STOP when you feel your frustration, fear, or anger rising. Then, breathe and calmly say, "I'm going to take a walk (or read, or call a friend, or pay some bills) – anything to stop you from getting sucked into the escalation of whatever typically happens next, whether it's a dramatic shouting match or a tense session of the silent treatment.

- Decide not to engage in pointless arguments. Remember: "No," is a complete sentence.

- Start a regular exercise program, regardless of whose "crisis" erupts as you're getting ready to go out the door to the gym or begin your home workout routine – deal with it later.

- Do not have late afternoon or evening visits with an actively drinking alcoholic or excessively drinking parent out of a sense of duty. You can time your visits (or phone calls) for early or midmorning when they've likely not started drinking, or they are more sober than they may be later in the day.

If You Loved Me, You'd Stop!

- Do not return a phone call message laden with guilt, such as, "You haven't called me today...where are you?...it must be nice to be so busy...."

- Refuse to give any more money to your child (or the loved one with alcoholism) but instead agree to pay rent and utilities directly to the payee (not through a deposit to your child or loved one's account) as long as they're in treatment and/or recovery.

- Buy a bus pass for your loved one who thinks they need a car that you should buy and maintain for them.

- Require other family members to help with chores, driving, shopping, and the like. Really, you don't have to do it all; others really are capable of doing and helping and will be grateful to be given the chance. [Often, it's guilt over what our children or other family members are going through that makes us want to make it up to them by "doing it all" so "at least they don't have to do chores, too!" But doing it all is extremely stressful, and we know what stress does to us – it becomes toxic. It harms our physical and emotional health and ruins the quality of our lives.]

- Take a nap instead of doing one more thing on your list of things to do.

- Let the alcoholic or alcohol abuser take FULL responsibility for ALL of the consequences of his or her actions and/or inaction.

- Talk with your loved one about their drinking and how it's affecting you (and the children, if applicable) – and talk in a way that is not designed to necessarily resolve anything, but to at least start calling it like it is. That means using some of the tools and suggestions shared in Chapters 11 and 12 in order to communicate in a way that is true for you, non-threatening and non-judgmental. Remember, too: Do *not* talk about these issues with loved ones while they've been drinking, and do not engage in conversations with an expectation or demand that they'll stop or change their drinking patterns.

I Was in the Car When He Got the DUI...

Why You Don't *Ever* Want to Ride in a Car if Your Loved One Drinks Too Much

I was in the car when Alex got a DUI. We'd been at a holiday dinner event at a multi-storied club, and I'd watched him like a hawk throughout the evening. I was convinced he'd only had one glass of wine with dinner, so I was okay with the idea of him driving us home after the event.

He went to get our coats, and it was one of those affairs that take forever to say all the good-byes, so I didn't register exactly how long he'd been gone. He explained, as he was helping me into my coat, that he'd gone to the bathroom and then ran into a couple of people on the way out as the reason for his delay.

We drove out of the city – which requires several turns, short streets and stoplights – and still nothing registered. Then, we got onto the freeway, and shortly thereafter, I asked him if he was okay. He was having a hard time staying within the lines. Almost immediately after the words left my mouth, the police pulled him over, gave him the "walk-the-line/touch your nose" test and took him to jail, allowing me to drive myself home.

Later, I learned he'd found a bar elsewhere in the club and had quickly "slammed back" several drinks during the time he was "getting our coats."

If You Loved Me, You'd Stop!

Hints About Setting Boundaries

Setting boundaries is hard, really hard – especially in the beginning. There is no doubt about it. It's hard because it's the opposite of what you've been doing for a long time. BUT, it's also reasonable because your loved one has the choice to change their drinking pattern (as in the case of alcohol abuse) or get treatment for their alcoholism. And you absolutely have the right to choose to live a safe, healthy, peace-filled life.

You don't have to stay physically and emotionally sick or have the very quality of your life destroyed so your loved one can keep drinking. You only have one life to live, too.

So, here are a few ideas to help you with setting boundaries:

Only set boundaries you can and will keep. "You cannot simultaneously set a boundary and take care of another person's feelings," says Jim Hutt, Ph.D., MFT (think about this one for a minute…). Other people may not like the boundary, but it is one you must set for *you*. For example, if you say, "Drink again, and I'm leaving," you must be prepared to leave. That means you'll first have to take the time to figure out things like what you'll need to bring with you, where you'll go, and how you'll leave. One woman I was working with kept giving her loved one this ultimatum. He knew she wouldn't follow through because it was her house they were living in, so she couldn't leave him! If you keep changing the boundaries you set, your loved one will know they can get you to change your mind the next time, which allows the dysfunction to continue.

Saying what's on your mind is setting a boundary. You don't have to have the whole solution to a problem before speaking your mind. For example, instead of, "Drink again, and I'm leaving," you might say, "Sometimes my fear that you will drink again, overwhelms me. It's really hard for me to trust and believe that this time will be different than the times before." And then use your other tools, like taking a moment to BREATHE, finding a yoga class, or taking a walk. You do not have to keep talking, if you don't want to.

When you use a statement like the one just suggested – instead of stating a boundary you're not ready to keep like, "Drink again, and I'm leaving," – you stop the denial and make your health and welfare more important than their "right" to drink. It also allows you to share your feelings about a conflict, but not get into an argument.

Know the "Red Flags" That Indicate It's Likely Time to Set a Boundary

- When you are feeling anxious or ashamed or afraid or inordinately angry, it is generally a signal that it's time to set a boundary. That boundary could take the form of using one of your reaction stoppers to stop yourself from going further with your reaction until you figure out the real cause of your anxiety or other feelings or to come up with a better response.

- When you find yourself wanting to get someone to do something *you* think they should do, like go to the gym because you think they need the exercise, it's likely you are "focusing over there" to avoid thinking about or addressing what's really bothering you. Try to catch yourself and figure out what's going on. And, it may be that you *do* have a good idea that might help that person – in which case you need to just say, "I have a suggestion, would you like to hear it?" And if they say, "No thanks," you have to honor their boundary and not plow ahead with giving your suggestion, anyway.

- When you keep trying to make your point in all sorts of different ways, you are probably trying to control the situation and its outcomes. Instead, set the boundary, say it once and then stop. Don't worry, the other person heard you. And if you say it only once, just think, you're free to do lots of other things! It keeps you from being their target and deflecting you with saying things like, "All you do is, nag, nag, nag."

- When you are complaining or rehashing the same transgression over and over or you keep repeating the same scenario looking for validation of the "rightness" of your part in a situation, it is usually time to set a boundary. Quite possibly the boundary may be for you to apologize for your part in whatever recurring "conflict" or "argument" happens with your loved one. And if the situation calls for your apology, do so without the "but ___," or "but you _____" as a way of getting the other person to recognize their part in the situation or to apologize back to you. That frees you to move on. Remember, don't expect your loved one to apologize or to "hear" you. Boundaries are about taking care of your business and allowing other people to take care of theirs.

- When you find yourself feeling defensive or telling "little white lies" to justify your behaviors or thoughts, it's time to remember you don't have to get another's approval for what you think or feel. Your boundary in the example above could be stopping yourself until you can sort things out, and then speaking your truth – and if you owe an apology, then go back and make one.

- When you find yourself judging or gossiping, it can be a sign that you are assigning your thoughts and feelings to what someone else has said or done. Or you might be focusing "over there" as a way of assuring yourself that you aren't that bad. In either case, stop and ask yourself, "Is this my business?" And, if it turns out to be a case of assigning your thoughts and feelings to what someone else has said or done, you can go back and clarify what *they* meant and then regroup.

When A Person with Alcoholism Tells You Who They Are, Take Their Word for It

The writer, Maya Angelou, once made this statement that is among her most famous quotes: "When someone shows you who they are, believe them the first time." In that spirit, I want to share with you the following anonymous "Open Letter to My Family," written by a person with alcoholism and distributed by a treatment center.

Don't allow me to lie to you and accept it for the truth. In so doing, you encourage me to lie. The truth may be painful but get at it.

Don't let me outsmart you. This only teaches me to avoid responsibility and to lose respect for you at the same time.

Don't let me exploit you or take advantage of you. In so doing, you become an accomplice to my evasion of responsibility.

Don't lecture me, moralize, scold, praise, blame or argue when I'm drunk or sober. And don't pour out my liquor. You may feel better, but the situation will be worse.

Don't accept my promises. This is just my method of postponing pain. And don't keep switching agreements. If an agreement is made, stick to it.

Don't lose your temper with me. It will destroy you and any possibility of helping me.

Don't allow your anxiety for me to compel you to do what I must do for myself.

Don't cover up or abort the consequences of my drinking. It reduces the crisis but perpetuates the illness.

Above all, don't run away from reality as I do. Alcoholism, my
illness, gets worse as my use continues. Start now to learn, to understand.

Don't Forget About the Condition of Your Loved One's Brain During Early Recovery

It is not uncommon for a loved one in early recovery to forget they have "brain trained" you to expect lies, excuses, broken promises, rationalizations, and the like.

They are usually so thrilled with their sobriety (and rightly so), they expect you to be just as thrilled. They may expect you to show it by letting "bygones be bygones" and often act out in hurt or anger when you question where they've been, for example. They forget (or choose not to consider) the reason you question where they've been is because "disappearing acts" generally meant they were drinking.

Know that you can, and should, expect to see a long period of consistent, trustworthy behaviors before you let down your guard and fully trust again. It's going to take quite some time for your loved one to heal and rewire their brain.

How will you know when it's okay to trust, again?

When your loved one no longer gives you the vibe (or outright says), "Cut me some slack, I stopped drinking, didn't I?" Or: "I'm going to meetings, what more do you want?" and instead says something like, "I know it's going to take time for you to trust me, again. I understand. Really, I do." That's when you will know your loved one is "in recovery." And that is what will make you open your heart (and your brain) to trusting, again. But it will take time, and that's okay.

Above all, understand that it is not your responsibility to NOT set a boundary for fear it will make your loved one relapse. What you say or do – or don't say or do – does not keep a person from relapsing. It's entirely up to our loved ones to do whatever they need to do to not drink and to heal their brains.

If You Loved Me, You'd Stop!

Chapter 14
What to Say to Children, Extended Family, and Friends, Plus Other Concerns

This chapter offers some suggestions on how to deal with a number of the worrisome matters you likely still have or have had to ignore or let go, like setting boundaries with your loved one to protect your children or addressing custody concerns in your Will. When you take charge of these kinds of things, you feel more in control and therefore less anxious. By the way, these matters *are* your business, no matter what your loved one may say, and they are another way to set boundaries that are good for your peace of mind. This, of course, is important to *reclaiming* YOUR life.

Understand Every Family Member Tells a Different Version of "Life at Home"

In families with a loved one who has alcoholism or where there is alcohol abuse, it is common for family members to have wildly different recollections of their lives in the same household. There is often disagreement about what happened or what's happening, how bad it was or is, who was right, and who was wrong. For example, the oldest child may recall mom as a wonderful, loving mother who baked cookies all the time, and the youngest of five might remember her as a "drunk" whose behaviors were so awful, he refused to bring his friends home. These kinds of differing memories can cause family members to argue amongst themselves – all vying for one or the other to see it from their perspective or agree with their recollections and thereby validate their experiences.

It's important to understand that each family member is correct. First of all, each individual sees things from their own perspective because of their uniqueness as an individual.

Secondly, the number of years and the stage of brain development during which those years were spent with the actively drinking alcoholic or alcohol abuser will also change a child's perspective. In other words, the family dysfunction influences on the oldest child may not have been nearly as severe as they were for the younger children. Not only this, but the way the children recall their time with the parent who doesn't have a drinking problem will differ, as well. That parent's stress reactions and coping behaviors also worsened as the alcoholism or alcohol abuse progressed.

Recognizing all of this helps family members accept they each have their own version of "life at home," and all of them are "right."

Help Your Children

Often, we assume that because our children have friends, play sports, get along with their teachers, have decent grades, and/or work, then all is well with them. But, growing up with a loved one's alcohol abuse or alcoholism affects *all* members of the family.

Talk to Them

The first step in helping your children is to have open, age-appropriate conversations with them about what has been going on and what you are doing to make things better for yourself and for them.

Use the information you've read in this book to help you with these conversations. Chapter 4 explained how the brain wires, maps, and develops. Chapter 5 described ACEs (Adverse Childhood Experiences) and how experiencing secondhand drinking can cause additional ACEs for a child. Chapter 6 explained the risk factors for developing alcoholism.

Your child potentially has one of the risk factors already – genetics. They likely have others and/or ACEs as a result of living with parental alcohol use disorder and experiencing secondhand drinking.

So, talking with your child over time will help them understand all of this. As importantly, it will help them see alcoholism for what it is, a brain disease, not something to be ashamed of. This talking should be done in stages, of course, which are explained next.

What to Say and When

Initially, your conversation with your children should be something very simple, along the lines of one of these examples:

- Things may have felt pretty chaotic, tense, and weird around here when it comes to the way _____ acts when they've been drinking alcohol. And it's not just the way _____ acts, it's the way *I* act when I'm trying to keep everybody safe. Anyway, I've been doing some research and have learned so much I never knew. Mostly, it's that drinking alcohol, among other things, can change the way a person's brain works. It's a chemical in alcohol that makes that happen. And it's those brain changes that make _____ behave the way they do and say the things they say. I'm just starting to learn about it, but I want you to understand that I know things have not been "normal" around here. I don't want you to be scared. Just know, I am doing what I can to figure this out so things can get better."

- If your children start asking questions you can't answer, tell them you don't know the answer but that you are learning as much as you can and will keep them informed. Assure them things will change for the better.

- If your loved one is at a treatment center that offers the services of a family therapist to help the family, then you can ask that person to guide you through this kind of a conversation.

Then, as you get more certain of your own thoughts and beliefs, sit down with your children to have a more detailed, open discussion about what has been going on. Allow your children to tell you about the scary behaviors they've experienced and how awful it's been without interrupting, correcting, dismissing, or minimizing what they have to say – even if it's about *your* behaviors! (And, don't be surprised if they don't know what [or have much] to say in the beginning. They probably don't have words for it, yet.) On your end, this kind of conversation will require:

- an age-appropriate description of alcoholism (or alcohol abuse) that helps them understand it is the brain changes caused by the chemicals in alcohol, brain wiring and mapping, and other things that cause their parent or sibling to say and do things that are unsettling or scary or weird

- a very clear message that alcoholism is a disease that can be treated (or in the case of alcohol abuse, drinking pattern can be changed) – that their parent or sibling can get better and be fun and happy and "normal," again, with the right kind of help

- a very clear message that there is absolutely NOTHING they do that causes their parent or sibling to drink or behave the way they do when they drink – not their fighting, not their bad attitude, not their poor grades, not their messy room, and certainly not because they're not showing enough of or the "right" kind of love – none of it!

Other Suggestions

Keep it simple. Again, recall Chapter 4 and how the Cerebral Cortex (especially the prefrontal cortex) is the last to develop. Because that "thinking" part of the brain is not yet fully engaged in children (depending on their age), long, detailed explanations can't/won't sink in. Your explanation can be as simple as, "_____'s brain changes when he drinks too much, which is what causes him to say and do things, like _____."

The National Association for Children of Addiction (NACoA) has two great sections on their website that can help with key points to cover in these kinds of conversations. One is *Just 4 Kids*, and the other is *Just 4 Teens*. *NIDA For Teens* is another great online resource. You might also suggest your child visit these sites on their own.

Have these early conversations with all children present in the beginning but also have them one-on-one. Remember, it's not uncommon for each child to have different memories or interpretations of what's happened/is happening.

As time goes on, initiate new conversations centered on the changes that are happening or whatever else they might want to discuss. This is important. It lets your children know they are free to break the crippling rules: Rule #1) drinking is not the problem, and Rule #2) don't talk about it and attack, minimize, or discredit anyone who does.

And, as you identify and understand your own stress reactions and coping behaviors (rage, sadness, silent-treatment, minimizing, excusing), you should also talk to your children about those, as well. Acknowledge how unsettling, confusing, or scary those may have been. Additionally, if you have toxic stress-related physical and mental health impacts, explain those, as well as why they happen. You may even use the secondhand drinking/secondhand smoking comparison because most children are well aware of secondhand smoking, and what it does to a person's health.

In time, help your children look at some of their stress reactions and coping behaviors – getting into fights or not being able to concentrate at school, for example, or arguing with a teacher or being rude to/lashing out at you. They, too, may have their own toxic stress-related physical and emotional health impacts, like anxiety, depression, stomach problems, or headaches. Help them know these are the result of their frustrations over their inability to make things better. Talking about your unhealthy stress reactions and coping behaviors and/or physical and emotional health problems will make it okay for them to talk about theirs. Once out in the open, you can decide together what might help your children repair their own brains so they can be more of who they "know" they are and find ways to be happier. You can also help your child learn ways to calm themselves, an important first step in healing their brains. If you haven't looked at it already, check out the YouTube video, *Just Breathe*, I previously mentioned.

And For the Siblings of a Child With an Alcohol Use Disorder

Parents, understandably, put a laser focus on the child with an alcohol use disorder (or other drug use disorder). This is their child, and they are trying to save their child's life! But time and again when I'm giving presentations to family groups – groups that include the adolescent with the substance use disorder, their parents, and their siblings – I see in the eyes of the other siblings, sentiments similar to those so eloquently shared in this anonymous poem:

> *I am the other child.*
> *The ok one*
> *I am the sober child.*
> *The one on the sidelines.*
> *I am the observer.*

The one watching him slowly killing our parents.
I am the angry one.
The one who's pissed because he's destroying our family.
I am the sad one.
The one losing her first best friend.
I am the reassuring one.
The one holding her Momma as she cries.
I am the torn one.
The broken one trying to hold everyone together.
I am the confused one.
The one who wonders how we became so unimportant and
invisible.
I am the other child.
The ok one.

It's important to remember that the time it's taken for an adolescent's alcohol (or other drug) use disorder to develop to the stage where parents are seeking treatment, there's been a lot of family dysfunction. No one knew what they were dealing with or how to stop it or how to help it. So, if your loved one is your child, I truly wish you all the best as you incorporate the information shared in this book to help your son or daughter and to help yourself. And I urge you to talk with your other children, as well. Do things with just them – especially one-on-one, if you can squeeze in that kind of time – when "all-things addiction and your other child" are forbidden conversation. Let them know you "see" them and know they're hurting, too. Let them know things will change and things will get better for everyone.

Additional Suggestions

Try your best not to get negative; not to smear the person with the alcohol use disorder. Remember, it is a brain disease/brain changer, and you'd want your children to feel free to love their sibling/parent with alcoholism the same way you'd want them to feel free to love their sibling/parent if they had cancer or heart disease.

It might also be helpful to arrange for your children to talk with someone outside the family system. Consider scheduling a few sessions with a therapist who is trained and experienced in working with children/siblings of people with alcohol use disorders. Another resource might be a trusted pediatrician. For young people ages 13 and up, you might suggest Alateen. The main thrust of all these suggestions is for you to help your children see that it's okay and safe to break the two primary, crippling "Rules" of dysfunctional families with a loved one who drinks too much.

Unleashed on Innocents

Often, we take out our fury towards our loved one out on our children. We may snap at our children or rush them through their bedtime routine or yell at them to stop "making noise" – all activities that might have been fine with us just the day before.

As you learn to recognize you're furious with the alcoholic/alcohol abuser, not your children, you can sit down with them and say, "I'm sorry I yelled at you. You weren't doing anything wrong. I was mad at Daddy because he was drinking and saying mean things to me last night. I should have talked to Daddy instead of yelling at you because I was so mad at him."

You will be amazed at how this helps your children. You validate what they sense is not making sense. You acknowledge your spouse's drinking is a problem that affects you. You also acknowledge that the way you handled your reaction to your spouse's drinking affected them, and that's not fair, either.

Boundaries to Set for Your Children's Sake

Create a safety plan they can follow should they ever feel threatened by the alcoholic or abusive drinker.

This might include you talking to a friend or neighbor and asking for their permission to allow your children to go to their house, anytime, day or night, if they feel scared. Make sure your children have the friend/neighbor's name and phone number and put it in a place where they can always access it. Take your children with you to the "safe" home so all of you can discuss this safety plan and how it might work. Your children must know it is not their responsibility to make it okay for the alcoholic or alcohol abuser to drink and treat them badly. Everyone in the family should feel safe and protected.

No driving with the alcoholic or abusive drinker – ever. With this boundary in place, your children don't have to try and determine if Dad or Mom has been drinking. This will require you and your children to work out alternative methods for your children to get to their destinations, as well as ways of saying, "No thank you," to solicitations by the alcoholic or abusive drinker. For example, if Dad asks, "Do you want to go with me to get an ice cream?" the children know they can say "No." Having said all this, it is a very touchy issue. For no matter how much explaining and talking with the alcoholic/alcohol abuser you may do, they may not be able to uphold the agreement. And, no matter how much you explain and talk with your children, your children may not be able to uphold the agreement. Acknowledging the difficulty of this dilemma for your children, however, is an important step, as is simply having a discussion about it, even if there is no resolution.

Anchor your child's days with some kind of structure. This might include age-appropriate chores, a bedtime story, breakfast together (since dinner can be iffy when the alcoholic/alcohol abuser is actively drinking), or a weekly outing (one they choose). The goal is to pursue any activity or daily ritual (like at bedtime) that lets your child feel a sense of consistency – that what is good today will also be good tomorrow. This allows them to begin to "trust," too.

Teach them the basics of how to identify when drinking has crossed a line. By this I mean the very basics covered in Chapter 2 of this book – such as low-risk limits, standard drink sizes, and how the body processes alcohol – so they can know when the loved one's brain has been changed by drinking.

Teach them the basics of alcoholism. Talk about how the adolescent brain develops so they understand what goes on with puberty and why things can be so confusing until their prefrontal cortex more fully develops. Explain it's not so much about "just say, 'No,'" as it is about letting your brain fully develop before you decide whether to drink alcohol. Talk about the risk factors for developing alcoholism (or other drug addictions), because let's face it, they have at least one – genetics.

Take Charge of Your Children's School Experiences and Medical and Dental Care

Often a parent with an alcohol use disorder who has been in charge of the children's school activities, tracking of grades, and medical/dental appointments (such as age-required medical check-ups, immunizations, bi-annual dental visits and the like) may have let their follow-through slip as their drinking progresses. It is important for you to gently insert yourself into this custodial role for your children's sake.

Ask your child's teacher to see report cards, for example, or to put you both on the email exchanges from school. Call the teacher and/or school counselor and schedule a meeting to touch bases and let them know what is going on at home. Nothing too deep. You don't have to provide all of the details to school personnel but giving them a general sense of what's happening in your family will help that teacher/counselor understand your child's slipping grades or behavioral issues, and thereby handle those differently. Remember, with nearly 80 million Americans affected by secondhand drinking, it's very likely your child's teacher/counselor knows what your child is going through.

Call your child's doctor or dentist for a health status update. If you're not comfortable explaining why you're the one checking, now, then don't. You are their parent, and you have a right to call.

One other thing to be aware of is it's also likely your children have been exposed to some horrific behavior on the part of their parent with alcoholism or alcohol abuse – especially if that parent is the one who cares for them after school. That parent may have yelled or raged at or hit your children, threatened them with further discipline if they told anyone, left them unattended, and/or drove the car with them in it after (or while) drinking. This may have led your child to withdraw from after-school activities and friendships. Again, the alcoholic/ alcohol abuser would never intentionally do any of this – truly – it's just the consequence of their brain impairment. Nonetheless, as long as they abuse alcohol or drink alcoholically, you'll need to do double duty to protect and support your children at home and after school, even if you are simultaneously working outside the home.

One suggestion is to arrange for another responsible adult or after-school program to help fulfill these roles and state your reasons and actions in a conversation with your loved one when they've not been drinking. Know that you do not have to defend yourself. This is an example of setting a reasonable and much-needed boundary for yourself and your children. And, in setting it, you validate for your children that what they've experienced is not "normal," not to be tolerated, and not anything caused by something they were or were not doing. And, you free them of the worry about what might happen if _____.

Life Insurance / Wills / Who Takes the Children if Something Happens to You

One of my biggest fears was that something might happen to me before my children turned eighteen and graduated from high school. Who would be their guardian given whom the courts would legally favor? How would my life insurance proceeds be controlled so they lasted until my daughters graduated from college?

One woman in a similar situation shared her views and what she did:

❖ *I added a codicil to my Will that explained the situation and stated my wishes for a guardian. Not that a court would necessarily grant my wishes, but I made them known. The point is, you should have a voice and give your children a voice if you are not there to speak for them. Additionally, I set up a living trust to include my life insurance policy and then made my children the beneficiaries of my trust, stipulating how I wanted the non-related trustee to disburse funds on their behalf. This way, the money they were to inherit would be used by the trustee to issue checks for expenses directly to whichever entity was charging them in order to avoid their inheritance being misappropriated by their alcoholic father.*

These kinds of issues should <u>definitely</u> be reviewed with a trusted legal and/or financial advisor – hopefully someone who understands alcohol use disorders.

Recognize the Difference Between "Parenting" and "Manipulating" and "Parenting with ACEs"

One of the most difficult things for me was to grasp the difference between "parenting" and "manipulating" (one of my common coping behaviors) when it came to my children. I desperately wanted to help them avoid my mistakes and to succeed as far as they possibly could in school, in sports, and with friends, so they would have "all their options open." Subconsciously, I was desperate they be okay in spite of all they'd experienced. And, in this desperation, I was unknowingly manipulating them with a vengeance to do what *I* thought they needed to do.

I coached, coaxed, nagged, and "helped" them constantly, practically tracking their every move, always being there to pick up the slack, making sure they had everything, making sure they completed everything on time, etc., etc., etc. I didn't realize that in so doing, my unspoken message was, "Here, let me do it because I don't think you can." Sometimes it was, "I don't think you're good enough." It was all done with the best of intentions, but I robbed them of some important opportunities to make their own mistakes and learn from those mistakes.

Fortunately, this was one of the first changes I worked on with my therapist, and thankfully, it seems I was able to change some of my coping behaviors in time to have made something of a difference before my daughters left for college. My therapist helped me understand that letting them do things for themselves was really giving them back their gut feeling – the voice we all have (or are trying to find, again) – that tells us what's right and what's wrong for us. The therapist helped me appreciate that my children will make mistakes – likely some big ones – and that's okay. Mistakes guide us to make better decisions next time.

And by the way, it took many years of practice for my new coping behaviors to be consistent enough that my daughters could really trust me, again. This was understandable given their early, formative years through their early twenties were as much affected by my stress reactions and coping behaviors as by our loved ones' drinking and/or alcoholism-related behaviors. They also had their own secondhand drinking experiences and ACEs, as well. As I've said before, it's a family disease.

Something else here is the idea of "parenting with ACEs." Parents, like myself and my mom, who experienced adverse childhood experiences before age 18 don't just get over those experiences as adults, as I explained in Chapter 10 in the section, "Look at Your Brain History." As a parent with untreated ACEs, it's easy to subconsciously be parenting from a place of fear, anxiety, frustration, or anger because you're being triggered by things your child is doing or not doing; things you're afraid will get them into trouble or harm them the way you'd been harmed as a child. (Of course, there is no way you'd have known it was ACEs or childhood trauma you were dealing with until you learned about the research I explained in Chapter 6). But that kind of parenting is simply passing ACEs from one generation to the next. As I also mentioned, you may want to look online for ACEs Connection Community – *Parenting with ACEs* for additional support and advice.

What to Tell Neighbors, Extended Family, and Friends

When you followed the fundamental "rules" of dysfunctional families with a loved one with an alcohol use disorder, you had to stay silent about the drinking behaviors and problems at home. But now that you are reclaiming your life, do you go around telling everyone about all of the messy details? That happens sometimes, so don't worry if you suddenly find yourself telling others more personal details than you ever dreamed of. Or, you may find yourself being very open on some days and others not. It can be confusing.

So, what *do* you tell neighbors, extended family, and friends? Short answer – only what you are comfortable talking about. Sadly, this is all still so shrouded in secrecy and shame that we may continue to be embarrassed or afraid to talk about it. Not only this, but the presumption is we have to protect the anonymity of our loved one. But remember, if your loved one had cancer, you'd be talking about it openly, and others who care about you would be there to help in whatever way they could.

This is not to say that you *should* talk openly, rather it's to say it's *okay* if you do.

As for what to say, if anything, keep it brief (unless it's someone you typically share everything with), something along the lines of what you might tell your children early on. This effort is not about making your neighbors, friends, or extended family feel better about or forgive your loved one, nor is it about getting their approval. It is simply a means of letting them know there is a reason for what you and your family have been going through and are working to change.

Another solution is to say something like, "I don't know how to fully explain this, yet, but I'll send you a link to a resource that I've found helpful." Then send them the link to the National Institute on Alcohol Abuse and Alcoholism (NIAAA's) website, *NIAAA Alcohol Treatment Navigator – What Is Alcohol Use Disorder*. Another link you may want to send is to NIDA's website, *Drugs, Brains, and Behavior: The Science of Addiction*. (You might even send them a copy of this book.)

You'll likely be surprised to find out they already know, or know someone who has an alcohol use disorder, or have someone in their family with an alcohol use disorder. Between the almost 16 million with an alcohol use disorder and the nearly 80 million experiencing secondhand drinking – the odds of this being the case are high.

Cover Your Assets

Know where you and your family stand financially. "Why?" you may ask.

If your alcoholic or alcohol abusing loved one is drinking and driving or spending money on alcohol and whatever else might accompany their drinking behaviors, you need to be sure you are not financially exposed or at risk of losing everything. This is crucial. Do not accept the brush off that he or she "handles it at the office" or that asking for information is proof you don't trust him/her. No matter how much you trust your loved one, remember, you are dealing with someone whose brain has been seriously changed. They may tell you just about anything to protect their ability to handle the family finances to their advantage.

Having said this, achieving a complete understanding of your family finances will likely be very hard for you to do early in your recovery. But it is hugely important to you and your children that you understand and protect your assets. Many of the actions suggested below will require you to talk with your loved one when they've not been drinking. And know that you don't have to make the point, "I'm doing this because of your drinking." These are realistic actions any spouse might take. And know, you will likely have to practice (a lot) with a trusted friend or therapist on what you plan to say, and how and when you'll say it. Here are some places to start:

Savings, checking, and utilities accounts. Be sure your name is on the accounts. With regards to savings and checking accounts, agree neither party may withdraw more than $X amount without the other person's signature. Make sure the signature card at the bank reflects this requirement. And, ask your bank to also lower the limit on ATM (debit) cards so only small amounts can be taken out at any one time. As for utility accounts, you need to understand that unless your name is on the account, you cannot talk to an account representative – period.

Order your credit reports. Make sure they are clear and your credit rating is good. Ask a bank employee how to do it or use one of the services available via the Internet that provides all three major credit reporting agency's reports (Experian, TransUnion, Equifax). If you find credit cards you weren't aware of, call the credit card company immediately. It's not uncommon for an alcoholic/alcohol abuser to open a credit card without your knowledge in order to purchase items they do not want you to know about. They simply include your name on the application as a second, authorized card holder. Tell the credit card company you did not authorize your signature and you want to be removed from the account entirely.

Know what you're signing before your sign your tax returns. If you have been signing your joint tax returns on the day they are due and not fully understanding what's in them and how the various line-items are calculated, you can and should find out. Insist you be allowed to sit down with the tax preparer, and also insist that in the future, this appointment with the tax preparer is scheduled well in advance of the April 15 due date. (Note: You can also file for an extension, if need be, instead of being rushed at tax time).

Ask your loved one if you have any interests in community property. For example, do you own an interest in the family home. If so, how is it legally titled? If not, why not? These are hard questions to ask – especially when you love and trust the other person – but they are critical to your financial future and security. You just never know what the future holds, and if you are the stay-at-home parent, your retirement, health benefits, and financial security is entirely in the alcoholic's or alcohol abuser's hands unless you insist otherwise.

Think about how you might handle what happens if your loved one gets a DUI (a.k.a. DWI). Who will drive him/her to and from work if he loses his/her license? How will you afford the legal fees and the increased car insurance costs?

Consult an attorney or financial advisor. It is possible to pay an hourly rate to talk with an attorney and/or financial advisor (as opposed to giving them a retainer) about your concerns and what you can legally do about them. Family law attorneys would deal with child-related issues, and trust/estate planning attorneys would deal with estate planning issues, as might a financial advisor. Take some time to consult a book or other resources on the subject and then make a detailed list of your questions and gather any applicable documents, such as bank statements, before you meet with an attorney or financial advisor. Nolo Press (now nolo.com) is a publisher of legal books covering many of these topics, including wills, trusts, and divorce. They can be an excellent place to start.

Take charge of paying the bills. By taking this step, you'll know where the money is going. If you do not want to be responsible for paying bills, do insist you see all bank and credit card statements.

❖ *Once, I had the experience of opening the door to find my neighbor standing there with a homemade pie and the foreclosure notice that had been taped to the door. I should have insisted on knowing the details about the part of our finances my husband "handled at the office."*

If Divorce and/or Child Custody is An Issue

If you are considering divorce, you'll likely have to "educate" your family law attorney about all of the realities of dealing with a loved one who has an alcohol use disorder. While some attorneys are obviously more aware than others, do not assume they know or understand even some of the basic issues you've learned about in this book. It's also possible that the attorney will likely have to "educate" the family court about all of this as well. But you can do that using the resources I've shared throughout this book.

On the flip side, if your ex-spouse had been in treatment for an alcohol use disorder and is now in recovery and seeking shared custody, it's important you understand that your ex should be given some level of custody or visitation for your children's sake. And that's because recovery is entirely possible as you learned in Chapter 7. If, however, you're not sure your ex is solid in their recovery, there are safeguards you can require before such custody is granted. Those safeguards could include having your loved one get a medical evaluation by an addiction specialist (a doctor who is certified by the American Board of Addiction Medicine, for example), requiring random drug testing by an outside vendor, or working with a Guardian ad Litem who understands all of this to help you work out a shared custody plan that's safe for your children. (A Guardian ad Litem is a person the court appoints to investigate what solutions are "best for the children.")

Have Some FUN!

Often, we miss the opportunities to just have fun as we work to come to terms with the consequences of a loved one's drinking. We get so bogged down in trying to get "well" – whether that be by attending meetings, reading recovery books, going to therapy sessions, talking, worrying, and/or struggling against a desperate urgency to start feeling better, NOW. So it's important and very okay to have FUN in spite of it all.

Fun doesn't have to be complicated or take loads of planning. Turn on some music and dance around the house, take a run, join your children in *their* world, eat a whole pint of your favorite ice cream, read a book. "Fun" means we don't talk about any of the problems caused by drinking behaviors; we don't even think about them (even if we have to pretend at first). It is a time to completely separate ourselves from all of it and immerse ourselves in the joy of having some fun. Abandoning ourselves for a few moments or 20 minutes or an hour, when we do something that has nothing to do with any of this recovery "stuff," can do us a world of good.

This is especially true when children are involved. Taking time for fun helps everyone start to believe that life really will get better, and trust me, it really does. Recall that recovery for all concerned is about rewiring neural networks and brain maps. In this case, the "fun" brain maps are those involving the pleasure/reward neural networks – the ones that rely on dopamine, the neurotransmitter that allows us to experience feelings of happiness and pleasure. And it's likely those are the neural networks that have not been used much, lately!

So, having fun is a great way to do this kind of pleasure/ reward neural network re-wiring. The more you do it, the more grooved those kinds of neural networks will become, and the more likely they will become your new brain maps. Best of all, those are the neural networks that can help you experience happiness and joy by engaging in the simple pleasures available throughout the day.

A Few Final Words...

Be Patient with Yourself

It will take time to unravel the stress reactions and coping behaviors that were absolutely necessary for you to survive the progression of your loved one's alcohol use disorder, so keep these in mind...

- Be especially wary of resentments – yours and your loved one's.

- Remember your loved one was incapable of logical thinking. They were incapable of understanding any of these kinds of connections: "I drink, I start picking on my wife/husband." "I drink, I get in a fight and go to jail." "I drink, I hurt my children." Instead, their thinking was, "I *must* drink, I drink." Thus, every time your loved one promised they would stop – tears, pleading and all – they meant it. But the neural networks that would have allowed the follow-through on those promises could not override the neural networks that drove every action to the point where your loved one had to drink again. It will take your loved one some serious time and commitment to their own treatment and recovery journey to unravel these neural networks.

- Keep your expectations low – not "off" – but not a beautiful Norman Rockwell family painting either, and certainly not a picture of a "perfect" family on social media or advertisements. For example, try not to put stock in the hope that *this* holiday will be the one you've always dreamed of – because it can't be until a whole lot of recovery happens for all of you. But it will certainly be better than it was before!

- Count to 10 or 100, take a walk, or head to the bathroom and lock the door when it feels as if you'll explode. Do anything to break the moment so you can collect your wits about you (and give your neural networks an opportunity to switch from Limbic System reactions to Cerebral Cortex responses). Know this suggestion is not meant to imply that you should stop or repress an emotion or feeling. In fact, it is imperative that you allow yourself to "have" your emotions and feelings. Rather, it is to buy yourself time to decide how you want to respond to them, if at all.

- If a worry keeps poking into your thoughts, don't run from it. Face it. Even if "facing" it is simply to jot down a note or mark your calendar with a time-period when you can/want to think about and/or take care of the worry. That can be in a day, a week, or even a month or two down the line. We don't have to have the answers or solutions immediately, but getting it out of our minds temporarily frees us to enjoy the moments in our day.

- Enjoy the parts you can. When you aren't so caught up with trying to stop what is beyond your control, you can focus on a child, on yourself, or on your own admiration of the meal you have prepared. Try to be "mindfully" engaged in whatever it is you are doing and focus on that.

- Above all, know that you are to be commended for your courage and strength to stay with it and do everything you have done to keep things together. You are not at fault. You had no alternative given you were dealing with something you did not understand. But now that you know what and why it happened and what lies ahead, you can take actions that will allow you to make changes that work for *you*.

Don't rush yourself and do not judge yourself harshly. You will make lots of mistakes and sometimes feel as though it will never, ever get better. But, it does. Really. Just do what you can, when you can, because any change, no matter how small, is a step away from the craziness and towards a life that's beyond anything you can presently imagine!

And remember:
Your brain IS your power to change.

Join Me in Breaking the Cycles by Changing the Conversations

Recall the early 1970s. Many adults smoked cigarettes, we didn't wear bike helmets, infant car seats hadn't been invented, having cancer was still something to hide, and we rarely used our seat belts. And think about how we viewed and treated HIV-Aids when it struck!

All of that changed drastically in just 20+ years – simply because people started reading and sharing the emerging research about these issues and taking action as they gathered knowledge. Today, bike helmets are mandatory for children under 18, seat belts are mandatory for every passenger, fire departments install infant car seats, cancer is openly discussed, and HIV-Aids is recognized as a condition that can be prevented and treated. Today, there are 1.1 million Americans living with HIV and 15.5 million living with all forms of cancer. That means the medical science and treatment protocols were/are there to diagnose and treat them so people can live fuller and longer lives – because cancer and HIV are now viewed as medical conditions.

That's what new information AND talking about it can do. It allows us to change things for the better. It is my hope we can cause similar dramatic shifts when it comes to alcohol use disorders and their impacts on family members and friends, namely secondhand drinking.

There are almost 16 million Americans struggling with alcohol use disorders, but only 10 percent of those with alcoholism get the help they need. There are nearly 80 million Americans struggling with secondhand drinking and very, very, very few get the help they need. But the science is now available to boldly, unequivocally state, alcoholism is a chronic, often relapsing brain disease that can be prevented and treated. The science is now available to boldly, unequivocally explain why repeatedly dealing with a loved one's drinking behaviors causes toxic stress consequences that can also be prevented and treated. But we have to share this information AND we have to talk about it.

It's time.

It's time to change the conversations and break the cycles of the devastating consequences of alcohol use disorders and secondhand drinking. In this manner, we free more than one-fourth the American population to fully live their lives, and we free the next generation.

Help Shatter the Stigma, Misinformation, and Shame

I shared the following post on my blog on May 8, 2013. It is titled, "The Shame of Addiction."

I saw it again last night as I faced an audience of people in treatment for substance use disorders, most commonly known as addiction, and their family members, all of whom were present to hear my lecture.

I saw the crushing emotional pain that surrounds this family disease on their faces, in their body language, in the way they did or did not look me in the eye or venture a tentative smile.

For the people with substance use disorders, it crossed the spectrum: shame, defeat, anger, embarrassment, defiance, sadness, regret, fear. Shame. For the family members, it crossed the spectrum: shame, defeat, anger, embarrassment, defiance, sadness, regret, fear. Shame.

Some were numb, some still detoxing, some only there because it's what they were supposed to do. For some, there was hope. For others, it was a last-ditch effort. For some, it just was.

Later that evening, after the program, one young girl sobbed the pain of having her alcoholic father scream at her that very afternoon, yelling at her to, "Shut the @#!* up!" when she tried to explain why the person giving her a ride to visit him could only stay two days and not the three he demanded. He'd ended the call telling her not to come at all, that he was done.

Between sobs, the young girl pleaded, "How does a father do this? How can a father threaten to cut his daughter out of his life for something over which she has no control? And I know he'll do it, and I don't want that. God, I hate this @#!*ing shit – he's been doing this my whole life! How does a father do this!?!?!"

It was that young girl, especially, who tore my heart open. They all do to some degree. But sometimes there's one that really hits me harder than others, for one reason or another. After decades of my own experiences with family members and friends who abused or were dependent on alcohol, a decade of my own secondhand drinking recovery work and years of trying to help others on both sides of this family disease, I think it was her raw, gut-wrenching, core-stripping pain that left me crushed by my powerlessness to help her in that moment. It took me back to my own moments of that kind of pain.

So I wrapped her in my arms. She let me, and in time, she wrapped me back. And I held her tight, while she sobbed through her rage and her pain. But I had no words. There are no words at times like that because there are no words that can possibly touch the pain and make sense of the nightmare.

But when I got home, I wrote this post in the hopes that she will read it someday, when her pain is less raw, on a day when she will be able to let these words into her heart – actually into her brain – because it's in her thoughts that words such as these must sink in order for her to ease her pain.

Six Suggestions to Shatter the Stigma, Misinformation, and Shame

1. Know it is not your Dad – the real person he was before his disease corrupted the very neural networks and neural network opportunities he needs to show you, his daughter, the love, respect, understanding, pride, and joy you so rightly deserve. He has a brain disease – one that is difficult to understand without understanding the disease. For this, consider these two websites: *"The Addiction Project,"* created by NIAAA, NIDA, the Robert Wood Johnson Foundation and HBO, and *Drugs, Brains and Behaviors: The Science of Addiction,"* created by NIDA.

2. Know it is not You – his daughter – you are the anyone or anything that interacts with his diseased brain that is now missing most of its normal functionality. It is not *you* – his daughter. The decades of chemical and structural changes that have occurred as a result of his disease make it so he cannot, nor will he ever, be the Dad you want him to be as long as he drinks any amount of alcohol and does not treat his disease. You are sadly the unwitting partner in "The Dance of the Family Disease of Addiction."

3. Know neither you nor your Dad is alone. Your dad is one of the 21+ million Americans struggling with alcohol or drug abuse or

addiction – of which only 10% get the help they need. You are one of the one in four children who lives in a family with a parent addicted to alcohol or drugs. Yet this disease is so shrouded in secrecy and shame, we often feel alone and struggle to sort and live through the host of conflicting emotions that comes with this family disease.

4. Understand that all you can do to help your Dad is to help yourself. Believe it or not, this will break the cycle because your exchanges are a cycle – they are "The Dance." More importantly, it will help you live a sane and joyful life in spite of your Dad's untreated brain disease. This help can be through therapy work with a counselor trained in addiction and its impacts on family members, a 12-step program for family members, mindfulness practices, and believe it or not, nutrition, exercise, and sleep. On this route, you will meet people who know the road you've traveled and are trained and/or have the personal experiences and recovery that can support you in your journey. Above all know – you are powerless over his brain on alcohol.

5. And when you can – when you are able – forgive. Forgive him because he knows what he's doing and hates himself for not being able to control his drinking, for not remembering but knowing something bad must have happened, for not having any friends or a job, and for only having estranged family ties. He hates himself because he cannot, for whatever reason, take the necessary steps to start treating his disease – likely because of the secrecy and shame that still surrounds it.

Forgive him to set yourself free, and know, that forgiveness does not mean erasing the pain or accepting the behaviors. It means letting go of the hope of a different past or a different outcome. Your Dad has a brain disease – a disease that robs him of his capability to think, feel, say, and do the things a father does when that father does not have this disease. Forgive in the sense you were both doing the best you could with what you knew at the time, which was a big fat zero. Forgive for your sake.

6. Know there is always hope. This brain disease can be successfully treated and people can live happier lives in recovery.

And Lastly

...know that I'm here and will do what I can to help you find resources and information. My confidential email is lisaf@BreakingTheCycles.com. There is no charge.

And to anyone else reading this post who finds themselves in a similar situation, I extend the same offer to you.

Together We *Can* Shatter the Stigma, Misinformation, and Shame!

Acknowledgements

This book would not have been possible without the thousands of stories, personal experiences, and conversations I've had this past 16 years with family members, friends, persons in recovery or seeking recovery, clinicians, therapists, treatment professionals, law enforcement officers, educators, health care providers – the swath of society so deeply affected by or involved in dealing with the impacts of a person's substance use disorders. These people's experiences, concerns, courage, research, insights, and recovery helped me focus my research in order to identify the most current information and qualified sources to answer the questions we all have had at one time or another.

I want to thank Catherine Bitler for so generously helping me over the years to simplify, while maintaining the integrity of, the research so that it is easily understandable by people seeking answers. And for the readers of an advanced copy of this book, please accept my heartfelt thanks for taking the time to read it and share your endorsements. And to my editor and friend, Mary Claire Blakeman, thank you – not only for your astute editorial suggestions and insights but for your support as I weathered the ups and downs of writing this book.

I want to thank the scientists, medical professionals, researchers and others on the front lines of the incredible advances in understanding the human brain, how alcohol and toxic stress can hijack the brain, what adverse childhood experiences can do to a child's developing brain, what it takes to change a drinking pattern or treat and recover from addiction, and so, so much more. It is this research and these discoveries that are changing how we view and treat alcohol and other drug use disorders and, as importantly, how we can help those who are so deeply, deeply affected – namely family members and friends.

Lastly, this book would not have been possible without the secondhand drinking recovery work I did with Jim Hutt, Ph.D., MFT, and Caroll Fowler, MFT, LMFC. I will be forever grateful to them (and so will my daughters!). I want to thank my family and friends – some of whom go back to the beginning – who have listened as I ranted and raved about the same kinds of problems, over and over, and yet supported me in ways I never imagined. Thank you with all my heart for "then" and for hanging in there as I've changed, and we move forward in new, fun, more light-hearted directions.

And to you, the reader, thank you. Thank you for taking your time to read this book, and hopefully finding new insights that can help you break the cycles by changing the conversations in your own life and with others who care.

About the Author

Lisa Frederiksen has 40+ years of personal experience with secondhand drinking, a concept she first introduced in 2009. Working to overcome its impact, she's spent the last 16 years studying and simplifying 21st Century brain and scientific research on topics related to those experiences. These topics include alcoholism, drug addiction, alcohol and other drug use disorders, mental illness, co-occurring disorders, the family member's experience, toxic stress, adverse childhood experiences, codependency, brain development, and childhood trauma.

This work has culminated in her latest book – 10th Anniversary Edition *If You Loved Me, You'd Stop! What You* Really *Need To Know When Your Loved One Drinks Too Much.*

Lisa founded BreakingTheCycles.com in 2008 to change, and in some cases simply start, the conversations on the topics just mentioned. She has appeared as an expert guest on a variety of television, radio, and Internet radio programs, as well as authored hundreds of blog posts and articles for other publications. She is a nationally recognized keynote speaker with over thirty years' public speaking experience and the author of twelve books, including *Loved One In Treatment? Now What!* and *Secondhand Drinking: The Phenomenon That Affects Millions.* She consults with individuals, families, and organizational clients throughout the United States and from as far away as Kenya, Mexico, and Ireland about these topics.

For more about Lisa Frederiksen, visit BreakingTheCycles.com and LisaFrederiksen.com.

Selected Bibliography

As you can imagine, there are scores of pages of resources I have studied and used over the years to develop my knowledge base for the topics I cover in this book. This is a selected bibliography to give you a sampling of the resources that may help you further answer your questions.

ACEs Connection. "Communities." [A list of all groups (communities) working on some aspect of ACEs, such as parenting, juvenile justice, education, early childhood, etc.] https://www.acesconnection.com/groups.

ACEs Too High. "ACEs Science 101: ACEs Science FAQs." https://acestoohigh.com/aces-101/(a https://acestoohigh.com/aces-101/ (accessed 2.3.19).

ACEs Too High, "Got Your ACEs Score?" https://acestoohigh.com/got-your-ace-score/ (accessed 1.22.19).

Alcohol Research Group (ARG). "Overview." https://arg.org/research/overview/ (Accessed 1.4.19).

American Academy of Pediatrics. "Substance Use Screening and Brief Intervention for Youth." https://www.aap.org/en-us/advocacy-and-policy/aap-health-initiatives/Pages/Substance-Use-Screening.aspx (accessed 2.3.19).

American Psychological Association. "Stress effects on the body." https://www.apa.org/helpcenter/stress-body (accessed 4.3.19).

American Society of Addiction Medicine (ASAM). "Resources: Definition of Addiction." https://www.asam.org/resources/definition-of-addiction. (accessed 4.23.19).

Anda, Robert, MD, MS and Co-Principal Investigator Adverse Childhood Experiences (ACE) Study. "The Health Impacts of Growing Up with Alcohol Abuse and Related Adverse Childhood Experiences: The Human and Economic Costs of the Status Quo." National Association of Children of Addiction. http://www.nacoa.net/pdfs/Anda%20NACoA%20Review_web.pdf (accessed 5.7.19).

Babor, Thomas F., Higgins-Biddle, John C., Saunders, John B., Monteiro, Maristela G. *AUDIT: The Alcohol Use Disorders Identification Test, Guidelines for Use in Primary Care*. Second Edition. World Health Organization Department of Mental Health and Dependence, 2001. https://www.who.int/substance_abuse/publications/audit/en/.

Beattie, Melody. *Codependent No More, How To Stop Controlling Others and Start Caring For Yourself*. Second Edition. Center City, MN: Hazelden, 1992.

Bellis, Mark et al. "The impact of adverse childhood experiences on health service use across the life course using a retrospective cohort study." *Journal of Health Services Research & Policy* 2017, 22(3): 168–177. doi:10.1177/1355819617706720.

Bettinardi-Angres, MS, RN, APN, CADC and Angres, Daniel H., M.D. "Understanding the Disease of Addiction." *Journal of Nursing Regulation* July 2010, 1(2): 31-37. https://www.ncsbn.org/Understanding_the_Disease_of_Addiction.pdf (accessed 5.23.19).

Black, Claudia, Ph.D. *Unspoken Legacy, Addressing the Impact of Trauma and Addiction Within the Family.* Las Vegas: Central Recovery Press, 2018.

Brown, Stephanie and Virginia Lewis, Ph.D. *The Alcoholic Family in Recovery, a Developmental Model.* New York: The Guilford Press, 2009.

Brown, Stephanie and Virginia Lewis, Ph.D., with Andrew Liotta. *The Family Recovery Guide, a Map for Healthy Growth.* Oakland: New Harbinger Publications, Inc., 2000.

Carter, Rita, Aldridge, Susan, Page, Martyn, Parker, Steve. *The Human Brain Book,* New York: DK (Dorling Kindersley Limited) Publishing, 2009.

Center on the Developing Child at Harvard University. "Resilience." https://developingchild.harvard.edu/science/key-concepts/resilience/ (accessed 3.2.19).

Center on the Developing Child at Harvard University. "Toxic Stress." https://developingchild.harvard.edu/science/key-concepts/toxic-stress/ (accessed 4.12.19).

Centers for Disease Control and Prevention. "Adverse Childhood Experiences (ACEs)." https://www.cdc.gov/violenceprevention/childabuseandneglect/acestudy/index.html (accessed 4.15.19).

Centers for Disease Control and Prevention. "Alcohol and Public Health." https://www.cdc.gov/alcohol/ (accessed 1.14.19).

Dayton, Tian, Ph.D. "Remembering the Children Trapped by Addiction." ACEs Connection, May 13, 2019.

https://www.acesconnection.com/blog/remembering-the-children-trapped-by-addiction (accessed 5.20.19).

Dayton, Tian, Ph.D. *The ACoA Trauma Syndrome: The Impact of Childhood Pain on Adult Relationships.* Deerfield Beach, Florida: Health Communications, Inc., 2012.

Dennis, Michael and Christy K Scott. "Managing addiction as a chronic condition." *Addiction Science & Clinical Practice* 2007, 4(1): 45-55. https://www.ncbi.nlm.nih.gov/pmc/articles/PMC2797101/ (accessed 6.12.19).

Doidge, M.D., Norman. *The Brain That Changes Itself, Stories of Personal Triumph from the Frontiers of Brain Science.* New York: Penguin Books, 2007.

Doidge, Norman, M.D. *The Brain's Way of Healing.* New York: Penguin Books, 2015.

Felitti, Vincent J., MD, FACP, Anda, Robert F., MD, Nordenberg, Dale, MD, Williamson, David F., MS, PhD., Spitz, Alison M., MS, MPH, Edwards, Valerie, BA, Koss, Mary P., Ph.D., Marks, James S., MD, MPH. "Relationship of Childhood Abuse and Household Dysfunction to Many Leading Causes of Death in Adults, The Adverse Childhood Experiences (ACE) Study." *American Journal of Preventative Medicine* May 2018, 14(4): 245-258. doi: 10.1016/S0749-3797(98)00017-8.

Felitti, Vincent J. "The Relation Between Adverse Childhood Experiences and Adult Health: Turning Gold into Lead." *The Permanente Journal* Winter 2002, 6(1): 44-47. https://www.ncbi.nlm.nih.gov/pmc/articles/PMC6220625/pdf/permj-6-1-44.pdf (accessed 4.3.19).

Fisher, Sebern F. *Neurofeedback in the Treatment of Developmental Trauma, Calming the Fear-Driven Brain.* New York: W.W. Norton & Company, 2014.

Fletcher, Anne M. *Inside Rehab, The Surprising Truth About Addiction Treatment – And How to Get Help That Works.* New York: Viking, 2013.

Foote, Jeffrey, Ph.D., Wilkens, Carrie, Ph.D., and Kosanke, Nicole, Ph.D., with Stephanie Higgs. *Beyond Addiction, How Science and Kindness Help People Change, A Guide for Families.* New York: Scribner, 2014.

Frederiksen, Lisa. "Global Research on Alcohol's Harm to Others – Secondhand Drinking." SHD Prevention.com, September 21, 2015. https://shdprevention.com/global-research-alcohols-harm-others/ (accessed 3.2.19).

Galanter, M.D., Marc and Herbert D.Kleber, M.D. *The American Psychiatric Publishing Textbook of Substance Abuse Treatment, Fourth Edition.* Washington, D.C. American Psychiatric Publishing, Inc., 2008.

Grisel, Judith. *Never Enough, The Neuroscience and Experience of Addiction.* New York: Doubleday, 2019.

Harris, Nadine Burke, M.D. "How childhood trauma affects health across a lifetime." TEDMED, 2014. https://www.ted.com/talks/nadine_burke_harris_how_childhood_tra uma_affects_health_across_a_lifetime?language=en (accessed 11.4.18).

Kolb, Ph.D., Bryan and Whishaw, Ian Q., Ph.D. *An Introduction to Brain and Behaviors.* Second Edition. New York: Worth Publishers, 2006, 2001, p. 79.

Lander, Laura, Howsare, Janie, and Byrne, Marilyn. "The Impact of Substance Use Disorders on Families and Children: From Theory to Practice." *Soc Work Public Health* 2013, 28(3-4): 194-205. doi:10.1080/19371918.2013.759005.

Lemonick, Michael D. with Alice Park, "The Science of Addiction," *TIME,* July 16, 2007, p. 46.

Manejwala, Omar, M.D. "How Often Do Long-Term Sober Alcoholics and Addicts Relapse." *Psychology Today Online,* February 13, 2014. https://www.psychologytoday.com/us/blog/craving/201402/how-often-do-long-term-sober-alcoholics-and-addicts-relapse (accessed 3.24.19).

McKay, James R., Ph.D. and Hiller-Sturmhöfel, Susanne, Ph.D. "Treating Alcoholism as a Chronic Disease: Approaches to Long-Term Continuing Care." *Alcohol Research Current Reviews* 2011, 33(4): 356-370. https://www.ncbi.nlm.nih.gov/pmc/articles/PMC3625994/ (accessed 5.25.19).

Mee-Lee, David, M.D., Editor. *The ASAM Criteria, Treatment Criteria for Addictive, Substance-Related, and Co-Occurring Conditions, Third Edition.* Chevy Chase, Maryland: American Society of Addiction Medicine, Inc., 2013.

Mental Health America. "Co-dependency." https://www.mentalhealthamerica.net/co-dependency (accessed 5.1.19).

If You Loved Me, You'd Stop!

Miller, John, M.D. "Optimizing Brain Health." Psychiatric Times July 11, 2019, 36(7). https://www.psychiatrictimes.com/brain-health/optimizing-brain-health (accessed 7.18.19).

Moe, Jerry. *Understanding Addiction and Recovery Through a Child's Eyes.* Deerfield Beach, Florida: Health Communications, Inc., 2007.

Nakazawa, Donna Jackson. *Childhood Disrupted, How Your Biography Becomes Your Biology, and How You Can Heal.* New York: Atria Books, 2015.

Nayak, Madhabika B., Ph.D., Patterson, Diedre, M.P.h., Wilsnack, Sharon C., Ph.D., Karriker-Jaffe, Katherine J., Ph.D., & Greenfield, Thomas K., Ph.D. "Alcohol's Secondhand Harms in the United States: New Data on Prevalence and Risk Factors." *Journal of Studies on Alcohol and Drugs* 2019, 80(3): 273-281. doi.org/10.15288/jsad.2019.80.273.

National Alliance on Mental Illness (NAMI) Hearts & Minds. "Mental Illness and Substance Abuse." January 2010. https://azdhs.gov/documents/az-state-hospital/nami-mental-illness-substance-abuse.pdf (accessed 3.13.19).

National Association for Children of Addiction (NACoA). "Children Impacted by Addiction: A ToolKit for Educators." Kensington, Maryland: NACoA, 2018. https://www.addictionpolicy.org/hubfs/Kit4Teachers_ALt_2018-4.pdf (accessed 3.18.19).

National Institute on Alcohol Abuse and Alcoholism (NIAAA). "Alcohol and Your Health, Research-based Information on Drinking and Its Impacts." https://www.niaaa.nih.gov/alcohol-health (accessed 5.21.19).

National Institute on Alcohol Abuse and Alcoholism (NIAAA). "Alcohol Facts and Statistics." Updated August 2018. https://www.niaaa.nih.gov/alcohol-health/overview-alcohol-consumption/alcohol-facts-and-statistics (accessed 11.30.18).

National Institute on Alcohol Abuse and Alcoholism (NIAAA). "Alcohol Use Disorder: A Comparison Between DSM-IV and DSM-5." NIH Publication No. 13-7999. Revised 2016. https://www.niaaa.nih.gov/publications/brochures-and-fact-sheets/alcohol-use-disorder-comparison-between-dsm (accessed 5.10.19).

National Institute on Alcohol Abuse and Alcoholism (NIAAA). "Genetics of Alcohol Use Disorder." https://www.niaaa.nih.gov/alcohol-health/overview-alcohol-consumption/alcohol-use-disorders/genetics-alcohol-use-disorders (accessed 1.23.19).

National Institute on Alcohol Abuse and Alcoholism (NIAAA). "Research: Major Initiatives." https://www.niaaa.nih.gov/research/major-initiatives (accessed 5.21.19).

National Institute on Alcohol Abuse and Alcoholism (NIAAA). "Rethinking Drinking." https://www.rethinkingdrinking.niaaa.nih.gov/ (accessed 1.4.19).

National Institute on Alcohol Abuse and Alcoholism (NIAAA). "Treatment Navigator." https://alcoholtreatment.niaaa.nih.gov/ (accessed 6.2.19).

National Institute on Drug Abuse (NIDA), National Institute on Alcohol Abuse and Alcoholism (NIAAA), Robert Wood Johnson Foundation. *Addiction.* HBO: HBO Original Documentaries, 2007.

National Institute on Drug Abuse (NIDA). "Drugs, Brains, and Behavior: The Science of Addiction." U.S U.S. Department of Health And Human Services, NIH Publication No. 18-DA-5605. April 2007, Revised February 2008, August 2010, July 2014, July 2018.

National Institute on Drug Abuse (NIDA). "Principles of Drug Addiction Treatment: A Research-Based Guide (Third Edition)." National Institute on Drug Abuse; National Institutes of Health; U.S. Department of Health and Human Services, Last Updated January 2018.

National Institute on Drug Abuse (NIDA). "Principles of Adolescent Substance Use Disorder Treatment: A Research-Based Guide." NIH Publication Number 14-7953, January 2014.

National Institute on Drug Abuse (NIDA), "Research Report Series: Comorbidity: Addiction and Other Mental Illnesses." NIH: National Institute on Drug Abuse. Revised September 2010, https://www.drugabuse.gov/sites/default/files/rrcomorbidity.pdf (accessed 1.12.19).

National Organization on Fetal Alcohol Syndrome (NOFAS). "Light Drinking During Pregnancy." https://www.nofas.org/light-drinking/ (accessed 5.17.19).

Office of the Surgeon General. *FACING ADDICTION IN AMERICA: The Surgeon General's Report on Alcohol, Drugs, and Health.* Washington, DC: U.S. Department of Health and Human Services, 2016.

Ratey, M.D., John J. with Erick Hagerman. *SPARK, the Revolutionary New Science of Exercise and the Brain.* New York: Little Brown & Co., 2008.

Redford, James and Pritzker, Karen. *ACEs Primer*. KPJR Films, 2016.

Redford, James and Pritzker, Karen. *Paper Tigers*. KPJR Films, 2015.

Redford, James and Pritzker, Karen. *Resilience, The Biology of Stress & The Science of Hope*. KPJR Films, 2016.

Ries, M.D., FAPA, FASAM, Richard K., et al, (editors). *Principles of Addiction Medicine, Fourth Edition*. Philadelphia: Lippincott Williams & Wilkins, 2009.

Selhub, Eva, M.D. "Nutritional psychiatry: Your brain on food." Harvard Health Blog, Harvard Medical School, November 16, 2015. https://www.health.harvard.edu/blog/nutritional-psychiatry-your-brain-on-food-201511168626 (accessed 2.12.19).

Smith, David E., M.D. "History of Medicine: The Evolution of Addiction Medicine as a Medical Specialty." *Virtual Mentor* 2011, 13(12): 900-905. doi: 10.1001/virtualmentor.2011.13.12.mhst1-1112.

Substance Abuse and Mental Health Services Administration (SAMHSA). "Mental Health and Substance Use Disorders." https://www.samhsa.gov/find-help/disorders (accessed 12.10.18).

Substance Abuse and Mental Health Services Administration (SAMHSA). "Working Definition of Recovery." https://store.samhsa.gov/system/files/pep12-recdef.pdf (accessed 2.13.19).

Szalavitz, Maia. *Unbroken Brain, A Revolutionary New Way of Understanding Addiction*. New York: St. Martin's Press, 2016.

The European School Survey Project on Alcohol and Other Drugs (ESPAD). "The 2015 ESPAD Report." http://www.espad.org/report/home/ (accessed 3.14.19).

The National Center on Addiction and Substance Abuse at Columbia
University (CASA). "Addiction Medicine: Closing the Gap between
Science and Practice." June 2012.
https://www.centeronaddiction.org/addiction-
research/reports/addiction-medicine-closing-gap-between-science-
and-practice (accessed 3.18.19).

The National Child Traumatic Stress Network (NCTSN). "About
Childhood Trauma." https://www.nctsn.org/what-is-child-
trauma/about-child-trauma (accessed 4.25.19).

Tisch, Rosemary. "Celebrating Families!" National Association of
Children of Addiction: Celebrating Families.
http://celebratingfamilies.net/ (accessed 2.1.19).

van der Kolk, Bessel, M.D. *The Body Keeps the Score: Brain, Mind, and
Body in the Healing of Trauma.* New York: Penguin Books, 2014.

White, Cissy. "Understanding ACEs, Parenting to Prevent & Heal ACEs
(English, Dari & Spanish)." ACEs Connection, Parenting With
ACEs. January 28, 2019.
https://www.acesconnection.com/g/Parenting-with-
ACEs/blog/parent-handouts-understanding-aces-parenting-to-
prevent-and-heal-aces-english-and-dari (accessed 7.1.19).

White, William L. *Slaying the Dragon, The History of Addiction
Treatment and Recovery in America.* Normal, Illinois: Chestnut
Health Systems Publication, 1998.

Wood, Evan, M.D., Ph.D., FRCPC, Samet, Jeffrey H., MD, Volkow,
Nora D., M.D. "Physician Education in Addiction Medicine."
Journal of the American Medical Association October 23, 2013,
310(16): 1673-74. doi: 10.1001/jama.2013.2880377.

If You Loved Me, You'd Stop!

Endnotes

Chapter 1
[1] U.S. Department of Health and Human Services: Office of the Surgeon General, "The Surgeon General's Report on Alcohol, Drugs, and Health, Key Findings: The Neurobiology of Substance Use, Misuse, and Addiction," 2016, https://addiction.surgeongeneral.gov/key-findings/neurobiology (accessed 1.7.19).

Chapter 2
[2] National Institute of Health: National Institute on Alcohol Abuse and Alcoholism (NIAAA), "Alcohol Use Disorder: A Comparison Between DSM-IV and DSM-5," NIH Publication No. 13-7999, Revised 2016, https://www.niaaa.nih.gov/publications/brochures-and-fact-sheets/alcohol-use-disorder-comparison-between-dsm (accessed 5.10.19).

[3] Centers for Disease Control and Prevention (CDC), "Fact Sheets – Alcohol Use and Your Health," Last Reviewed January 3, 2018, https://www.cdc.gov/alcohol/fact-sheets/alcohol-use.htm (accessed 1.4.19).

[4] Breaking The Cycles – Changing the Conversations with Lisa Frederiksen, "Help for Families of Addicts | Alcoholics – Interview with Authors Jeffrey Foote and Nicole Kosanke," *BreakingTheCycles.com*, March 2, 2014, https://www.breakingthecycles.com/blog/2014/03/02/families-of-addicts-alcoholics-interview-authors-jeffrey-foote-nicole-kosanke/ (accessed 1.20.19).

[5] Dayton, Tian, Ph.D., "Remembering the Children Trapped by Addiction," *ACEs Connection*, May 13, 2019,

https://www.acesconnection.com/blog/remembering-the-children-trapped-by-addiction (accessed 5.20.19).

[6] National Institute on Alcohol Abuse and Alcoholism (NIAAA), "Alcohol Facts and Statistics," August 2018, https://www.niaaa.nih.gov/alcohol-health/overview-alcohol-consumption/alcohol-facts-and-statistics (accessed 1.17.19).

[7] National Institute on Alcohol Abuse and Alcoholism (NIAAA), Rethinking Drinking, "How much is too much?" https://www.rethinkingdrinking.niaaa.nih.gov/How-much-is-too-much/Is-your-drinking-pattern-risky/Whats-Low-Risk-Drinking.aspx (accessed December 12, 2018).

[8] National Institute on Alcohol Abuse and Alcoholism (NIAAA), Rethinking Drinking, "What's a 'standard' drink?" https://www.rethinkingdrinking.niaaa.nih.gov/How-much-is-too-much/What-counts-as-a-drink/Whats-A-Standard-Drink.aspx (accessed 1.4.19).

[9] Centers for Disease Control (CDC), "Fact Sheets – Alcohol Use and Your Health," https://www.cdc.gov/alcohol/fact-sheets/alcohol-use.htm (accessed 5.12.18).

[10] Centers for Disease Control (CDC), "Alcohol and Public Health: Frequently Asked Questions," Last Reviewed March 29, 2018, https://www.cdc.gov/alcohol/faqs.htm#excessivealcohol (accessed 5.12.19).

[11] *Ibid.*

Chapter 3
[12] World Health Organization (WHO), "AUDIT, The Alcohol Use Disorders Identification Test for Use in Primary Care," Second Edition, pg. 2,

http://apps.who.int/iris/bitstream/handle/10665/67205/WHO_MSD_MS
B_01.6a.pdf;jsessionid=7A62466DFCAC1253968C87E3E9A8BD91?se
quence=1 (accessed 1.5.19).

[13] *Ibid.*, pgs. 17, 19 and 20.

[14] National Institute on Alcohol Abuse and Alcoholism (NIAAA),
"Alcohol & Your Health, Alcohol Use Disorder,"
https://www.niaaa.nih.gov/alcohol-health/overview-alcohol-
consumption/alcohol-use-disorders (accessed 3.14.19).

[15] World Health Organization (WHO), "AUDIT, The Alcohol Use
Disorders Identification Test for Use in Primary Care," Second Edition,
pgs. 5-6,
http://apps.who.int/iris/bitstream/handle/10665/67205/WHO_MSD_MS
B_01.6a.pdf;jsessionid=7A62466DFCAC1253968C87E3E9A8BD91?se
quence=1 (accessed 1.5.19).

[16] Office of the Surgeon General (US); National Institute on Alcohol
Abuse and Alcoholism (US); Substance Abuse and Mental Health
Services Administration (US). "The Surgeon General's Call to Action To
Prevent and Reduce Underage Drinking. Rockville (MD): Office of the
Surgeon General (US); 2007. Appendix B: DSM-IV-TR Diagnostic
Criteria for Alcohol Abuse and Dependence," Available from:
https://www.ncbi.nlm.nih.gov/books/NBK44358,
https://www.ncbi.nlm.nih.gov/books/NBK44358/ (accessed 5.20.19).

[17] *Ibid.*

[18] *Ibid.*

[19] Office of the Surgeon General, "FACING ADDICTION IN
AMERICA: The Surgeon General's Report on Alcohol, Drugs, and
Health," HHS Publication No. (SMA) 16-4991, 2016, pg. 2-2,
https://addiction.surgeongeneral.gov/sites/default/files/surgeon-generals-
report.pdf (accessed 5.15.19).

[20] National Institute on Drug Abuse (NIDA), "Drugs, Brains, and Behavior: the Science of Addiction > What is Drug Addiction?" Updated July 2018, https://www.drugabuse.gov/publications/drugs-brains-behavior-science-addiction/drug-misuse-addiction (accessed 5.17.19).

[21] National Institute on Drug Abuse (NIDA), "Drugs, Brains, and Behavior: The Science of Addiction > How Science Has Revolutionized the Understanding of Drug Addiction," Updated July 2018, https://www.drugabuse.gov/publications/drugs-brains-behavior-science-addiction/preface (accessed 5.16.19).

Chapter 4

[22] Kolb, Ph.D., Bryan and Whishaw, Ian Q., Ph.D., *An Introduction to Brain and Behaviors, Second Edition,* New York: Worth Publishers, 2006, 2001, p. 79.

[23] Sukel, Kayt, "The Synapse – A Primer," The Dana Foundation News, March 15, 2011, http://www.dana.org/News/Details.aspx?id=43512 (accessed 1.11.19).

[24] Doidge, M.D., Norman, *The Brain That Changes Itself, Stories of Personal Triumph from the Frontiers of Brain Science,* New York: Penguin Books, 2007, p. 63.

[25] *Ibid.,* p. 48.

[26] National Organization on Fetal Alcohol Syndrome (NOFAS), "Light Drinking During Pregnancy," https://www.nofas.org/light-drinking/ (accessed 5.17.19).

[27] National Institute on Drug Abuse (NIDA), *Drugs, Brains, and Behavior: The Science of Addiction, Why is adolescence a critical time for preventing drug addiction?"* https://www.drugabuse.gov/publications/drugs-brains-behavior-science-

addiction/preventing-drug-misuse-addiction-best-strategy (accessed 6.1.19).

[28] National Institute on Drug Abuse (NIDA), "Research Report Series: Comorbidity: Addiction and Other Mental Illnesses," NIH: National Institute on Drug Abuse, p. 5, Revised September 2010, https://www.drugabuse.gov/sites/default/files/rrcomorbidity.pdf (accessed 1.12.19).

[29] National Institute on Drug Abuse (NIDA), "Drugs, Brains, and Behavior: The Science of Addiction," NIH: National Institute on Drug Abuse, Last Updated July 2018, https://www.drugabuse.gov/publications/drugs-brains-behavior-science-addiction/drugs-brain (accessed on 1.16.19).

[30] Doidge, M.D., Norman, *The Brain That Changes Itself, Stories of Personal Triumph from the Frontiers of Brain Science,* New York: Penguin Books, 2007, p. xx.

Chapter 5

[31] Lemonick, Michael D. with Alice Park, "The Science of Addiction," *TIME,* July 16, 2007, p. 46.

[32] National Institute on Drug Abuse (NIDA), "Drugs, Brains and Behavior – The Science of Addiction," NIH Pub No. 14-5605, Printed April 2007, Revised February 2008, August 2010, July 2014, https://www.drugabuse.gov/sites/default/files/soa_2014.pdf (accessed 1.18.19).

[33] National Institute on Drug Abuse (NIDA), "Drugs, Brains, and Behavior: The Science of Addiction," Updated July 2018, https://www.drugabuse.gov/publications/drugs-brains-behavior-science-addiction/drugs-brain (accessed 1.19.19).

Chapter 6

[34] Office of the Surgeon General, FACING ADDICTION IN AMERICA: "The Surgeon General's Report on Alcohol, Drugs, and Health, Key Findings: The Neurobiology of Substance Use, Misuse, and Addiction," *HHS: Office of the Surgeon General*, 2016, https://addiction.surgeongeneral.gov/key-findings/neurobiology (accessed 1.7.19).

[35] Galater, M.D., Marc and Herbert D. Kleber, M.C., *The American Psychiatric Publishing Textbook of Substance Abuse Treatment, Fourth Edition,* Washington, D.C.: American Psychiatric Publishing, Inc., 2008, p. 94.

[36] Volkow, M.D., Nora, "The Hijacked Brain," part of "Addiction and the Brain's Pleasure Pathway: Beyond Willpower" series, Home Box Office, Inc. (HBO) in partnership with the Robert Wood Johnson Foundation, the National Institute on Drug Abuse and the National Institute on Alcohol Abuse and Alcoholism, 2010, http://www.hbo.com/addiction/understanding_addiction/12_pleasure_pat hway.html, (accessed September 2008). Note: this link is no longer live as the series has been rolled into an HBO Documentary titled, "Addiction."

[37] HBO Documentaries, "Addiction," created in partnership with the Robert Wood Johnson Foundation, the National Institute on Drug Abuse and the National Institute on Alcohol Abuse and Alcoholism, https://www.hbo.com/documentaries/addiction (accessed 1.4.19).

[38] Riggs, Paula, M.D., "Addiction." Home Box Office, Inc. (HBO) in partnership with the Robert Wood Johnson Foundation, the National Institute on Drug Abuse, and the National Institute on Alcohol Abuse and Alcoholism, 2010,

https://www.hbo.com/documentaries/addiction/addiction (accessed via HBO streaming of video titled, "Addiction," on 7.27.18, minute 38:50).

[39] HBO Documentaries, "Addiction," created in partnership with the Robert Wood Johnson Foundation, the National Institute on Drug Abuse and the National Institute on Alcohol Abuse and Alcoholism, https://www.hbo.com/documentaries/addiction (accessed 1.4.19).

[40] National Institute on Alcohol Abuse and Alcoholism (NIAAA), "Genetics of Alcohol Use Disorder," https://www.niaaa.nih.gov/alcohol-health/overview-alcohol-consumption/alcohol-use-disorders/genetics-alcohol-use-disorders (accessed 1.23.19).

[41] National Alliance on Mental Illness (NAMI), NAMI Hearts & Minds, "Mental Illness and Substance Abuse," January 2010, https://azdhs.gov/documents/az-state-hospital/nami-mental-illness-substance-abuse.pdf (accessed 3.13.19).

[42] Dennis, Michael, and Christy K Scott. "Managing addiction as a chronic condition." *Addiction science & clinical practice* vol. 4,1 (2007): 45-55, https://www.ncbi.nlm.nih.gov/pmc/articles/PMC2797101/ (accessed 6.12.19).

[43] The European School Survey Project on Alcohol and Other Drugs (ESPAD), "The 2015 ESPAD Report," http://www.espad.org/report/home/ (accessed 3.14.19).

[44] Center on the Developing Child at Harvard University, "Toxic Stress," https://developingchild.harvard.edu/science/key-concepts/toxic-stress/ (accessed 5.30.19).

[45] *Ibid.*

[46] Fellitti, Vincent J., MD, FACPA, Anda, Robert F., MD, MS, Nordenberg, Dale, MDC, Williamson, David F., MS, PhDB, Spitz, Alison M., MS, MPHB, Edwards, Valerie, BAB, Koss, Mary P., PhDD, Marks, James S., MD, MPHB, "Relationship of Childhood Abuse and

Household Dysfunction to Many of the Leading Causes of Death in Adults, The Adverse Childhood Experiences (ACE) Study," *American Journal of Preventative Medicine,* May 1998 Volume 14, Issue 4, Pages 245–258, DOI: https://doi.org/10.1016/S0749-3797(98)00017-8.

[47] Felitti, Vincent J. "The Relation Between Adverse Childhood Experiences and Adult Health: Turning Gold into Lead," *The Permanente Journal* vol. 6,1 (2002): 44-47.

[48] Anda, Robert, MD, MS and Co-Principal Investigator Adverse Childhood Experiences (ACE) Study, "The Health Impacts of Growing Up With Alcohol Abuse and Related Adverse Childhood Experiences: The Human and Economic Costs of the Status Quo," http://www.nacoa.net/pdfs/Anda%20NACoA%20Review_web.pdf (accessed 5.7.19).

[49] KPJR Films, "ACEs Primer," https://www.youtube.com/watch?v=ccKFkcfXx-c (accessed 5.4.19).

[50] Center on the Developing Child at Harvard University, "Resilience," https://developingchild.harvard.edu/science/key-concepts/resilience/ (accessed 3.2.19).

[51] National Association for Children of Addiction (NACoA), sliding header image, "1 in 4 children...," https://nacoa.org/ (accessed 5.9.19).

Chapter 7
[52] National Cancer Institute, "Cancer Statistics," Updated April 27, 2018, https://www.cancer.gov/about-cancer/understanding/statistics (accessed 4.3.2019).

[53] Brady, Kathleen, M.D., Ph.D., "Addiction." Home Box Office, Inc. (HBO) in partnership with the Robert Wood Johnson Foundation, the National Institute on Drug Abuse, and the National Institute on Alcohol Abuse and Alcoholism, 2010,

https://www.hbo.com/documentaries/addiction/addiction (accessed video through HBO streaming 7/27/18, minute 43:52).

Brown, Stephanie, Ph.D. and Virginia M. Lewis, Ph.D., with Andrew Liotta, *The Family Recovery Guide, A Map for Healthy Growth*, Oakland, CA: New Harbinger Publications, Inc., 2000., p. 34.

Ibid., pgs. 34-35.

Sources include: Maxwell, Ruth, *BREAKTHROUGH, What to do When Alcoholism or Chemical Dependency Hits Close to Home*," New York: Ballantine Books, 1986, pgs. 63-75, and Brown, Stephanie, Ph.D. and Virginia M. Lewis, Ph.D., with Andrew Liotta, *The Family Recovery Guide, A Map for Healthy Growth*, Oakland, CA: New Harbinger Publications, Inc., 2000, pgs. various throughout.

Galater, M.D., Marc and Herbert D. Kleber, M.C., *The American Psychiatric Publishing Textbook of Substance Abuse Treatment, Fourth Edition*, Washington, D.C.: American Psychiatric Publishing, Inc., 2008, pgs. 95-97.

McKay, James R., Ph.D. and Hiller-Sturmhöfel, Susanne, Ph.D., "Treating Alcoholism As a Chronic Disease: Approaches to Long-Term Continuing Care," *Alcohol Research Current Reviews*, 2011; 33(4): 356-370, https://www.ncbi.nlm.nih.gov/pmc/articles/PMC3625994/ (accessed 5.25.19).

HBO Documentaries, "Addiction," created in partnership with the Robert Wood Johnson Foundation, the National Institute on Drug Abuse and the National Institute on Alcohol Abuse and Alcoholism, https://www.hbo.com/documentaries/addiction (accessed 1.4.19).

Office of the Surgeon General, "FACING ADDICTION IN AMERICA: The Surgeon General's Report on Alcohol, Drugs, and Health," HHS Publication No. (SMA) 16-4991, 2016, pg. 2-2, https://addiction.surgeongeneral.gov/sites/default/files/surgeon-generals-report.pdf (accessed 5.15.19).

[61] Manejwala, Omar, M.D., "How Often Do Long-Term Sober Alcoholics and Addicts Relapse," *Psychology Today Online,* February 13, 2014, https://www.psychologytoday.com/us/blog/craving/201402/how-often-do-long-term-sober-alcoholics-and-addicts-relapse (accessed 3.24.19).

[62] Substance Abuse and Mental Health Services Administration (SAMHSA), "Working Definition of Recovery," https://store.samhsa.gov/system/files/pep12-recdef.pdf (accessed 2.13.19).

Chapter 8

[63] Brown, Stephanie, Ph.D. and Virginia M. Lewis, Ph.D., with Andrew Liotta, *The Family Recovery Guide, A Map for Healthy Growth,* Oakland, CA: New Harbinger Publications, Inc., 2000, p. 3.

[64] *Ibid.*

[65] Beattie, Melody, "About," *MelodyBeattie.com,* https://melodybeattie.com/about/ (accessed 6.2.19).

[66] Mental Health America, "Co-dependency," http://www.mentalhealthamerica.net/co-dependency (accessed 3.28.19).

[67] *Ibid.*

[68] *Ibid.*

[69] *Ibid.*

Chapter 9

[70] Center on the Developing Child at Harvard University, "Toxic Stress," https://developingchild.harvard.edu/science/key-concepts/toxic-stress/ (accessed 6.16.19).

[71] American Psychological Association (APA), "Stress effects on the body," https://www.apa.org/helpcenter/stress-body (accessed 5.27.19).

[72] Ratey, M.D., John J. with Erick Hagerman, *SPARK, the Revolutionary New Science of Exercise and the Brain,* New York: Little Brown & Co., 2008, p. 64.

[73] *Ibid.*, p. 65.

[74] *Ibid.*, p. 63.

[75] Carter, Rita, et al., *The Human Brain Book,* New York: DK (Dorling Kindersley Limited) Publishing, 2009, p. 127.

[76] *Ibid.*, p. 196.

Chapter 11

[77] Sources for these are varied and include: Brown, Stephanie, Ph.D. and Virgina m. Lewis, Ph.D., with Andrew Liotta, *The Family Recovery Guide, A Map for Healthy Growth,* Oakland, CA: New Harbinger Publications, Inc., 2000; various treatment centers at which I've spoken, Dr. James Hutt, and the hundreds of family members in recovery with whom I've worked or spoken with.

[78] *Ibid.*

[79] Carter, Rita, et al., *The Human Brain Book,* New York: DK (Dorling Kindersley Limited) Publishing, 2009, p. 45

[80] Ratey, M.D., John J. with Eric Hagerman, *SPARK, The Revolutionary New Science of Exercise and the Brain,* New York: Little, Brown and Company, 2008, pg. 5.

Chapter 13

[81] *Ibid.*, pg. 39.

[82] Al-Anon Family Groups, "Al-Anon Faces Alcoholism 2007, Are You Troubled by Someone's Drinking?" Virginia Beach, VA: Al-Anon Family Group Headquarters, Inc., 2006.